# Our Continent

## A Natural History
## of North America

# Our
# Continent
## A Natural History
## of North America

NATIONAL
GEOGRAPHIC
SOCIETY

# OUR CONTINENT
### A NATURAL HISTORY OF NORTH AMERICA
### PUBLISHED BY
### THE NATIONAL GEOGRAPHIC SOCIETY
ROBERT E. DOYLE, *President*
OWEN R. ANDERSON, *Secretary*
MELVILLE BELL GROSVENOR, *Editor-in-Chief*
GILBERT M. GROSVENOR, *Editor*

*Editorial Consultant*

**EDWIN H. COLBERT**
Curator of Vertebrate Paleontology, Museum of Northern Arizona
Curator Emeritus, The American Museum of Natural History

*Chapters by Dr. Colbert and*

**WILLIAM J. BREED**
Curator of Geology, Museum of Northern Arizona

**ARCHIE CARR**
Graduate Research Professor, University of Florida

**EDWARD S. DEEVEY, JR.**
Graduate Research Curator, Florida State Museum

**STEPHEN JAY GOULD**
Professor of Geology, Harvard University

**CHARLES B. HUNT**
Adjunct Professor of Earth Science, New Mexico State University

**PAUL A. JOHNSGARD**
Professor of Zoology, University of Nebraska

**BJÖRN KURTÉN**
Professor of Paleontology, University of Helsinki, Finland

**BATES McKEE**
Affiliate Professor of Geological Sciences, University of Washington

**JOHN H. OSTROM**
Professor of Geology, Yale University

**ROBERT O. PETTY**
Associate Professor of Biology, Wabash College

**JOHN S. SHELTON**
Consultant in Geology

**GEORGE E. WATSON**
Curator of Birds, Smithsonian Institution

**J. TUZO WILSON**
Director General, Ontario Science Centre, Canada

**JOHN A. MOORE,** Professor of Biology,
University of California, Riverside, served as consultant on animal life.

**PETER H. RAVEN,** Director of the Missouri Botanical Garden,
served as consultant on plant life.

First printing 525,000 copies
Library of Congress CIP data page 398

A VOLUME IN THE
NATURAL SCIENCE LIBRARY
PREPARED BY
NATIONAL GEOGRAPHIC BOOK SERVICE
JULES B. BILLARD, Director

Staff for this Book

SEYMOUR L. FISHBEIN
Editor

CHARLES O. HYMAN
Art Director

ANNE DIRKES KOBOR
Illustrations Editor

MARY H. DICKINSON
Chief Researcher

THOMAS B. ALLEN
ROSS BENNETT
JULES B. BILLARD
MARY SWAIN HOOVER
EDWARD LANOUETTE
DAVID F. ROBINSON
MARGARET SEDEEN
VERLA LEE SMITH
Editor-Writers

CONNIE BROWN
Design

ROBERT C. FIRESTONE
Production Manager

KAREN F. EDWARDS
Assistant Production Manager

LINDA B. MEYERRIECKS
BARBARA G. STEWART
Illustrations Research

SUZANNE P. KANE
JOAN PERRY
Assistants

MARTHA K. HIGHTOWER
JESSICA C. TAYLOR
Index

JOHN T. DUNN
JOHN R. METCALFE
WILLIAM W. SMITH
JAMES R. WHITNEY
Engraving and Printing

WERNER JANNEY
Style

CAROL BITTIG LUTYK
PAMELA MUCCI
SHIRLEY L. SCOTT
KAREN H. VOLLMER
ELIZABETH L. WAGLEY
ANNE E. WITHERS
Editorial Research

JOHN D. GARST, JR.
VIRGINIA L. BAZA
CHARLES W. BERRY
MARGARET A. DEANE
NANCY SCHWEICKART
SNEJINKA STEFANOFF
ALFRED ZEBARTH
LEO B. ZEBARTH
Map Design and Production

Diagrams, maps, and sketches by

LISA BIGANZOLI
WILLIAM H. BOND
JAIME QUINTERO
TIBOR TOTH
of the National Geographic Staff;
and TONY CHEN

Photographs by

JEN and DES BARTLETT
DON BRIGGS
DAVID CAVAGNARO
WILLIAM R. CURTSINGER
ENTHEOS
WILLIAM A. GARNETT
DAVID MUENCH and others

Paintings of prehistoric life by

ZDENEK BURIAN
JAY H. MATTERNES

360 illustrations
342 in full color, 24 maps

PAGES 2-3: Still life from the
collections of the Smithsonian
Institution; Victor R. Boswell, Jr.,
National Geographic photographer.
OVERLEAF: Sunlit firs sentinel
an Olympics ridge; Entheos.

# Contents

*Ever the dim beginning,*
*Ever the growth,*
*    the rounding*
*    of the circle. . . .*
*Strata of mountains,*
*    soils, rocks, giant trees,*
*Far-born, far-dying,*
*    living long.*

SIERRA NEVADA CRESTS SHADOW A CLOUD BANK AT SUNSET, GALEN ROWELL

CANYON-WALLED COLORADO CAROMS TOWARD THE SEA; DON BRIGGS. RIGHT: ICE MELT IN YOSEMITE; ERNEST BRAUN, FROM "LIVING WATER" © AMERICAN WEST PUBLISHING CO.

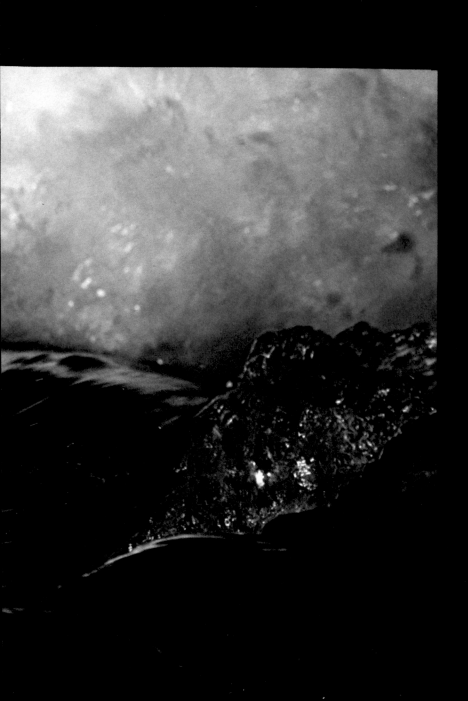
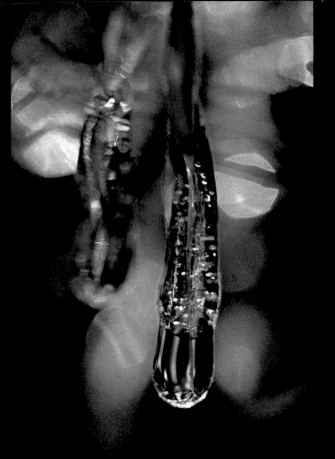

What wondrous stories
a water molecule could tell,
of wild peaks
visited on stormy nights,
of quiet rivulets
and raging rivers traveled.

DAVID CAVAGNARO

*Let the waters bring forth
abundantly the moving
creature that hath life,
and fowl that may fly
above the earth in the open
firmament of heaven.*

<small>GENESIS 1:20</small>

We too are the children
of the glacier. . . .
And when we find the first
wild flower in spring,
we sense that primal knowing—
somehow we too survived
the glacial snows.

ROBERT O. PETTY

I've known the wind . . . to shake
The late leaves down,
    which frozen where they fell,
And held in ice as dancers in a spell,
Fluttered all winter long. . . .
There was perfection

# Through the Mists of Time

Archie Carr

It was late afternoon when I walked out on the foot trail toward the crest of Water Rock Knob, up in the Balsam Range of the southern Appalachians. The world is in view up there; you have only to walk a short way and new openings through the firs let you see in any direction. Out to the west toward the Great Smoky Mountains and Tennessee the sun was low and the sky rosy. Back eastward toward Craggy and Mount Mitchell the darkening domes and peaks were mixing with the sky in a blue tumult of clouds and mountains. We had spent the day driving about the Balsams, admiring the incredible spectacle of October. The leaves of Appalachian October are one of the stunning natural assets of North America. I heard somewhere that you can find their equal in China. Be that as it may, the spectacle they make in the United States is so rare that not just American outlanders but even Swiss and Swedes and Germans congregate to view it. You don't count on finding a motel room in Buncombe County, North Carolina, in mid-October.

There is varied magic in Appalachian leaves, painting a different picture with every curve in the road. On the near slopes the crown-forms of individual trees mold the color. Farther away the yellow, scarlet, orange, and wine of the forest top blend into tawny flame that is textured, not by tree form or leaf shape, but by the sweeping away of the land itself. Up close in the roadside edges, foliage becomes separate leaves. Maples, dogwoods, grape, and sumac twinkle and dance with particulate color in any little breeze, and the decorated twigs of sourwood trees swoop out like plumed birds scattering.

As I threaded the ridgetop firs and birches, I heard a quiet conversation of birds in a rhododendron bush beside the trail—a pair of pine siskins puttering about in complete unconcern over my presence just a few feet away. While I stood there pondering their curious tameness, the western mountains were darkening fast, and above them the sunset was stealing the last color from the land. Patches of hoarfrost under the firs sparkled rosy reflections. Trunks of bare-twigged birches gleamed like worn columns of silver-plated copper. For a long time I stood there with the birds conversing beside me, looking out into the dark ocean of the mountains; they seemed vast beyond any possible limits, and full of mystery.

Timeless, they seemed. It is a cliché, but almost a ceremonial obligation, to refer to an imposing landscape as "timeless." I never know exactly what the word means in this context. One way you look at it, the word is not appropriate; because *timeless* suggests *changeless*, and change is universal in both the face of the earth and the living creatures that inhabit it. On the other hand, if you mean duration of existence as an earth feature, then the Appalachians certainly are among the timeless landscapes of the world.

I pondered the huge, slow-moving forces that had built the landscape out there under the fading sunset—the Smokies, and on beyond: the prairies, plains, and deserts to the west; and finally the towering young Western ranges that were elevated long after the Smokies had grown old. When I took geography as a boy, I was told that the Appalachians were "old, worn-down mountains," while the Rockies, by contrast, were "young, rugged mountains." I was also told that seas once covered Kansas, that towering ice has stood over Indiana, that Utah was once filled with dinosaurs. I accepted this on faith, but I clearly remember my vagueness over the scheduling of such events—the wearing down of mountains especially. I had observed that it took time for the tread of a bicycle tire or a path to the barn to wear. So in a general way it seemed reasonable to call Clingmans Dome old because it was smooth, and Pikes Peak young because of its being a sharp peak. Nevertheless, I had the feeling that the adjectives "old" and "young" were more metaphoric than exact. And even now, looking out into the endless undulations of the Smokies—the array of domes, knobs, runs, valleys, gaps, and ridges—the time it took to make and wear down the mountains seemed beyond any possible knowing.

Such events seem so remote that their bearing on the life and land of today may appear irrelevant to us. Nevertheless, the old forces are still at work in the world, and the living things are in some measure a part of the substance of the primordial soup in which life began. Seas have repeatedly come and gone in the midriff of North America. Continents have pulled apart, and wheeled in stately turnings that changed the shapes of oceans, shifted the very poles of the world, and laid the Equator across its belly in capricious ways. And still the land is wearing away, the rocks are going to pieces and then being laid down to make new rocks. Climates cycle and shift; everything alive is changing—adapting and surviving, or becoming extinct.

One great earth disturbance, culminating about 250 million years ago in the Permian Period of geologic time, churned up the Eastern mountain realm of Appalachia. Land masses rose everywhere during the Permian, and tropical climates began to change. During much of the preceding 65 million years—the period known as Carboniferous because tremendous coal deposits were laid down then—vast swamp forests had spread through North and South America, and in Eurasia as well. The trees in them were huge spore-bearing kinds related to the tiny club mosses of today; there were giant horsetails and scale trees more than a hundred feet tall, with trunks six feet in diameter. The first winged insects coursed the forests, and amphibians, newly derived from lobe-finned fishes, ventured ashore.

With the Permian, terrestrial life came under stress. Goaded by cold and drought, the plants made use of an important evolutionary innovation—the seed. By means of this they could go dormant when times were bad, and then grow fast on food stored in their seeds when good times returned. By then the earliest reptiles had already achieved the momentous development of the shelled egg, which made it unnecessary for them to go back to water to breed. This prepared the way for a feverish evolution of the reptiles, eventually including the dramatic radiation of dinosaurs, and the founding of other lines that led to birds and mammals.

The Appalachians of those distant days rose to heights far greater than any there now. Since then the piecemeal decay of the ages has weathered and smoothed the mountains; rivers have cut at their bases and broadened the valleys among them; and now, correctly if with some understatement, the geography books refer to the Appalachians as old and worn.

Even so, they are not the most ancient land on the continent. The oldest solid ground in North America is the Canadian Shield, the great sweep of tundra, lake, and pine forest that surrounds Hudson Bay. This is the nucleus of the continent. Some of the rocks there are Precambrian strata that date back to times when life on earth was just beginning. Until lately not much could be made of the rocks of the shield because whatever living things existed were naked and soft and left scarcely any fossils; but partly, also, because some of the sediments were surely laid down when the seas were wholly lifeless. By the time of the Cambrian Period, 600 million years ago, life had become a thriving enterprise, and Cambrian rocks contain fossils of all the major animal groups except the vertebrates. Though the Precambrian record of life is dim, momentous events had happened by the time it ended. Cells had organized themselves for maintenance and reproduction. Chlorophyll had developed, and a teeming array of blue-green algae was providing a food supply for animal life—and oxygen for it to breathe.

As the resources expanded, the diversification of life accelerated, and organized relationships among living creatures were established. Planet earth acquired a biosphere; and from then on through the ages, ecology and evolution have proceeded hand in hand. When you walk through a forest today, it is not just a pointless clutter of plant and animal life but an organized enterprise of interdependent beings. And some of the molecules that circulate among these beings have come down from little creatures whose remains are fossils in rocks that date to the start of biological time.

The problem of conceiving the immense time spans involved in geological processes was what postponed until only yesterday our conception of organic evolution by natural selection. There was plenty of evidence around to show that the earth is ancient, and that later forms of life were related to earlier ones. Wherever there were sedimentary rocks—sandstone or limestone or shale—there were likely to be fossils in them. Wherever the edges of these rock strata were exposed in the wall of a gorge or a road cut, each above the others in horizontal layers, a time sequence was clearly involved; the old layers were obviously those on the bottom and the young ones those on top. Maybe if all the venturesome thinkers of a few centuries ago had grown up in the Badlands or in the Grand Canyon, the connection between fossils, rock strata, erosion, and time would have added up to something much sooner than it did.

Unfortunately, however, sedimentary strata don't always lie suggestively one on top of the other. They are often tilted, or wrinkled; or they stand side by side, or some are even missing completely. So with Archbishop James Ussher of Ireland insisting that the earth was created in 4004 B.C., and with the best minds of the day accepting his dating, and with the story of Noah's flood to account for any fossil creature in an inappropriate habitat, it was no wonder that dinosaur footprints in Connecticut rocks were attributed to "Noah's Raven," or that the fossilized skeleton of a big salamander was gravely named *Homo diluvii testis*— Man, witness to the Flood. The idea of the vastness of earth-time had to await the pronouncement, late in the 18th century, of a Scot named James Hutton that the earth-changing processes of the past were the same as those at work today.

So you can see the past in the face of the present. Time molds the natural world. It shapes the land, and the smallest pebbles in it. The kinds of animals and plants have evolved through time and will continuously change as more time passes. And the complex web of ecological relationships among them will also change.

Though the biological landscapes of North America are varied and magnificent, the continent is not markedly different in these respects from Europe and Asia. All of North America's temperate and arctic biomes—its major life areas— occur also in Eurasia, and many of its animals and plants likewise have close Eurasian kin. Other features are shared with South America. The similarity of North American and Eurasian life reflects the intermittently open road to Asia across Bering Strait, and also old ties with Europe before the Atlantic Ocean grew to its present size. The present-day Central American isthmus and land connections that came and went in earlier times account for the strong biogeographic similarities between North and South America.

In spite of these ancient highways for dispersal and interchange of life, our continent has distinctive representatives of most major groups of vertebrate animals. The most striking are fishes. The gars and bowfin, for example, both of which look like revived fossils, belong to orders found only on this continent. Bluegills and black bass seem so indispensable a blessing to us that it is hard to imagine a land without them; but except where it has been artificially introduced, the family they belong to lives nowhere else. There are other American fishes, less well known but just as distinctive. The mooneyes, for example; and the whole order to which the pirate perch and the trout perch belong, and the rice fish and related species of blind cave fishes. The redoubtable snapping turtle family is almost wholly North American, though it trickles down through the isthmus to northern South America.

I remember feeling resentful when I first learned that we share with China the alligator and the paddlefish, members of groups as old as the dinosaurs or older. It seemed a bizarre miscarriage of zoogeography. However, there are a number of plant types that have similar distribution, and so do the huge aquatic salamanders of the group to which the American hellbender belongs. So the thing to do, I suppose, is to stop fretting about having to share such forms with the Orient, and instead meditate on the stupendous historical events that produced the curious separation. That is to say, a two-foot hellbender writhing at the end of your fishing line in an Eastern stream is in itself an electrifying sight—one that has been known to cause people unaware of hellbenders to jump out of boats. But knowing that you would have to go clear to the other side of the world to see the like of the animal adds drama to the moment.

It is interesting to go back to the early chronicles to see what New World productions impressed the colonists. One American species that evoked universal comment was the turkey. There are only two peculiarly North American families of birds, and the turkey is one of them. The other is the wrentit, which lives only on the Pacific Coast.

Another source of excitement was the broadleafed forest that stood just back of most of the landing places along the Atlantic seaboard. A part of the impact was nostalgia—the forest looked much like the remnants of the old Robin Hood woods of England. But in Europe the forest lay in fragments, while in the New World it was virgin. It was the most diverse temperate forest in the world, and it reached its climax in the southern Appalachians. The few tracts still unlogged surely rank with the most magnificent vegetation on earth.

If I had to list the most spectacular landscapes of North America, four would quickly come to mind. One is Grand Canyon; another, the valley of Yosemite. A third is Appalachia in October. The fourth would certainly be the coniferous forests of the West Coast: the incredible coast redwoods; the sequoias of the Sierra Nevada; and the soaring architecture made by Douglas fir, Sitka spruce, western hemlock, and western cedar along the coast and on the Olympic Peninsula.

Sequoias are the world's most massive trees; redwoods are the tallest. Another famed record-breaker among Western conifers is the bristlecone pine, a stunted, gnarled tree with threadbare foliage. In one place in the White Mountains of California, 17 of these trees are at least 4,000 years old. This tiny, archaic grove almost provides a living link with the paleontologic past. The parents, at least, of these bristlecone pines could have been alive when ground sloths and other Ice Age animals were still afoot in the land. For me that thought helps close the gap between us and the recent past of North America.

It is probably naive to complain about the loss of animals through natural extinction, but it is hard to keep from doing so. Especially when the lost species are grand old beasts whose bones in the rocks make you drool over the thought of having them around today. Of course, you can get so carried away with the continuity idea that you start seeing ghosts. You find yourself grieving over the lack of brontosaurs slogging through Corkscrew Swamp. You get to dreaming what a thrill it would be to the football crowd in the Orange Bowl if a pterosaur—one of the newly found Texas breed for instance, with wings 60 feet from tip to tip—should sail in from somewhere and start cutting the fool with the little airplane towing big letters that spell out "Tony's Pizza." Such talk is moonshine I suppose; but the point is, the world of those great animals was not another world at all. It was the same world we live in now, cut off only by the flow of time.

You don't have to go back to the dinosaurs to see changes in American nature. As geologic time goes, some of the most dramatic changes occurred only a little while ago; and what brought them about is not well understood. Where did the huge old ground sloths go, for example? And why are the elephants gone from my Florida farm? Florida is too new for dinosaurs, but the imperial mammoth, one of the biggest elephants that ever existed, once roamed places so like the Southeastern landscapes of today that their passing makes no sense at all. When I cross Paynes Prairie I can almost see them, over toward Persimmon Point, standing in a big band in the maiden cane, ponderous and peaceable, flapping their ears and waving bundles of long grass into their mouths.

Something strange and fateful happened in North American nature between six and twelve thousand years ago. It was not just elephants and ground sloths that disappeared. Extinction spread among Ice Age mammals everywhere. Did Indian hunters kill them off? Or the rigors of Ice Age climates? Able paleoecologists are at outs with each other over the causes.

Simple-minded people will sometimes tell you that because extinction is natural, we ought not bother about the whooping crane. "Why should we be concerned with endangered species," you'll hear, "when most of the species that ever lived are extinct." There is of course no similarity between the obsolescence that accompanies long-term evolutionary competition or environmental change, and the dismal kinds of extinction perpetrated by modern man. Natural extinction is a necessary result of the flow of biological time — of the natural progression of geology, climate, and evolution which causes well-adapted creatures of one period to go out of style and either die out or change into something else in the next. The process is an orderly and inevitable one, not a blot on the record of civilized man, as the disappearance of whooping cranes would be.

When the water goes down at the shore of Smoky Hollow, near my house in Florida, you can sometimes see together on the smooth mud the tracks of three small, venturesome animals: armadillos, raccoons, and opossums. All are mammals, all are more or less omnivorous, and all love the night. Each has survived the slings and arrows of geologic time, and has come through space and time to Smoky Hollow by a different path. So it is with the plants and animals that make up any biotic community. Though knit together by myriad ecological ties, all are of different origins and ages. All have achieved the tour de force of evolutionary survival, but as the future unfolds and their habitats change, they must change also, or else move on to new places in which the old environment remains. Otherwise they will simply die out.

Whatever the causes of Ice Age extinctions, by the time the European colonists arrived, the continent was back on its ecological feet, and had become a rich and splendid wilderness in which Indians lived with nature in harmony and balance. Today the harmony and balance have diminished. Daniel Boone would have trouble finding his way about the countryside. Yet there is much of wild nature left to cherish, and our will to keep it seems to be growing. People nowadays often speak of a "quality of life" that our land must provide if the future is to be worth living in. I have not heard the phrase defined very clearly, but I hope the quality they mean is a self-perpetuating harmony with the magnificent remnants that have survived the long, long journey through the mists of time.

# The Shaping of the Continent

J. Tuzo Wilson

Across the vast vault of night, astronomers with their telescopes can gaze at an array of billions upon billions of stars, Shakespeare's "burning tapers of the sky." They have discovered many with fantastic properties—stars that gleam ten trillion times more brightly than our sun, objects so dense a teaspoonful would weigh as much as 600 million automobiles, mysterious black holes whose incredible gravitational pull sucks in the dust and stuff of space, never to be seen again. They have catalogued that jumbled throng of stars into an orderly sequence by variety and age, as if they had looked at a crowd of people and sorted them into infants, children, young adults, the middle-aged, and the elderly.

Astronomers calculate that the oldest stars formed with the universe itself about 13 billion years ago. They consider that the birth occurred when a primordial mass exploded with a titanic bang, sending particles flying in every direction. These clouds of gas and matter have been condensing ever since to form galaxies of stars and planets. Some 4.6 billion years ago, scientists believe, our own sun coalesced from such a swirling nebula of gas and dust. As gravitation pulled the mass together, collisions, compression, and radioactivity heated it until temperatures at the center reached millions of degrees. Hydrogen atoms fused to form helium, kindling a source of energy —nuclear fusion—that has kept the sun ablaze ever since. It has fuel enough to continue for billions of years more.

The condensing solar cloud spawned orbiting bodies of various sizes. These collided and accumulated until there grew the planets and satellites we know today. Meteorites strike the earth as that collection process still goes on. From analysis and dating of these extraterrestrial rocks, along with other clues read in the heavens, scientists conclude that the composition of the solar system is remarkably uniform— persuasive argument for a common origin 4.6 billion years ago.

The oldest known earth-rocks, discovered in Greenland, date back some 3.8 billion years. Rocks nearly as old have been found in Minnesota, Labrador, and South Africa. All resemble the youngest of rocks, suggesting that the earth was not very different in composition then from now. Older ones may turn up, but one explanation for the age span between meteorites and our oldest rock may be that the earth took a long time to form. Evidently it passed through a molten stage. As it cooled, heavier matter rich in iron settled to the center; lighter rocks like basalt and granite rose to the surface, eventually forming a crust. Volcanoes brought gases and water vapor from deep within to create an atmosphere and the seas. Continents developed, and the earth took shape as a unique member of a family of planets.

So far this is a familiar description; but a new view of the world and its workings suggests that our seemingly fixed earth is always changing. Continents drift about— bumping into each other to thrust up mountains, breaking apart to shape new lands.

OVERLEAF: *Earth retches, and steam and exploding lava streak the skies as the islet of Surtsey grows from the sea near Iceland in 1963. Such pyrotechnics hint of the powerful forces at work in our restless, hot-hearted planet—pushing continents around, building mountains, opening and closing oceans.*

SOLARFILMA

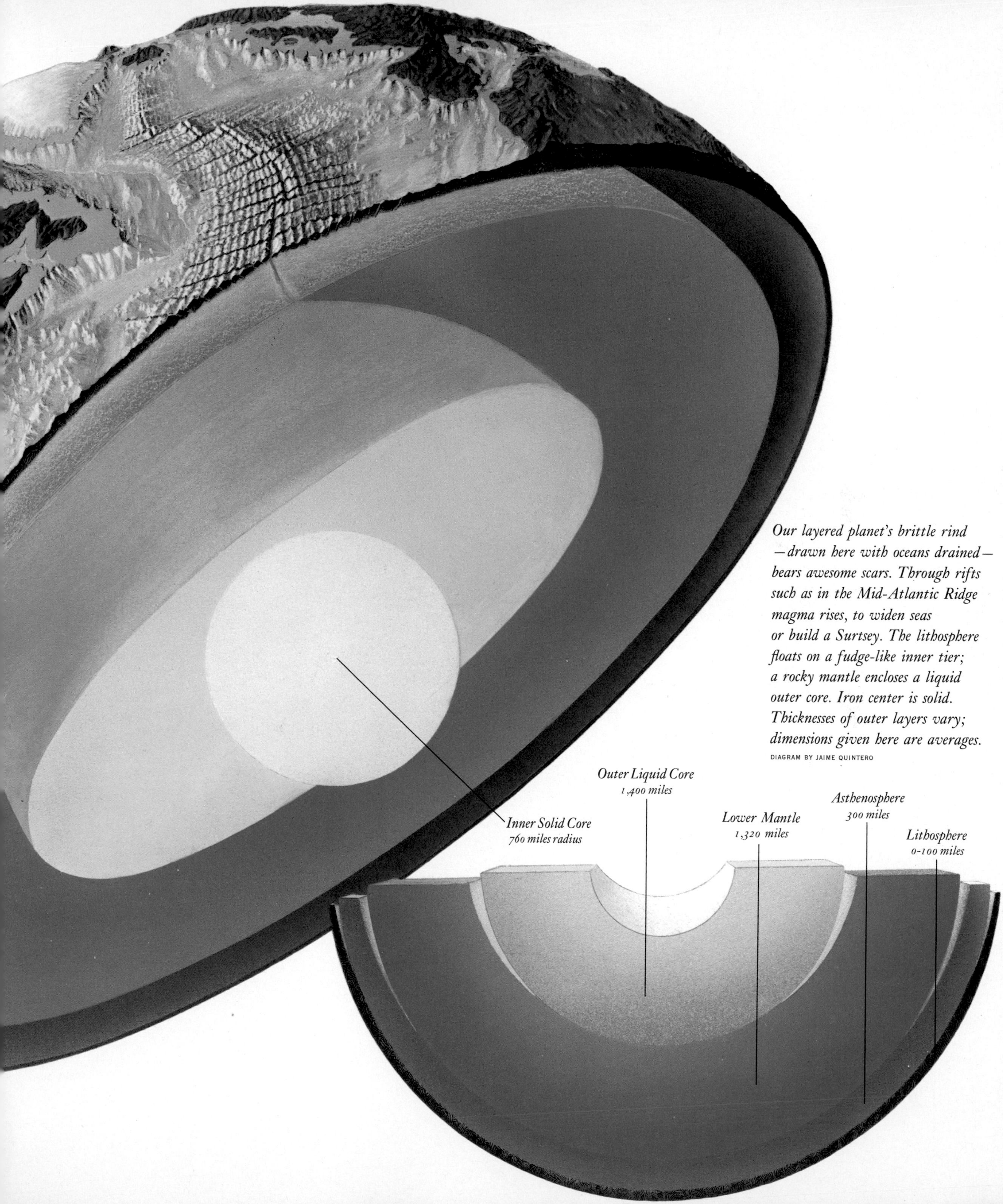

Our layered planet's brittle rind —drawn here with oceans drained— bears awesome scars. Through rifts such as in the Mid-Atlantic Ridge magma rises, to widen seas or build a Surtsey. The lithosphere floats on a fudge-like inner tier; a rocky mantle encloses a liquid outer core. Iron center is solid. Thicknesses of outer layers vary; dimensions given here are averages.

DIAGRAM BY JAIME QUINTERO

Inner Solid Core
760 miles radius

Outer Liquid Core
1,400 miles

Lower Mantle
1,320 miles

Asthenosphere
300 miles

Lithosphere
0-100 miles

Ocean basins appear and disappear. These awesome events take eons, but the earth in its own slow way is a very dynamic body.

This concept—that oceans and continents are not fixed and permanent, but that lands are mobile and seas ephemeral—constitutes one of history's great leaps in scientific understanding. Because of it, old ideas have been overturned, old textbooks have had to be rewritten. It has done for geology what Copernicus's realization of a sun-centered solar system did for astronomy, what Darwin's theory of evolution did for biology, what Einstein's theory of relativity did for physics. It is a true scientific revolution. We are fortunate it has occurred in our times, barely a decade ago.

We know that our vibrant planet has a layered structure. Seismic waves from explosive charges or from the tens of thousands of quakes that shake the earth every year help tell us so. Some of these waves pass through liquids, others cannot. Boundaries between layers bend certain kinds of waves, reflect others. Speeds vary as the waves travel through different types of material. From this and other evidence we conclude that our globe somewhat resembles a soft-boiled egg. It has a thin, brittle, shell-like crust; a thick, solid section, called the mantle, representing the white; and a partly liquid core equivalent to the yolk.

Earth's original heat and the energy from decay of radioactive elements are thought to keep the interior at temperatures of perhaps 8,000° F. The core, like the charge of a blast furnace, is largely liquid iron, but great pressure at the very center compresses a dense inner core to solid iron. The mantle is rigid and consists of iron-rich silicate rocks. Like the lining of a blast furnace, these silicates do not melt as easily as iron. Pressure keeps the lower part of the mantle hard; higher up, the hot rock becomes slightly plastic. This layer is called the asthenosphere, from the Greek *asthenes*, for "weak." Nearer the surface the earth is cooler and becomes more rigid again, forming the layer called the lithosphere, from *lithos*, for "stone." This includes the top of the mantle and the entire crust—the latter averaging some 20 miles thick under continents and about 3 miles under ocean basins.

Realization that the lithosphere and asthenosphere differ in their resistance to deformation provided an understanding of how continents drift. The asthenosphere behaves like a pliable, red-hot poker—or like ice, which in a cube from your refrigerator is crystalline and brittle, but in a mass as large as a glacier can shift and flow. This was first appreciated when it was observed that the asthenosphere can yield under loads. Glacial sheets of the Ice Age weighted down the land; measurements show that much of North America has risen since they melted. Continents, formed of relatively light rocks, can float high on the asthenosphere, but the heavier basalt of ocean floors cannot. The continents can wander about, for the new view of an ever-changing earth holds that the lithosphere is cracked into huge plates which move over the layer

---

*"What stranger miracles are there?" Walt Whitman asked about the seas. As if in echo, scientists found in mid-ocean deeps clues to how far-off continents drift about. Camera lens here curves the horizon.*

BILL FARRELL, FOR THE AMERICAN BUREAU OF SHIPPING

29

# Stone Ships That Sail Over the Seas of Time

Cracked into perhaps a score of pieces, earth's lithosphere includes our familiar crust of continents and ocean basins. Ponderously slow churnings in the semi-plastic interior are thought to drive the plates in endless driftings. Where plate edges grind together, earthquakes (yellow dots) most frequently occur. Where plates split apart, molten rock may surge to the surface and solidify; one great rift along which this happens (bright-red lines) meanders about the globe for 40,000 miles. Dark-red lines mark "subduction" zones where the edge of one plate dips below another—to melt in the depths and breed volcanoes. Orange lines locate "transform faults"—regions where plate edges slip sideways past each other.

Scientists believe plate movements have carried the continents across the face of the earth since early in its history. Two hundred million years ago all were joined in one huge mass which got the name Pangaea, meaning "all lands," from the writings of Alfred Wegener—father of the continental drift theory. Pangaea was washed by a universal ocean—Panthalassa ("all seas")—of which the Pacific is a remnant. By 135 million years ago Pangaea had divided into northern Laurasia and southern Gondwana, with an embryo Mediterranean between them, and India and an Australia-Antarctica split off. About 65 million years ago the Atlantic had developed and India drove toward Asia, eventually to bump up the Himalayas.

Today ocean-floor spreading shoves North America farther from Europe by an inch a year; parts of the Pacific creep four times as fast. In 50 million years, if movements continue unchanged, Africa will have begun to break apart, the Mediterranean will be squeezed into a large lake, and a bit of California, detached from the mainland, will have drifted toward the Aleutian Trench.

DIAGRAMS BY JAIME QUINTERO

*200 million years ago*

*135 million years ago*

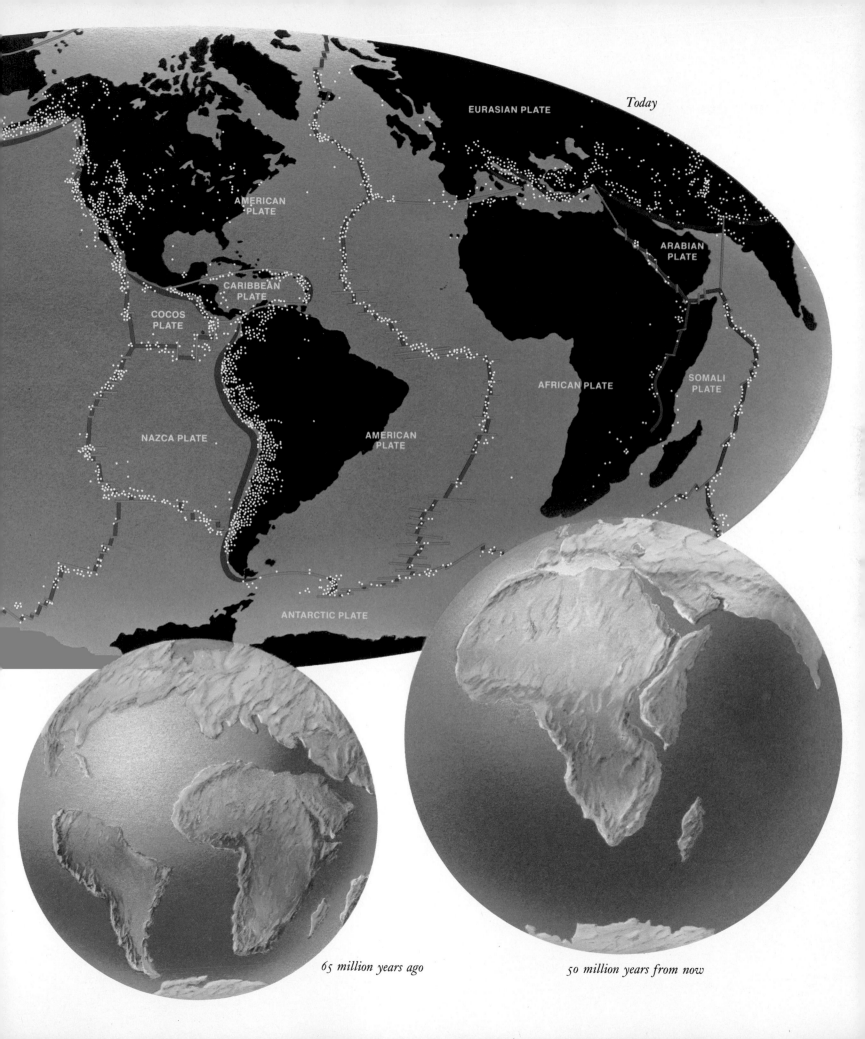

EURASIAN PLATE

*Today*

AMERICAN PLATE

CARIBBEAN PLATE

COCOS PLATE

ARABIAN PLATE

AFRICAN PLATE

SOMALI PLATE

NAZCA PLATE

AMERICAN PLATE

ANTARCTIC PLATE

*65 million years ago*

*50 million years from now*

below. Where plates separate, molten rock wells up, cooling and solidifying to form new crust. Elsewhere plates are pushed together, and one may be forced beneath another to soften and merge in the hot depths. This theory can explain how mountains are formed, what causes earthquakes and volcanic eruptions, why Antarctica once had fern forests—questions inadequately explained by old ideas. Piecing the theory together has been one of the great detective stories in the history of science.

Almost as soon as outlines of the New World began to appear on maps, imaginations were provoked by the jigsaw-puzzle fit of opposite coasts of the Atlantic. In 1782 wise old philosopher Benjamin Franklin wondered if "the surface of the globe would be a shell" capable of swimming on an internal fluid. Other scientists held that the Old and New Worlds had been rent asunder by a cataclysmic event, probably involving the Flood described in the Bible. Then in 1908 an American geologist, Frank B. Taylor, proposed that the continents were moving about slowly, propelled by tidal action. And by 1912 the German meteorologist Alfred Wegener had marshalled arguments to support the first comprehensive view of continents in motion.

Wegener not only showed that the edges of the continental shelves match, but he also demonstrated that rocks and fossils on opposite shores of the Atlantic dovetail remarkably. "It is just as if we were to refit the torn pieces of a newspaper . . . and then check whether the lines of print run smoothly across. If they do, there is nothing left but to conclude that the pieces were in fact joined in this way," he wrote. He argued that if continents can move vertically, it is logical to suppose that they can also move laterally. He cited evidence of great climatic changes: fossils of subtropical forests in now-arctic Spitzbergen, salt beds from seas that dried when North America must

*Stark crack across an arid plain north of Los Angeles, California's San Andreas Fault marks a boundary where two slabs of earth's crust rub together. Pulverized rock—debris of millenniums of grinding—clogs the cleft. When segments slip, earthquakes wrack the land; one jump—of up to 21 feet—gutted San Francisco in 1906.*

*The west side of the 700-mile fault system is part of the earth's Pacific plate and drifts northwest relative to the rest of North America. The movements are those of a transform fault, one of four types of plate action. Sea-floor spreading adds a square mile of new ocean bottom to earth's surface each year. Subduction sires huge ocean trenches deeper than six Grand Canyons. Continental collisions buckle up mountains, and beyond the juncture may create weak spots that become new subduction zones.*

DIAGRAMS BY JAIME QUINTERO. OPPOSITE: JAMES P. BLAIR, NATIONAL GEOGRAPHIC PHOTOGRAPHER

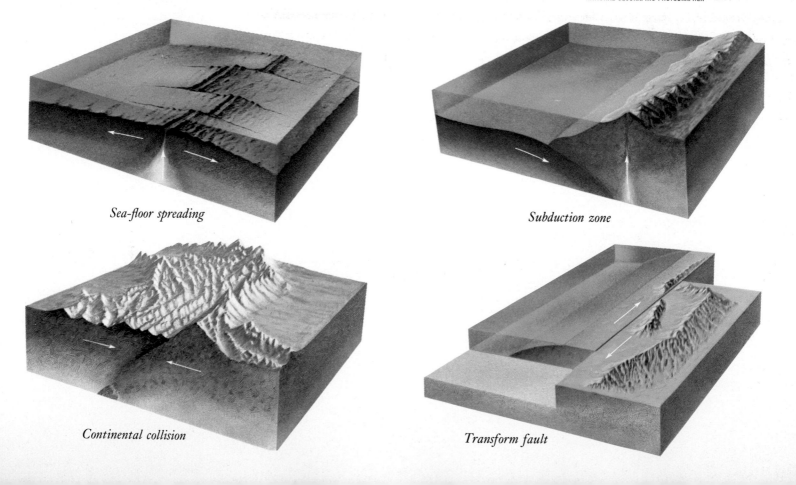

*Sea-floor spreading*

*Subduction zone*

*Continental collision*

*Transform fault*

have lain in the torrid zone, debris left by glaciers in lands now near the Equator.

But Wegener's suggestion that stone continents plow through stone floors of the oceans like stately ships seemed too preposterous to accept. Sir Harold Jeffreys, then the world's most influential geophysicist, spurned the drift theory as "quantitatively insufficient and qualitatively inapplicable." Other scientists used minor flaws in the argument to deride the whole concept. When Wegener died in 1930—a casualty on a hazardous meteorological expedition into the middle of the Greenland ice cap—few persons had accepted his unorthodox views.

For a quarter of a century Wegener's theory lay largely ignored. Then discoveries made after World War II by the application of new scientific devices forced a renewed interest. Echo sounders using principles designed to detect submarines gave exact charts of ocean floors. Magnetometers were devised that could be towed on the ocean surface to record weak magnetism in rocks beneath the ooze miles below. Instruments were designed to pinpoint the source of earthquakes, to make delicate readings of gravity, to measure heat flow from the earth's interior—it was as if earth's skin at last could be peeled back for a look at what lay beneath. Until then, earth scientists had been like doctors of old who, lacking stethoscope or X-rays, could examine only the outsides of their patients.

But proof that continents are in motion did not come immediately, as an inspiration in the mind of one genius. Evidence built up piece by piece. Each advance had to struggle against entrenched ideas; each scientist had to abandon cherished views.

As did most scientists, I scoffed at the idea until I recognized it as the only theory that could clear up the confusion existing in geology. I remember when, as a new convert in 1960, my arguments were greeted with skepticism and a few boos from geologists and members of the American Geophysical Union. Not until after 1965 was evidence clear enough to win over most doubters in the scientific community.

Two broad areas of investigation provided the strongest support. One involved study of magnetic records frozen in ancient rocks—paleomagnetism. The other was tracing an underwater mountain system that winds about the globe.

Until a century ago we knew virtually nothing about the floors of the oceans except that they were very deep. Then soundings compiled by Matthew Fontaine Maury, a U. S. naval officer, and by the British exploration ship *Challenger* revealed the presence of an underwater ridge bisecting the Atlantic. In time, other expeditions found other ridges in other seas. By 1956 Maurice Ewing and Bruce C. Heezen, professors at Columbia University, could show that all the ridges are connected into a single mighty mountain range. Far larger than any chain on land, the mid-ocean ridge sprawls as much as 3,000 miles wide, and its crest rises a mile or more. Some peaks

*Flaunting fiery garb, Hawaii's Mauna Ulu—"growing mountain"—cloaks itself with lava. Thus volcanoes build, changing earth's face, recycling mineral riches. They also destroy—witness Thera, whose explosion about 1500 B.C. may explain the fall of Minoan civilization and bolster legends of a lost Atlantis.*
DON REESER

## Variations on a Mountain Theme

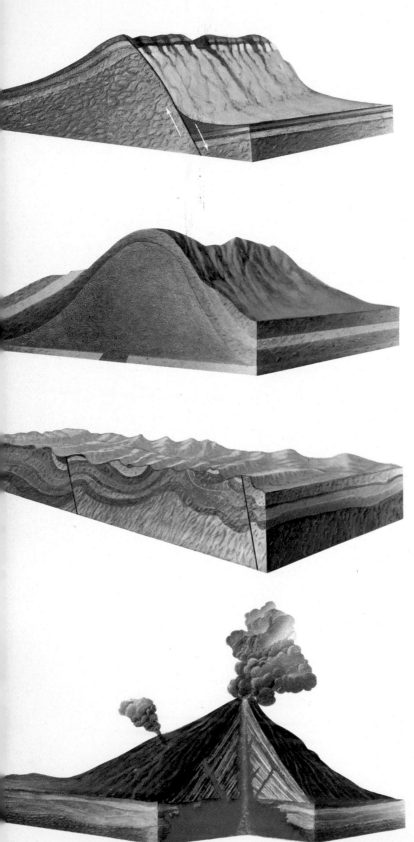

*California's Convict Lake filches snowmelt from crags of the Sierra Nevada—awesome result of one of earth's mountain-making processes.*

FAULT-BLOCK MOUNTAINS *grow when crustal masses tilt or slip along a fault. Movement—in inches at a jerk—raises blocks like Wyoming's Grand Tetons or the 400-mile-long Sierra Nevada. Erosion carves the upturned scarp, or face, and builds a pediment of rubble at the base.*

*Welling forces from below push up earth layers into* DOME MOUNTAINS *—the Black Hills of South Dakota, for example. Where outer strata weather away, curving "hogback" ridges result. The Teapot Dome of a 1920's scandal speaks of the oil often found in such formations.*

*Like a rug shoved against a wall, sections of earth's surface may be squeezed and tortured into* FOLDED MOUNTAINS. *Lower layers cock up; fracturing often occurs. As erosion wears away softer strata, valleys develop. The rhythmic patterns of valley and ridge in the Appalachians are a classic example.*

*Piles of cinders, shields of spilled magma, layers of stone and dust form earth's* VOLCANIC MOUNTAINS. *Such symmetrical summits as Fuji, Rainier, and Hood rise as composite cones—tiered ribs of lava and ash. Some 1,000 active peaks dot the globe.*

DIAGRAMS BY JAIME QUINTERO. OPPOSITE: WILLIAM A. GARNETT

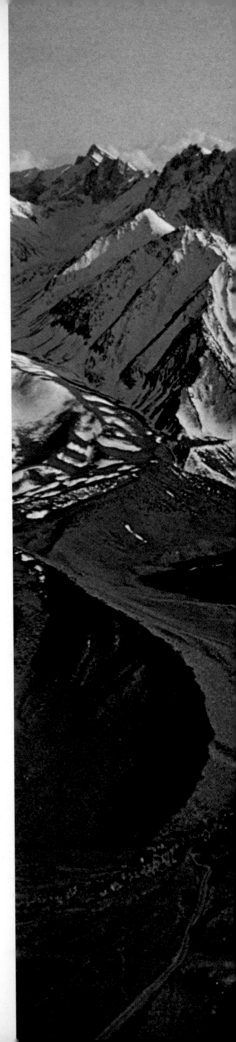

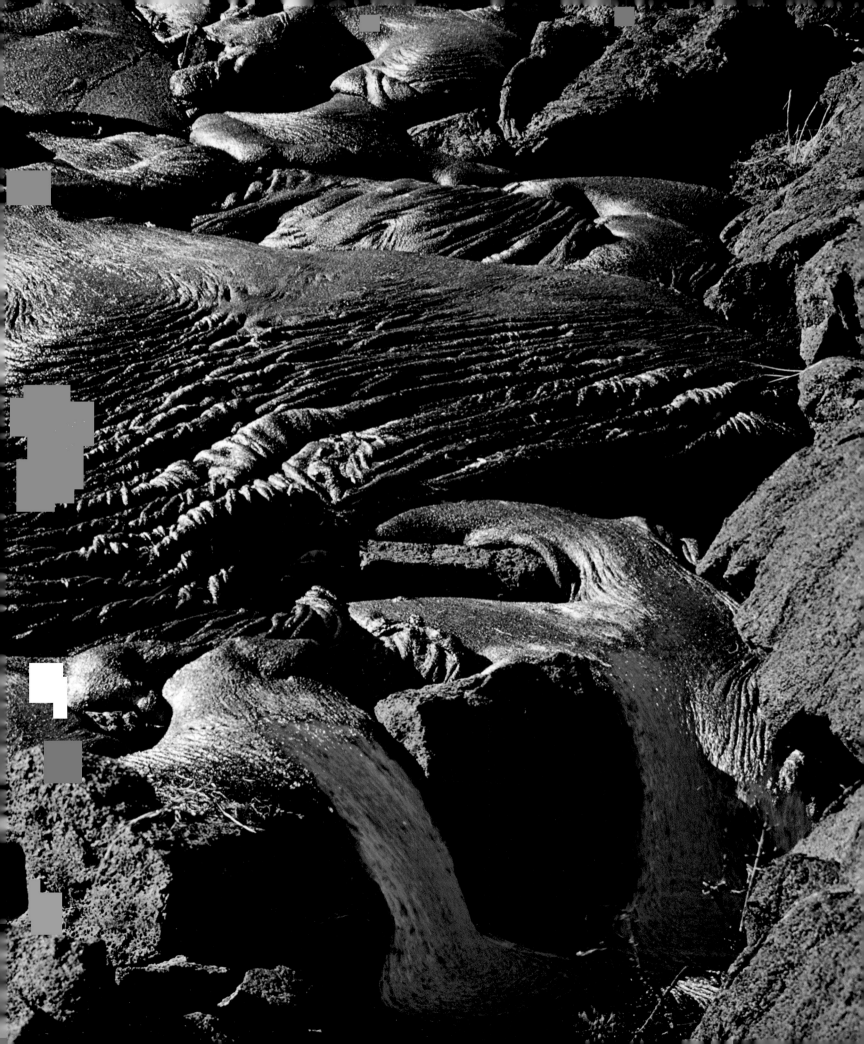

climb above the ocean surface to form such islands as Easter or the Azores group.

Another Columbia scientist, Marie Tharp, called attention to the continuity of a great rift valley along the crest of the ridge. Earthquakes and volcanic activity, earmarks of a restless earth, concentrate at this gash. They focus too beneath enormous trenches found in the seas, and near young and active mountains—forming a "ring of fire" around the Pacific, branching across Himalayan and Alpine regions. Could it be that the earth is splitting along the rift, with material from the depths supplying new floor for the spreading ocean basins? Harry H. Hess of Princeton University and Robert S. Dietz of the U. S. Navy Electronics Laboratory advanced this theory in 1960-61. Since earth's size is finite, new surface must be compensated for elsewhere. Could this take place, the scientists postulated, where mountains pile up and in the deep ocean trenches? Paleomagnetism provided some evidence.

Most people know that some rocks, called lodestones, are natural compasses; few are aware, however, that many rocks become weakly magnetized at the time they are formed—during cooling in the case of lavas and during deposition in the case of sediments. Tiny mineral crystals align themselves with the earth's magnetic field, and thus become permanent indicators of the direction the poles lay when the rocks solidified. Oddly, these poles have often reversed—north has become south and south north at least 170 times in the past 76 million years.

Two British scientists, Frederick J. Vine and Drummond H. Matthews, analyzed the data from hundreds of readings of this magnetism in the rocks on ocean floors. These showed a pattern of zebra-like stripings parallel with the central rift. Vine and Matthews reasoned that if new floor is born where rift valleys spread, the lines on one side—including the record of polar flip-flops—should be a mirror image of those on the other. Rock samples collected from ocean bottoms proved the scientists right.

It was logical to assume that rocks created through sea-floor spreading ought to be progressively older the farther they lie from the mid-ocean ridges. Determining the age of rocks is a technique easy to understand. If a mineral contains a radioactive element, uranium for example, and the rate at which uranium decays into lead is known, then the ratio of lead to uranium in the mineral is a measure of its age. The relationship is a little like sand pouring through an hourglass. Dating rocks gathered from many locations has confirmed the initial supposition: The continents are old and complex, the ocean basins are young and of relatively simple structure.

Further evidence for the drift theory comes from the similarity of fossils found on widely separated continents. Robust, far-ranging creatures such as mammals might have traveled from one place to another by now-drowned land bridges, but the similarities were hard to explain for forms like earthworms, freshwater fishes, land snails, or tropical plants which are killed by sea water or by cold. Then in the late 1960's a discovery in Antarctica shook the geological world.

In gravel deposits on wind-exposed peaks, an expedition found fossilized bones. Edwin H. Colbert, one of the world's foremost authorities on ancient reptiles and

*Red tongues lick from a hellish maw in Hawaii Volcanoes National Park. Lava and its underground duplicate, magma, create one of the three basic categories of earth's crustal rocks. Geologists often call this type "igneous" for its fiery origin.*

*Sedimentary rock like the shales of Utah's Book Cliffs (above) builds through the slow deposits of time— 35 feet in a million years in ocean deeps. Reburied in earth's interior, these layers are changed by heat and pressure to metamorphic rock such as this Death Valley marble.*

ROBERT REYNOLDS. ABOVE AND OPPOSITE: DAVID MUENCH

amphibians, identified them as belonging to a mammal-like reptile called *Lystrosaurus*. An almost toothless, dog-size vegetarian, it lived like a hippopotamus in freshwater swamps from 350 to 200 million years ago. Others of its kind had ranged across South Africa, India, and China. In no way could *Lystrosaurus* have swum the seas between these lands. More Antarctic finds produced added similarities to Africa and India in fossilized bones, skeletal imprints, and plant remains—too broad a variety to have come by chance. The continents must once have been joined.

Thus the theory of crustal drifting called plate tectonics took shape. It pictures the lithosphere as fractured into six major and about a dozen minor plates; on them continents and ocean basins sail—not like Wegener's ships, but more like rafts frozen in sheets of ice. Sluggish convection currents in the interior are thought to drive the plates, rather in the way that the simmering of thick soup shifts scum on the surface. Conveyor-belt fashion, the plates grow at mid-ocean ridges and diminish where they subduct—dip again into the interior. Light continental plates are not dragged down; they tend to override the denser oceanic sheets. Mountains form as friction rumples the overlapping edge, or where two continental masses crush together. Where oceanic plates lap, arcs of islands such as the Aleutians or Philippines rise. As plates subduct or sideslip—they also can move horizontally alongside each other—friction sets earthquake shudders rumbling. Subducted plates melt—to rise as fuel for volcanoes above.

The process appears to have started early in earth's history. Continents began as small blocks which jostled and united, broke apart and reformed again. Gradually they assembled in large masses whose traces we find in the heart of every continent today. Those continents themselves have married and divorced more than once in the past. Fossil finds hint that a proto-Atlantic existed. Beginning some 500 million years ago that ocean slowly closed, and island arcs and undersea shelves were shoved against a continental mass. The collision of land masses raised the mountain range that exists today as the Appalachians and that appears also as the highlands of Scotland and Scandinavia. This united region lay not far from the Equator; swamps spread whose vegetation produced the coal beds of Pennsylvania and those of Great Britain that powered the Industrial Revolution 300 million years later.

About 180 million years ago the present Atlantic began to open, fracturing along a slightly different seam than had the ocean it replaced; bits of Georgia were left in Africa, and pieces of Europe stuck to Canada and New England. By then lava had spewed out to form the Hudson River Palisades. Rift valleys tore open, to become lakes and swamps; their red mud bottoms, now hardened into Connecticut Valley rock, still bear dinosaur footprints. The Great Glen Fault which slices Scotland, cradling Loch Ness and Loch Linnhe, crops up again as a series of cracks from Newfoundland to Massachusetts. There one important fracture has been named, in a geologist's bit of whimsy, for a lake Indians called Chargoggagoggmanchaugagoggchaubunagunga-maug. Scientists call it the Lake Char Fault for short. *(continued on page 47)*

*Tawny ripples footprint the wind in desolate Monument Valley astride the Arizona-Utah border. One of nature's sculpturing tools, wind can sandblast rock strata or move mountains—4,000 tons of soil may ride in a cubic mile of storm; in the 1930's, Colorado farmland blew out into the North Atlantic.*
DAVID MUENCH

PAGES 42-43: *The San Juan River cuts a snow-frosted layer cake in southern Utah. Originally winding atop flat plains, the stream kept its gooseneck meanders as the land uplifted. Biting off loops can isolate buttes or create bridges.*
*Called "liquid conveyor belts," rivers tumble sand, gravel, and rocks as potent forces of erosion.*
DAVID MUENCH

PAGES 44-45: *Filings from craggy flanks lane-stripe the icy highway of Kaskawulsh Glacier in Canada. Where more snow falls than melts in a year, such frigid sheets form. Compaction turns the flakes to hard crystalline ice. Debris, dragged along as moraines, scours the land or drops when the glacier melts to form such drumlins as Bunker Hill or terminal deposits like Long Island.*
DEWITT JONES

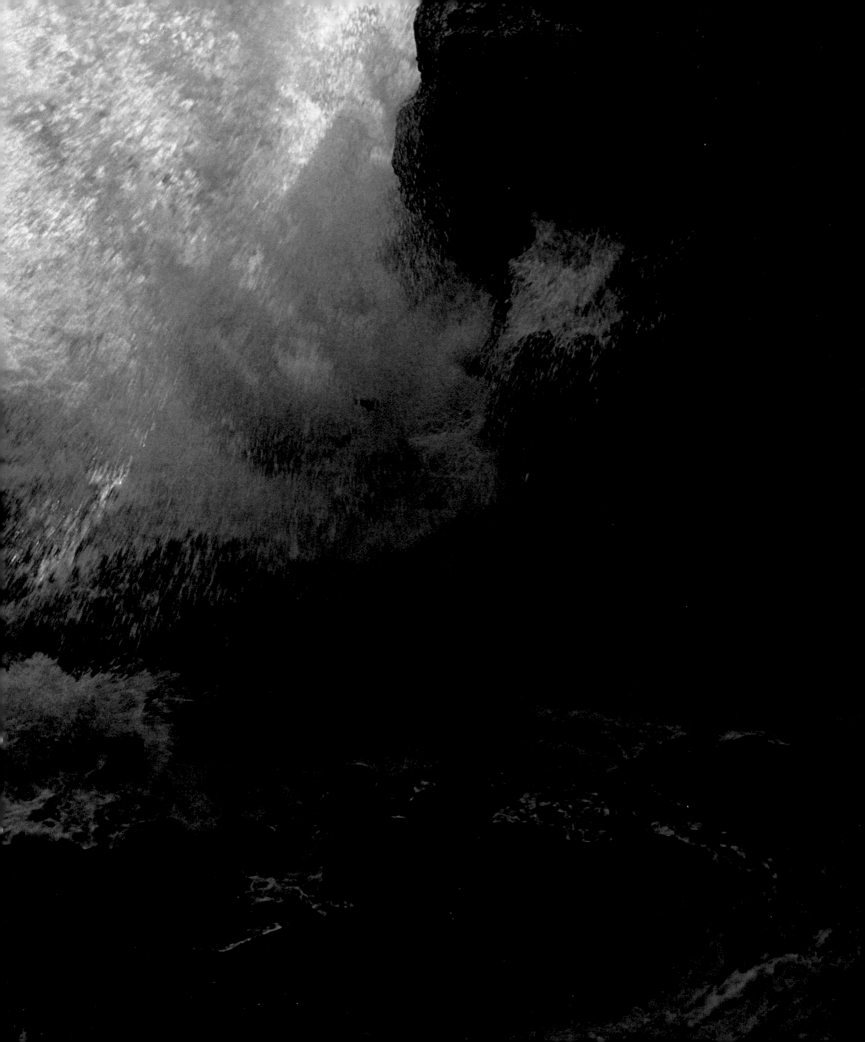

While plate movements have been operating to shape continents, other forces have been active reshaping them. Erosion has been constantly at work—leveling the raw summits of such mountains as the Appalachians, wearing down the rocks of the Canadian Shield. Sediments carried by wind and river filled the Midwestern plains and dropped along the Atlantic Coast. Seas rose to inundate them. The North American plate, moving westward, is thought to have overridden part of the Pacific floor, crumpling up the Sierra Nevada and Coast ranges. Landmarks such as Mount Baker, Lassen Peak, and Crater Lake still hint of volcanic fury below. Some studies suggest that a section of mid-ocean ridge known as the East Pacific Rise, sliding under the continent, may account for the uplift of the Colorado Plateau and the Rockies, and for the geysers and sulphurous pools of Yellowstone National Park.

We can see a new ocean being born today where a tongue of the Pacific separates Baja California from mainland Mexico. A great fracture, alive with volcanic activity at its southern end, continues overland through California as the earthquake-prone San Andreas Fault system. It dips into the sea to skirt Canada and the Alaska panhandle.

Other plate movements buckled up the region tapering from southern Mexico to Panama, forming the land bridge between the two Americas that dammed off waters once flowing freely between Atlantic and Pacific. Some scientists speculate that this interruption of temperature-moderating currents may have changed the weather enough to trigger an ice age. The forces continue: railroad trackbeds in Costa Rica rise an inch or so a year; an earthquake brings death to 22,000 people in Guatemala.

Along young mountain ranges, such as the cordillera that includes the Cascades and the Andes, active volcanoes tend to lie between 60 and 160 miles inland. The reason: At that distance the leading edge of the subducted plate, slanting downward, finally reaches depths hot enough for melting to begin, and magma rises to the surface. In the oceans, other activity raises volcanic islands. They grow where an unusual quantity of lava pours out of a mid-ocean ridge, creating an Iceland or a St. Helena. Or they occur where a chimney-like hot spot, or "plume," spews through a break in the ocean floor. The location of the plume stays fixed, but the plate creeps across it. In time the volcanic island is carried away—to be replaced by another, and then another, like puffs of smoke borne along by the wind passing over a chimney. The Hawaiian Islands are just such an assembly-line archipelago. The youngest, Hawaii at the easternmost end, still has active volcanoes and rocks only a million or two years old. The other islands become progressively older until in the Midway group, at the western end, rocks 25 million years old are found.

Of the many varieties of lava, two are common. Basalts—hard, dense, and dark— occur oftenest where tectonic forces lay down the ocean floors. Andesites—lighter in color and with less iron and more silica than basalt—predominate in areas of subduction and mountain-building. The name comes from the volcanically active Andes. Other lavas include glassy obsidian, spongy pumice whose bubbles of trapped gas make it so light it floats, and rocks formed in wall-like "dikes" or sheet-like "sills" in

*Pitiless teeth of time, waves gnaw a rocky spur on Vancouver Island, British Columbia. Sand and other comber-tossed material aid the abrasion. So does air—compressed into pores and cracks of the rock by the water's surge and exploding outward when the breaker passes. Storms magnify the oceans' power; waves smashing with forces of as much as seven tons per square foot have been known to hurl gigantic boulders over 20-foot seawalls. Thus work the titanic agents ever wearing down—and rebuilding— our never-passive planet.*

cracks beneath the surface. Magmas solidifying in such deep reservoirs cool so slowly their minerals have time to grow into coarse crystals. Granite is an example. Often geologists use the term "igneous"—from the Latin *ignis*, for "fire"—to class lavas and deep-seated rocks that once were molten. Igneous rock is one of the three groups into which traditional geology divides the earth's stony building material. The others are called sedimentary and metamorphic.

Sedimentary rock forms from deposits of sands, clays, and gravels laid down by the action of water, and sometimes by wind or glaciers; plant and animal remains also pile up. Usually these sediments collect in horizontal layers; compaction and chemical change transform them to stone. Sedimentary rocks lay a veneer over more than two-thirds of the earth's surface, with shales, sandstones, and limestones most common.

Metamorphic rocks live up to their name, which comes from the Greek words *meta*, meaning "change," and *morphe*, "form" or "shape." These are pre-existing rocks which writhings and foldings have reburied in the earth. Subjected anew to heat and pressure, they recrystallize and develop coarse grains of new and different minerals. The process can be likened to making a cake. If you stir together some sugar and flour and butter, you can still, with patience, sort out and separate grains of sugar, unchanged. But bake the mixture, and the ingredients combine so that the sugar no longer exists in its old form. Thus it is with metamorphic rock: limestone turns to marble, shale becomes slate, bituminous coal becomes anthracite, and so on. Both kinds of deep-seated rocks—those which formed from liquids while trapped in the depths and those which metamorphosed there—are occasionally classed as "plutonic."

By whatever name, rocks are the backbone stuff of the crust on which we live. Mountain-building and folding of sedimentary layers raise them from deep in the earth or from under the sea. Such forces as faulting—slippage of huge blocks up, down, or sideways along great fractures in the surface—may expose them. So does that relentless conqueror, erosion. Its sculpturing forces include glaciers that grind, rain and rivers that nibble, and weak ground acids that dissolve. Plant roots and ice force rock crevices apart. Wind and wave carve with buffeting might. Gravity flattens. Every boulder that rolls down a hillside, every glacier that slowly creeps, every grain of sand washed by a river down to the sea is being pulled by gravity to lower levels. A 10,000-foot peak that loses two inches of its height in a thousand years disappears at a rate indiscernible in our lifetimes, but will wear flat in 60 million years. This has happened frequently throughout geologic time.

Yes, the age of the earth is vast, and there are more eons for its sculpturing—and reshaping—than our short lives can imagine. The forces that mold its face have been so uniform for billions of years that we can expect them to shape it for billions more to come. Though they may be cataclysmic and destructive—resulting in continents that split, mountains that erupt, oceans that appear and disappear in slow motion—we must esteem them. For this is what has made our planet habitable, what has fitted it for the procession of life of which we are an inquisitive, late-coming part.

48

# The Kingdoms of Life

Like the story of the changing land, the history of the procession of life is written in the rocks, in precious fragments called fossils. Seeking to classify and name them, scientists adopted the convention devised by the Swedish naturalist Linnaeus two centuries ago—a system which assigns to each species a unique, two-part, Latinized name. Thus, in place of a babel of common names —*chien, hund, cane, perro*, dog—the universal language of science establishes but one, *Canis familiaris*, signifying genus and species. In a saga spanning some three billion years, encompassing unfamiliar life forms never named in popular tongues, the scientific name —hard for the layman to pronounce, even harder to remember—is usually the only one.

Scientists using the Linnaean system traditionally divide the realm of life into plant and animal kingdoms (though the distinction blurs with fungi and single-celled organisms). By subdividing each kingdom into successively smaller categories, such as phylum, class, order, and family, the system seeks to reflect degrees of kinship between groups of species, and to isolate features that make each species unique. In the animal kingdom *Homo sapiens* ("Man the wise"), a backboned creature, belongs to the phylum Chordata. Humans are in the class Mammalia because they are warm-blooded, have hair, and suckle their young. Complex brains, stereoscopic vision, and hands adapted for grasping place them in the primate order. The family Hominidae distinguishes humans and man-like ancestors from apes. At the genus and species levels, man is the only living large-brained organism that walks erect on two feet and can communicate through speech.

Fossils reveal not only what lived in the past, but also how living things changed across the span of geologic time. The evidence has been preserved in various ways. Minerals seeping in groundwater may petrify woody plants and animal bones or shells, turning them to stone. A shell may leave only its shape in a mold or cast. Or, in the process of distillation, the pressure of overlying sediments, coupled with decomposition, alters tissues, leaving a flat carbon residue—a carbon copy. Amber, a fossil resin, may preserve insects. Larger animals can become mummified in dry caves, frozen in icy wastes, or mired in peat bogs whose acid waters retard decay. Tracks, burrows, even dung, have been fossilized. But animals with hard parts and plants with woody stems are the most likely to become fossils. One scientist estimates that ten million such species may be preserved in the rocks. Perhaps a hundred thousand, or one percent, are known to science. In the history of life, many a volume remains to be read.

# The Procession Begins

Stephen Jay Gould

The early earth would have appeared to us as a singularly inhospitable place. Fiery gases flared from volcanoes pocking the young surface. Lava seared the land and scalded the sea. Lightning etched the sky. But, within the cauldron of the sea, simple molecules composed of four common elements—hydrogen, carbon, oxygen, and nitrogen—combined randomly to form ever more complex organic molecules. The originally sterile sea became an organic broth of amino acids, nucleic acids, carbohydrates—the brew from which all living things evolved.

We think this may be the way life started. Though we have little evidence of what went on billions of years ago, we do know what happened in 1953 within an apparatus set up by Stanley L. Miller, a University of Chicago graduate student. He passed steam through a mixture of methane, ammonia, and hydrogen. Then he struck the gases with "lightning"—a high-energy electrical spark. He condensed the steam to water and recycled it. And in the water he found amino acids.

Chemical evolution did not happen that simply. As biologist Norman H. Horowitz later pointed out, "The duration of this experiment was only a week. Nature had a couple of billion years and all the oceans in which to carry out the experiments, instead of a 500 cc. flask." Given that couple of billion years, "something as complicated as a protein molecule or a nucleic acid molecule could have been generated spontaneously by a random chemical combination."

When did this happen? We don't know. The earth, we believe, is about 4.6 billion years old, and the oldest fossils on record are remnants of simple bacteria and blue-green algae from rocks about 3 billion years old in the Transvaal of Africa. This earliest known evidence of life emerges from the Precambrian, which represents seven-eighths of all time since the formation of earth's crust. So our search for the beginnings of life must start in that immense span. And our search cannot be restricted to North America. The insights of plate tectonics have taught us that continents move, fuse, and separate. To avoid a parochial focus on a single piece of real estate that did not include all the events of note, I will try to place North American happenings in the context of earth history.

Geologists believe that the earth's atmosphere formed primarily by the emanation of volatile material from the earth's interior—typically, in volcanic eruptions. By studying the chemical composition of what wells out of the earth today, we can get an idea of what made up the atmosphere before life evolved. The studies show that the Precambrian atmosphere had little or no free oxygen. This means that the first living things could not have stayed alive by respiration. But organisms that did not need to breathe could have survived—as bacteria do by the process of fermentation, or as algae do by using sunlight in photosynthesis.

Scientists theorized that traces of such organisms would be found in Precambrian rock, though the record was nearly blank. Searchers puzzled over reeflike structures of calcium carbonate or silica occasionally found in layers or mats in Precambrian limestone. Some authorities speculated that these stromatolites, as they were called, had been formed by algae. The issue was in doubt until 1954, when Stanley A. Tyler,

*Thunderbolts tread a watery stage, conjuring up what may have been the opening scene in the drama of life. The theory has lightning pour energy into a primeval sea rich in carbon-linked elements. Amino acids, building blocks of life, form.... Proteins develop and eventually join.... Finally, ever to reproduce, the cell is born.*
JOHN F. DEEKS

a University of Wisconsin geologist, and Elso S. Barghoorn, a Harvard paleobotanist, discovered Precambrian fossils in rocks known as the Gunflint Iron Formation. The fossils were in black chert—a flintlike rock composed of fine-grained silica that was found in outcrops along the shore of Lake Superior. Studies determined that the age of the fossil-bearing rock was about 2 billion years.

Dr. Barghoorn identified the microfossils as remains of the most primitive group of algae—the blue-greens, which still daub the earth. Most were three-dimensional "and many show exquisite anatomical details," he reported. He believed that the fossils, suspended in a solution that crystallized into chert, were preserved "much as a modern biological specimen is preserved by being embedded in plastic."

One group was named *Eoastrion*—dawn star—to signify the age and typical shape of those fossils. Most of the Gunflint finds were filaments 0.6 microns to 1.6 microns in diameter. (A micron equals one-thousandth of a millimeter or about 39 millionths of an inch.) Dr. Barghoorn said these filamentous organisms resembled present-day blue-green algae and iron-oxidizing bacteria.

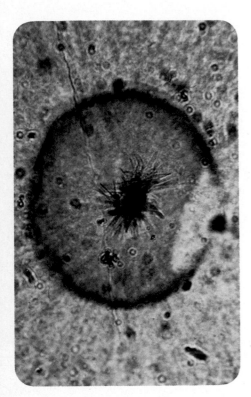

*A lion's mane jellyfish displays the filmy beauty that enhances a dark sea but makes no impression on time. Though ancient, jellyfish have left a scant record. Their bodies, lacking hard parts, rarely appear in fossils. Equally rare are hints of Precambrian life, such as this fossil colony of blue-green algae, enlarged 875 times. This relict from the Gunflint Chert is kin to algae we see—and smell—in stagnant water. Blue-green algae may be the ancestors of all multicellular organisms.*

ELSO S. BARGHOORN. OPPOSITE: WILLIAM R. CURTSINGER

As animals we may have trouble believing life goes back to forms so primitive that they can be designated as neither animals nor plants. Aren't all organisms either animals or plants? Probably not. A far more basic difference is spelled out by two words—procaryote and eucaryote—whose common syllable, *caryo* (from the Greek for "kernel"), refers to the nucleus of a plant or animal cell. Procaryotes (roughly, "before nuclei") include bacteria and blue-green algae. Their cells lack structures we call organelles. Besides having no nucleus, a procaryote has no separate chromosomes, carriers of genetic information. All other plant and animal cells have organelles and are called eucaryotes ("with a true nucleus").

With the eucaryotic cell came sex. Efficient sexual reproduction requires that hereditary material be packaged into chromosomes. Such packaging permits the evolution of a mechanism for producing a sex cell—an egg or sperm—with half the genetic material of a normal cell. Chromosomes come in pairs, and each sex cell contains one member of each pair. The fusing of two sex cells restores the original amount of genetic material, and sexual reproduction is accomplished.

There is a significant biological difference between reproduction and sex. Reproduction keeps a species in existence. In terms of speed and number of progeny, no system is more efficient than the one used by bacteria; they reproduce simply by splitting apart. In such asexual organisms, an offspring is exactly like its parent, unless a mutation occurs. But mutations are rare—and evolution is thus limited. The function of sex is to mix the genetic material of two individuals, thereby increasing variations in their offspring. Parent and offspring are never exactly the same. Such variability is the raw material of evolution; without it, natural selection has nothing to choose from and evolution cannot occur.

We do not know how or when the originators of sex first appeared. The earliest undoubted eucaryotes are part of a rich fauna—worms, jellyfish, soft corals—in

Early life, cradled by the sea,
burgeons in a myriad of forms about
550 million years ago, midway in the
Cambrian Period. Jellyfish swim
over strands of algae, a meadow
for primeval vegetarians.
Sponges passively eat their meals:
food particles borne by water that
is drawn through their self-anchored
bodies. Trilobites scuttle across
the seabed, jawless mouths plowing
up organic debris. Their carapaces
are shed as they grow.

The jellyfish form persisted,
as did the sponges' meshwork design
and skeleton of silica — still
found in glass sponges. Trilobites
live on in a detailed, extensive
fossil record. It ticks off
geologic chronology and provides
insights into an evolutionary saga
that spans the Paleozoic Era. Fossil
hunters once puzzled over these
"petrified butterflies" and named
one group "paradoxical animal."
Now Paradoxides (foreground), found
in western Europe and on the east
coast of North America, helps
prove the continents drifted apart.

PAINTING BY ZDENEK BURIAN

57

Australian rocks of late Precambrian age. As recently as one billion years ago there may have been no eucaryotic organisms. The existence of so many different ones a mere 300 million or so years later leaves us with another question: How could evolution have proceeded so quickly? (We must remember that one million years is a geologic instant; a few hundred million in this context is not a long time.)

There is precious little evidence for any complex life before the very end of the Precambrian. Then, beginning about 600 million years ago, as suddenly as the name of the event implies, came the Cambrian "explosion." In a rapid burst of evolution, animals with hard parts began replacing simple, soft-bodied organisms. Within a short span of a few million years most invertebrate groups had appeared.

Why did it happen? Perhaps the answer is that it could have happened earlier, but it just didn't. Or perhaps we can turn to ecology, which in its scientifically restricted sense is the study of animal and plant diversity. Steven M. Stanley of Johns Hopkins University has suggested that an ecological theory—the "cropping principle"—may provide the answer. A "cropper" gobbles up the food in a given area. Ecologists have discovered, contrary to most people's intuition, that the introduction of plant-eating croppers into a previously uncropped area increases rather than decreases the number of plant species in that flora.

A cropper tends to eat the most abundant food, thus freeing space for other species that otherwise would not be able to compete. A well-adapted cropper will decimate—but never destroy—its source of food, for destruction could mean starvation. Diversity rapidly begets more diversity as new herbivores evolve to exploit the different kinds of plants that become available. And carnivores evolve to feed upon the herbivores. The mats of algae formed in Precambrian times may well have been an uncropped, uniform ecosystem. One step—the evolution of an efficient single-celled plant-eater— might have started a chain of events: the swift, widespread, self-intensifying biology of diversity that took life beyond algae.

A major product of the Cambrian explosion was the trilobite, whose remains make up about 70 percent of the period's fossil record. The creature—named for its three-lobed body form—evolved into thousands of species: Some walked, some burrowed, and some swam; some had compound eyes and some were blind. Most were only an inch or two long. The largest, about 18 inches long and weighing some ten pounds, was the biggest animal that we know from Cambrian times.

Trilobites abound in a North American formation known as the Burgess Shale and called by some a window on the Cambrian Age. In this great array, however, trilobites take second billing to fossils of soft-bodied invertebrates—rare and precious pieces in the puzzle of life. Skeletonized animals make up more than 99 percent of the fossil record; few deposits preserve the soft parts of animals. But in this shale (named for Burgess Pass at Mount Wapta in the Canadian Rockies) such delicate marine organisms as jellyfish are preserved. Hydrogen sulfide, produced by decaying organic matter, may have poisoned the animals, whose bodies then drifted down into the

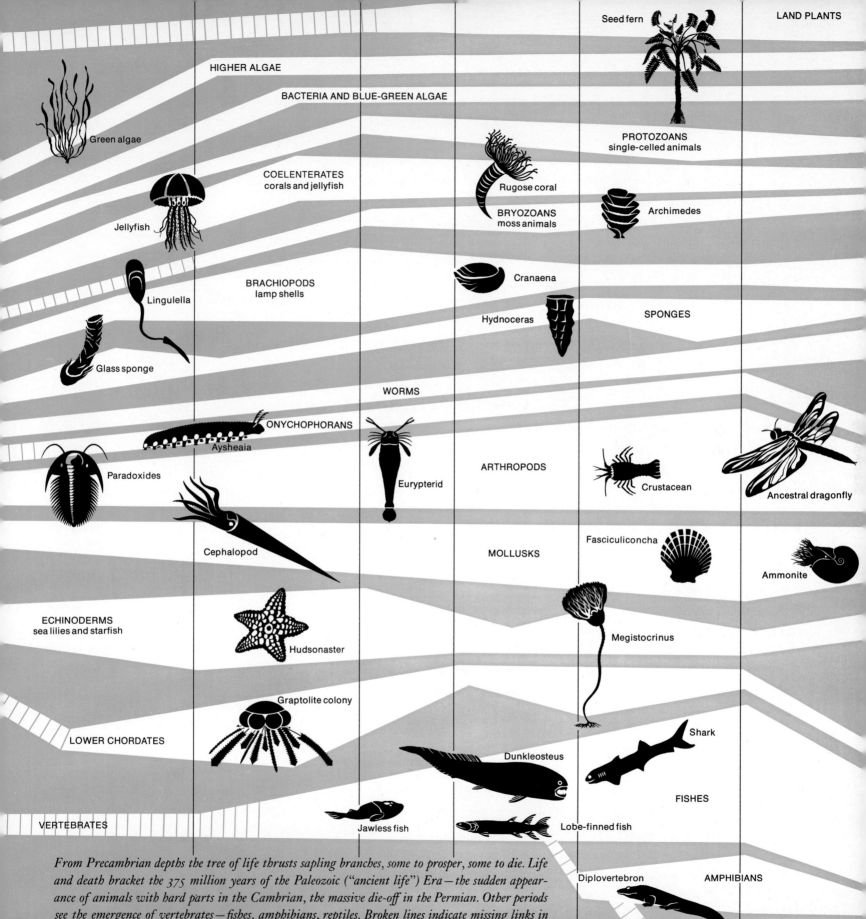

Seed fern          LAND PLANTS

HIGHER ALGAE

BACTERIA AND BLUE-GREEN ALGAE

Green algae

PROTOZOANS
single-celled animals

COELENTERATES
corals and jellyfish

Rugose coral

BRYOZOANS          Archimedes
moss animals

Jellyfish

Lingulella

BRACHIOPODS          Cranaena
lamp shells

SPONGES

Hydnoceras

Glass sponge

WORMS

ONYCHOPHORANS

Aysheaia

ARTHROPODS

Paradoxides          Eurypterid          Crustacean          Ancestral dragonfly

Fasciculiconcha

MOLLUSKS

Cephalopod          Ammonite

ECHINODERMS
sea lilies and starfish

Megistocrinus

Hudsonaster

Graptolite colony

LOWER CHORDATES          Shark

Dunkleosteus

FISHES

VERTEBRATES          Jawless fish          Lobe-finned fish

*From Precambrian depths the tree of life thrusts sapling branches, some to prosper, some to die. Life
and death bracket the 375 million years of the Paleozoic ("ancient life") Era — the sudden appearance of animals with hard parts in the Cambrian, the massive die-off in the Permian. Other periods
see the emergence of vertebrates — fishes, amphibians, reptiles. Broken lines indicate missing links in
the fossil record; the branches' widths mark the variety and abundance of species within groups.*

Diplovertebron          AMPHIBIANS

DRAWINGS BY LISA BIGANZOLI. SIZES NOT TO SCALE.

REPTILES

CAMBRIAN          ORDOVICIAN          SILURIAN          DEVONIAN          CARBONIFEROUS          PERMIAN

ooze; scavengers would not have been drawn to the poisonous waters. And so the animals would have been entombed intact.

One fossil—a member of the Onychophora, which means "claw-bearers"—typifies the kind of insight that the Burgess window provided. Living onychophorans are a peculiar group of soft-bodied animals halfway between segmented worms and arthropods—that vast group which includes insects, spiders, and crustaceans. The strange onychophorans, too obscure to be known by common names, have the velvety skin of a caterpillar and the claw-bearing legs of an arthropod—all jutting from a wormlike body. Were it not for the Burgess finds, we would have no record of the modern animals' fossil ancestors. Of 130 or so species in the shale a few are more puzzling; they neither resemble modern creatures nor seem to belong to any known fossil group.

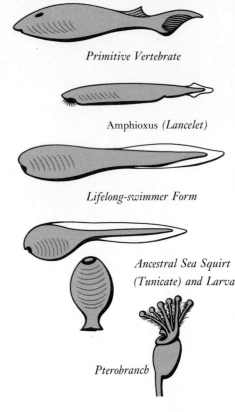

*Primitive Vertebrate*

*Amphioxus (Lancelet)*

*Lifelong-swimmer Form*

*Ancestral Sea Squirt (Tunicate) and Larva*

*Pterobranch*

Passing from the Cambrian to the Ordovician Period, the second of the six divisions of the Paleozoic Era, we find the sea dominated by two animal groups still with us today. Bryozoans, creatures of various shapes ranging from thick stems to clumps to fans that often form in mosslike colonies, flourished in the Paleozoic and remain abundant in species and numbers. The second group, the brachiopods, are often called "lamp shells"—for the shells of some resemble ancient Roman lamps, complete with wick hole. So thick in some deposits that their fossils make up most of the rock, they have dropped off from about 30,000 species to some 200 known today. Members of one hardy genus, *Lingula*, dwell in mudflats around the world. They are almost identical to their Cambrian ancestors.

The lamp shells and "moss animals" abounded in the placid shallows. Upon deeper Ordovician waters floated tiny organisms whose fossil imprint on rock looks like pencil marks; we call them graptolites—writing on stone. From these tracings we deduce that the graptolites lived in colonies, probably on stems attached to a float. They are related to distant ancestors of backboned animals.

In the Ordovician seas we also find cephalopods, whose name ("head-foot") suggests the animal's appearance: Its head was seemingly enwrapped by tentacles. The body protruded from a tapering shell. The big-eyed creature propelled itself by expelling jets of water. Most highly developed of all mollusks, the cephalopods have produced about 10,000 species. The 400 living today include squids and octopuses.

From New York to Michigan can be found remnants of complex reefs formed in the next period, the Silurian, which began 430 million years ago. The reefs consist primarily of corals and remains of creatures seemingly akin to sponges. Scorpion-like giants called eurypterids, some of them ten feet long, reigned in Silurian waters. They may have preyed upon small bottom-dwellers that are generally considered the oldest vertebrates. These are the ostracoderms. They had no internal bones, but were covered with bony plates; scientific speculation suggests that the hard covering developed as a kind of defensive armor.

Did the coming of vertebrate animals—our early ancestors—represent progress? Most people would say yes. But progress is not an inherent feature of Darwinian

*The past shows its face in the gape of a Great Lakes sea lamprey. Early, fishlike vertebrates also lacked jaws. But the toothy, suction-cup mouth—for attaching to fishes and draining their blood—is a modern accessory on an ancient model.*

*Three other living creatures— the pterobranch, sea squirt, and lancelet—show a possible underwater path to vertebrates. The plantlike pterobranch stays put, feeding via waving arms. The sea squirt feeds with gills and may begin life as a larva that swims, then plants itself. An ancestral form may have kept on swimming, its progeny evolving into primitive backboned creatures and a jawless, eyeless, brainless—but promising—animal that inspired an evolutionary ditty: "Good-bye fins and gill slits, Welcome teeth and hair; It's a long . . . way from Amphioxus, But we came from there."*

DIAGRAM BY LISA BIGANZOLI. OPPOSITE: JAMES L. AMOS, NATIONAL GEOGRAPHIC PHOTOGRAPHER

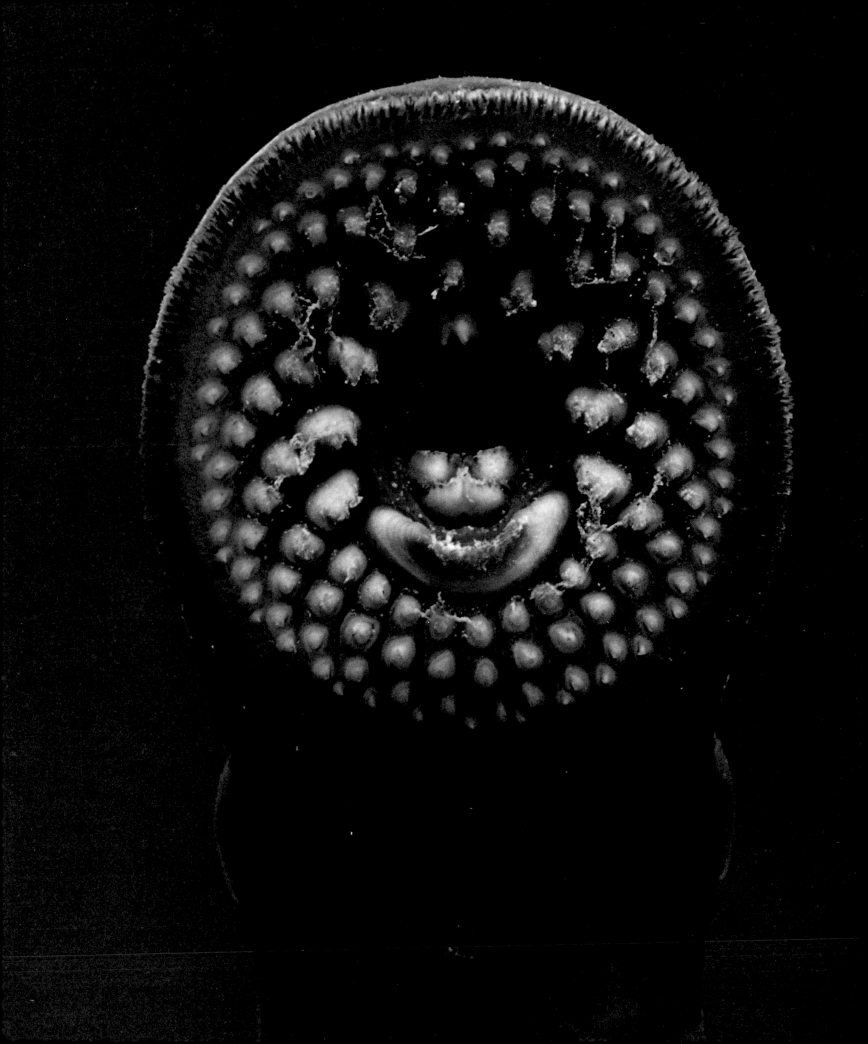

*At the premiere of jaws, the victim was the shark: Mouth agape, eyes on target, an 8-foot* Dunkleosteus *attacks a fleeing* Cladoselache, *one of the first sharks found in the fossil record. The predator, biggest and best-armed vertebrate in Devonian waters, is a placoderm, a type of fish that introduced both paired fins and jaws.* Dunkleosteus *had a head armored in bony plates; its serrated jaw, though toothless, sheared victims with a scissorlike cutting edge. By the end of the Paleozoic, the placoderms were extinct.*

*Cladoselache would also vanish. But with teeth and a skeleton of cartilage, it foreshadowed the lasting form of the shark, which would become the prime predator of the sea. With its kin, the skates and rays, it radiated into hundreds of species. Today's most fearsome, the great white, is related to a giant that prowled the continent's inland seas 18 million years ago. Its fossil teeth, nearly 6 inches high, would fit a 50-foot shark.*

PAINTING BY ZDENEK BURIAN

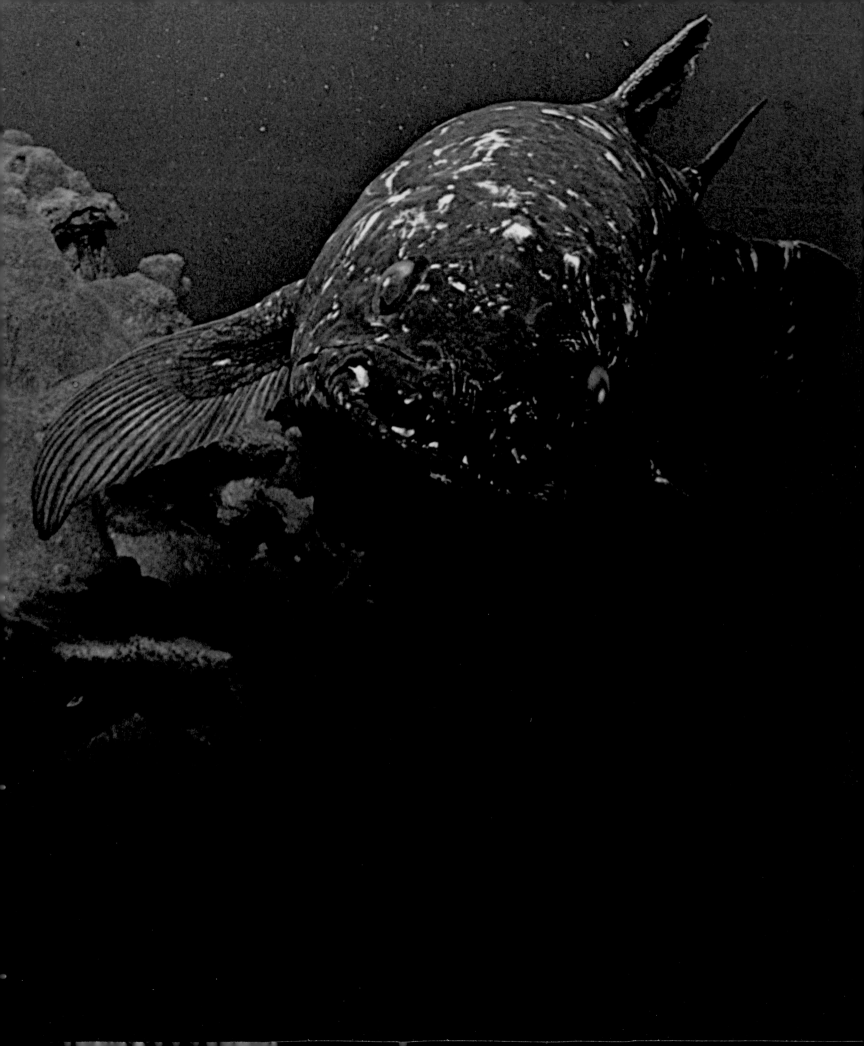

theory. Evolution means change only. In the panorama of Paleozoic life we tend to focus on backboned animals. Yet they include only a tiny fraction of the fossil record —which is essentially a story of marine invertebrates and their adaptation to changing local environments. The basic design for most invertebrate groups appeared early in the era, and for most of the Paleozoic not much happened in the way of new appearances within the established groups. I do not deny that what we may call progress often characterizes the history of particular groups. Animals may adapt by improving their general design (becoming warm-blooded, for example) rather than by specializing (developing webbed feet). If these general improvements accumulate over time, we may choose to speak of progress. Still, nothing in evolution guarantees progress.

The first well-documented vertebrate fossils—bony fragments of early jawless fishes—come from Colorado sandstone about 450 million years old. But the triumph of the vertebrate gets underway about 395 million years ago in the Devonian Period, the Age of Fishes. The origins of vertebrates are still largely a mystery to us. About the best we can do is point to the uncanny resemblance between larvae of two primitive groups: starfish and certain other echinoderms, and animals known as lower chordates. (Along the back of a vertebrate embryo runs a rod of cells called the notochord. As the animal grows, the notochord usually disappears and is replaced by that hallmark of vertebrates, the backbone. Some lower chordates, however, never outgrow their notochords.) A relationship between the starfish's family and vertebrates seems likely, but we do not know who was ancestral to what.

Our classification of vertebrates into fishes, amphibians, reptiles, birds, and mammals does not give us an appreciation of how varied is the design of fishes. Five classes of fishes had evolved by Devonian times: the jawless fishes (Agnatha), represented today only by the parasitic lampreys and hagfishes; the jawed armored fishes (Placodermi) and the spiny "sharks" (Acanthodii), both extinct; the true sharks, skates, and rays (Chondrichthyes); and the bony fishes (Osteichthyes).

A large and varied group make up the first fishes of the fossil record. All of them are jawless. Armored fishes with jaws and spiny "sharks" make their debut in the Silurian; sharks and early bony fishes are first found in Devonian rocks. Shales around Cleveland have yielded the amazingly detailed remains of the early shark *Cladoselache*. The shales preserve bodies—some as long as two feet—complete with a skeleton of cartilage, teeth, and impressions of the skin, muscles, and kidneys.

The evolution of jaws, the key innovation in early vertebrate history, established the basic design for all backboned animals that followed. We have no fossil evidence for the

*Through the murk of sea and time looms a coelacanth, living link in the evolutionary chain that hauled animals to land. Thought extinct until its scientific debut in 1939, the rare Indian Ocean fish was dubbed "Old Fourlegs" because its paddle-shaped fins—boned, muscular, and more flexible than ray fins—prefigured the limbs of land animals. An ancestral relative (below) shows within its lobed fins the skeletal form that evolved into the stubby limbs of an early amphibian (lower)—and ultimately into arms and legs.*

event, but comparative anatomy clearly indicates the path of transition. Our jaw is, anatomically, a modified gill arch, the V-shaped structure in fish that supports their gills. The "V" points toward the rear of the fish and is composed of several elongated bones. By their design the bones were admirably, if accidentally, "preadapted" to move forward and evolve into the vertebrate jaw. By similarly remarkable changes in function, reptilian jaw bones became mammalian ear bones, and the fish's swim bladder, used as an aid in maintaining buoyancy, evolved from the organ that would give vertebrates a lease on land—the lung.

But vertebrate pioneers were not the first inhabitants of land. The path already had been blazed. Indeed, if the land had been barren, it is hard to imagine what would have inspired a fish to crawl out of the water. Fossil evidence indicates that plants and arthropods had migrated to land by late Silurian times. The earliest land plants conducted food and water through what was hardly more than a bundle of tubes. The plants had no true roots, or leaves. But mats of green began to spread on moist soils; by the Devonian small plants were sprouting in abundance.

Not until a flash flood exposed fossil "tree stumps" in the Catskill Mountains of New York State in the 1860's did we realize how big those Devonian plants could become. Later, diggers for a dam there revealed more stumps, earth's first known forest: a landscape of trees, some of them probably 30 feet tall, their tapered trunks crowned by long, green, leaflike fronds.

The greening of North America in the period that followed, the Carboniferous, produced lush swamps that left a legacy: coal, which underlies all but a few U.S. states. In the Carboniferous, invertebrates flourished on land and in shark-prowled waters. (The petroleum industry has relied upon tiny marine animals of this time—single-celled protozoans with shells resembling wheat grains in size and shape—as index fossils for potential oil deposits.)

Arthropods—highly adaptable creatures with external skeletons and jointed limbs—had invaded the land long before vertebrates arrived to eat them. Among the new arrivals were insects, which probably arose in the Devonian. By the latter half of the Carboniferous, about 300 million years ago, the forests teemed with cockroaches four inches long and predatory ancestral dragonflies. The spread of arthropods continued through all eras, filling virtually every niche where life could be sustained: the crabs, crayfishes, lobsters, and shrimps of the sea; the air-breathers, such as spiders, mites, and ticks; and some 800,000 species of insects with us today. Counting all their classes, arthropods make up about 75 percent of the animal kingdom.

To find our place in that kingdom, we must look to the fishes. The class that includes fishes with bones (not cartilage, as in sharks) is divided into two major subsections: "ray-finned" fishes, which include most modern ones, and "fleshy-finned" fishes, which include lungfishes and the coelacanth—the fish that won fame as a living fossil. It was believed to have been extinct for about 70 million years until a South African trawler netted one in 1938 and it was shown to a museum curator. The

*Heir of a Carboniferous earth, Diplovertebron stands on two thresholds: water and land, fish and reptile. This early amphibian still feeds in its ancestral home, but walks on five-fingered limbs. Such steps soon changed species' life-support systems: Obsolete gill openings in the skull became sites for eardrums; water-pumping muscles switched to air-gulping— respiration amphibians still use.*

*In a pantomime of the past, a walking catfish hobbles on fins to scuttle to water. Similar treks in Devonian droughts may have put gasping fish on the amphibian road.*

ROBERT F. SISSON, NATIONAL GEOGRAPHIC PHOTOGRAPHER.
OPPOSITE: PAINTING BY ZDENEK BURIAN.

The forest primeval, crowding a shallow lake, flourishes in the long, moist Carboniferous. At death, plants will become deposits banked in earth—to yield dividends of coal. Delicate leaves crown a seed fern, an early seed-bearer, which stands in a tangle of climbing ferns and rotting trunks. (A tip of a seed fern's frond, dropped 300 million years ago, is preserved in this coal-bed fossil from Illinois.) Branches with lush leaves spiral up a tall Cordaites, relative of conifers. Tree-like club mosses, with crescent tops and scarred trunks, soar on the lake's far shore; some towered 100 feet. An ancestral dragonfly, one of the oldest flying insects, courses on 28-inch wings in a hunt for prey.

PAINTING BY ZDENEK BURIAN. FOSSIL FROM
PEABODY MUSEUM, YALE UNIVERSITY; FRITZ GORO

discovery excited scientists not only because of the fish's antiquity but also because the coelacanth is the closest living relative to the truly extinct "lobe-finned" fishes that evolved into land creatures—and, eventually, into us.

The fleshy-finned, always a small group among bony fishes, numbered in their ranks a minor assemblage of our lobe-finned ancestors. They were called the Crossopterygii, fishes with paired fins structurally unlike those of ray-finned fishes. Each fin, attached to the body by a shoulder girdle, had bones around a strong central axis. Such features had evolved only as favorable adaptations to water. Lungs offered a chance for supplementary breathing—gulping air at the surface of an oxygen-depleted pond, say. The fins probably helped in getting about on the bottom of the pond. But the adaptations turned out to be beautifully suited for transformation of a water creature to a land animal. The strong axis of bones in the lobe-fin became the basis for the major bones of our own limbs. The numerous thin rays of the ray-finned fishes could not efficiently support an animal's weight on land.

Danish explorations in late Devonian rocks of eastern Greenland in 1932 turned up the bones of the earliest known backboned animal with terrestrial adaptations. The discovery was not much of a land animal, a fact scientifically indicated by the "fish" in its name, *Ichthyostega*. The creature must have spent most of its time in the water, as the persistent tail fin on its three-foot-long body testified. It also possessed a lateral-line system, a network of nerves that serves as an "auditory" sense for detecting sound waves by the motions they induce in water.

The transition from water to land did not primarily involve a new way of breathing, for the lobe-finned ancestors of amphibians already possessed lungs. Nor did the migration to land free animals from their dependence on water, for amphibians still had to maintain a moist skin and needed to return to the water to lay eggs. But the transition did involve a remarkable reorganization of basic designs in locomotion. A fish propels itself with its tail fin and balances with its paired appendages. The amphibian balances with its tail and moves with its limbs.

Amphibians diversified during Carboniferous times, and a small group soon evolved

*One trapped in time, the other in a deadly flower, two insects bespeak the perils of their class. But they belong to a vast and hardy band that acquired an advantage— wings. In the air 100 million years before reptile or bird, they found a lasting niche; the vast majority of insects are winged. With one pair, this fly in amber—fossilized pine resin—is a type more modern than the four-winged damselfly snared by a sundew, a carnivorous plant.*
FRANK M. CARPENTER. OPPOSITE: E. R. DEGGINGER

into reptiles. The sail-backed pelycosaurs (pages 76-77)—as forerunners of mammal-like reptiles, our ultimate ancestors—roamed the lowlands of Texas in Permian times.

Meanwhile, back in the water, a great and mysterious extinction had begun to speed up. By the end of the Paleozoic, about 225 million years ago, at least half the families of marine invertebrates vanished in the short span of a few million years. The death toll included all trilobites and most bryozoans and brachiopods.

I believe that modern geology's theory of plate tectonics has solved at least partially the mystery of that massive extinction. In the late Permian all the continents came together to form the single supercontinent of Pangaea. For marine organisms, the consequences of such a union were profound and negative.

Previously isolated faunas came into contact and had to compete for the same resources, making widespread extinctions inevitable. The suturing of the continents eliminated shallow seas that had existed along the edges of the land masses. The sea level around Pangaea fell, drained off shallows around the edge of the supercontinent, and probably exposed the continental shelf. Thus did much of the favored environment for marine life vanish. The earth's climate may also have changed drastically. We do not know what complex combination of factors, inspired by the creation of Pangaea, actually caused the extinction. But it seems reasonable that the suturing itself was a primary cause of the great dying.

The Permian seas of Texas had teemed with one of the richest assemblages of Paleozoic life: brachiopods, massive sponges, great colonies of bryozoans, and coil-shelled predators that survive as the beautiful fossils we call ammonites. They had flourished for ages, yet most of these animals were gone when the Paleozoic curtain came down. The end of my story records a decimated world. But the seeds of rebirth had not died. The survivors found a world with ecological opportunities unmatched since Precambrian times. Life bounced back. And here we are.

---

*Amphibian life, as old as the Paleozoic, still thrives, as with these North American salamanders—though predators may find a paradise in the hatchery of water-borne eggs. With reptiles came the hard shell.*
EGGS OF AMBYSTOMA GRACILE (NORTHWESTERN SALAMANDER), 1/8 INCH; PAUL A. ZAHL.

AMBYSTOMA MACULATUM (SPOTTED SALAMANDER), 6 3/4 INCHES; ROBERT S. SIMMONS

# When Reptiles Ruled

Edwin H. Colbert

Near the mining town of Joggins, Nova Scotia, where 50-foot Bay of Fundy tides lap the cliff-rimmed shore, tree trunks have *stood* for some 300 million years. These upright trunks, known to local coal miners as "pots," are the remains of primitive scale trees and huge club mosses that grew in low, lush swamps—in those ancient days Nova Scotia lay near the Equator. When the trees died, mud piled around, holding them upright. Rot hollowed the trunks; animals crept or fell into them, were trapped, and died. Mud washed into the hollow trunks, entombing the skeletons. As time passed, trees and bones fossilized, and mud hardened into shale. Among the trapped animals was a slender, agile creature, about two feet long, which we call *Hylonomus.* It is perhaps the oldest reptile known.

The little reptile represented a minority group. When it was alive, far back in Carboniferous times, amphibians still generally dominated the continents. They were numerous and varied, some rather large, so *Hylonomus* and its reptilian relatives had to elbow their way through hosts of unfriendly creatures in order to establish themselves in restricted territorial enclaves.

But successful as the amphibians were (and as their many frog and salamander descendants still are), they had their limitations—principally the fact that they had to seek out water, or at least moist places, to reproduce. They laid unprotected eggs which were constantly bathed in watery surroundings. From these eggs were hatched little tadpoles which eventually lost their gills, sprouted legs, and came out of the water. The amphibian life cycle involved metamorphosis from a fishlike creature to a four-legged animal able to venture on land.

For *Hylonomus* no such metamorphosis was necessary. For this animal a new way of reproducing its kind had evolved. It laid an egg protected by a shell, and containing a fluid that formed a private little pond within which the embryo developed. And when the newborn reptile broke out of its dark crypt, it emerged as a tiny replica of its parents, ready to seek its living in a strange and hostile world.

Here indeed was a revolution in the history of life. No longer did land animals have to depend on ponds or streams or moist environments to continue the species. They were free to roam across the landscapes, low and high, and their eggs could remain viable in many environments. And roam they did, spreading over the face of the land. Less than a hundred million years after the time *Hylonomus* scuttled through the swamps, reptiles ruled the earth. Their reign was long and absolute, continuing through the Mesozoic Era. We find their remains widely dispersed across the lands of our modern world, an indication that they could move easily from one region to another. Little wonder, in times when there were no oceans to cross. The Age of Reptiles was well under way before the great landmass of Pangaea began the slow breakup into the continents we know.

The reptiles were bewildering in variety of form and ways of living, and frequently spectacular in size. Some forsook the land and returned to the ancestral sea. From the primitive "stem reptile" group known as cotylosaurs (*Hylonomus* was a member) arose a line that would lead directly to mammals. From the cotylosaurs, too, came the turtles

*The egg does it again: A new life shucks the shell and enters the outer world, as reptiles have done for hundreds of millions of years. Drought-resistant, rich in nutrient, protective yet porous enough to let air pass through, the shelled egg could thrive out of water. Reptiles became the first backboned animals to dwell on land lifelong, though not all abandoned water; this young marine turtle hurries home to the sea after hatching.*

*Turtles saw the rise and fall of dinosaurs, the triumphant spread of mammals, and hung on—Aesop's fable, plodding through time.*

ROBERT E. SCHROEDER

Deep in the heart of ancient Texas
strode Edaphosaurus, *an early
reptile rigged with a strange sail
conducive to solar heating.
The four-foot-high spread could
work both ways—absorbing warmth
in sunlight, shedding heat in a
shady nook. Researchers calculated
the effect: A sail-backed reptile
like this one might take 80
minutes to raise body temperature
6 degrees; without a sail, 200
minutes. Thus a cold-blooded
animal, its sail spread, could shake
the lethargy of night sooner,
get off to an earlier start on its
morning rounds.*

*The sail-backed beasts, called
pelycosaurs, were out of the main
line of the reptile dynasty; dinosaurs
sprang from other stock. But from
the tribe of* Edaphosaurus *came
the advanced mammal-like reptiles,
and from them—the mammals.*

PAINTING BY ZDENEK BURIAN

and an insignificant-looking tribe called eosuchians, whose descendants include the lizards and snakes. The latter are essentially lizards that lost their legs and became highly adapted as slithering predators. The unprepossessing eosuchians were also the progenitors of reptiles known as thecodonts, which in turn were ancestors of the crocodilians, of the flying reptiles, and of the marvelous beasts that above all others dominated the Mesozoic world—the dinosaurs.

Dinosaurs, more than any ancient animal, excite man's wonder: gigantic long-necked vegetarians, fierce predators with terrifying jaws, bizarre forms on two legs or four, with bony armor on their backs, with ducklike bills, or domed or horned heads. We call them all dinosaurs—derived from the Greek for "terrible lizard"—though many were peaceable giants, no threat to anything but the vegetation they munched, and some were no bigger than a chicken. We wonder, too, at their sudden dying. With the close of the Mesozoic, they disappear. For this reason, popular fancy has come to equate them with backwardness, with failure. Science knows better. They were among the most successful animals that ever existed. More than a hundred million years of history can hardly be marked up as a record of failure.

No human being ever saw a live dinosaur. We know them and their early reptile kin from their fossilized bones, from footprints frozen in rock, even from their eggs. For a paleontologist, bones have beauty and meaning. In the shape and structure of a bone we can sense its strength and function. On its surface we can see the attachments that linked it to muscle, how it combined with other bones to form a skeleton. In our minds we can flesh out the skeletons and see them alive in their time and place. It is a calling that reminds me of the words of the prophet Ezekiel, set down in a valley full of dry bones: "So I prophesied . . . and the bones came together, bone to his bone. And when I beheld, lo, the sinews and the flesh came up upon them, and the skin covered them . . . and the breath came into them, and they lived."

We have never found any eggs of *Hylonomus;* telltale characteristics of its skull identify it as a reptile, and hence an animal that laid shelled eggs. The oldest reptile egg found was laid a mere 280 million years ago near the base of today's Texas panhandle, west of Wichita Falls. Scarcely more than two inches long, it has the elongated shape typical of many kinds of modern reptile eggs. It had never hatched, and X-rays showed no signs of an embryo; likely the egg was addled. It comes from a site which has lured paleontologists for a century—the famous "red beds," where wind and rain rasp gullies and mesquite-clad slopes, exposing the fishes and amphibians and reptiles that populated Texas in Permian times.

They seem to have lived on a tropical delta and in a sea that stretched from central Texas to central New Mexico. At times drought afflicted them. Fossilized burrows reveal how lungfishes encysted themselves in mud to survive dry spells, just as they do today in Africa and South America. Two strange reptiles of the group called pelycosaurs dominated the scene. Both grew to about 11 feet long. *Dimetrodon* had the daggerlike teeth of a meat-eater, but *Edaphosaurus* had, in addition to marginal teeth,

*Anything strange in the picture opposite? It re-creates a landscape of the early Triassic, dawntime of the dinosaurs some 220 million years ago. Examine the tracks. Thousands of these "petrified hands" turned up in Europe, in Arizona and Utah—but no bones to match; science dubbed the mystery creature* Chirotherium *—hand animal. But the "thumb" is on the* outside. *Savants of the 19th century were puzzled; one pictured the animal as a cross-legged frog! Eventually, new studies changed the "thumb" to a divergent fifth toe. Many living reptiles show a like pattern.*

Chirotherium *was one of the primitive ruling reptiles called thecodonts. A late Triassic relative, the swift little European Saltoposuchus (above), had the two-legged stance and long, toothy jaws of the first dinosaurs.*

PAINTINGS BY ZDENEK BURIAN

plates of small teeth over much of the palate, suggesting a specialized diet—perhaps freshwater mollusks. On their backs both had tall spines that doubled their height. Those of *Edaphosaurus* had crossbars, like irregular yardarms of an old square-rigger. In life, obviously, skin stretched between the spines to form a sail.

What was the sail for? To make its owner look big and frightening to enemies? A camouflage device for hiding in the rushes? Some early paleontologists thought the sail was just what it looked like, and they envisioned the "ship lizards" blithely tacking back and forth on breezy lakes. Probably the sail had more to do with keeping the pelycosaurs comfortable. The living reptiles we know are cold-blooded, or ectothermic. With no internal mechanism to regulate body heat, they must depend on the temperature of the environment around them. It seems logical to suppose, therefore, that the pelycosaur sails served as thermoregulators. When cold beset *Dimetrodon* or *Edaphosaurus*, it could turn sidewise to the sun, so that the sail could absorb heat from the sunrays. When the animals became too hot, they could retreat to shade where the sail would act as a radiator to shed heat quickly. This would have greatly increased their efficiency and might explain their dominant role in the deltaland of Permian Texas. It is a nice idea, and nobody has come up with a better one.

In 1802 a farmer lad with the fine old New England name of Pliny Moody chanced upon three-toed fossil footprints near South Hadley, Massachusetts. The tracks were imprinted in red sandstone, rock congealed from sediments laid down some 200 million years ago in the Triassic Period, a fascinating time of transition in life history. During the Triassic, amphibians were still introducing new styles—frogs made their debut on earth, never to leave it; but much of amphibian life consisted of straggling holdovers from the labyrinthodonts, a group long past its prime. The reptiles, by contrast, had proliferated exuberantly, establishing innovative and vigorous lines of evolutionary development. Hardly a habitat on land existed without a reptile to occupy it. They lived on uplands, along rivers, in trees. Competition for space must have been intense; reptiles had even invaded the seas. Dinosaurs had made their appearance, unimpressive at first, but gaining size, pointing toward the giants of the future. With the Triassic, the first of the three great divisions of the Mesozoic Era, the Age of Reptiles was in full swing.

Pliny Moody had stumbled upon the first evidence of dinosaurs discovered in North America, but it would take more than half a century before anyone realized it. To the early 19th century it appeared that a gigantic bird had made the tracks, and they were christened the footprints of "Noah's raven." They fascinated the Rev. E. B. Hitchcock, who became president of Amherst College. For decades he trekked across Massachusetts and Connecticut, assembling a magnificent collection of similar tracks, still preserved at Amherst. In 1858 he published a monumental tome, beautifully illustrated with the footprints of these "ancient birds." But within a few years science concluded that there were no birds on earth when the tracks were formed; they were left by "birdfoot" dinosaurs of the Triassic.

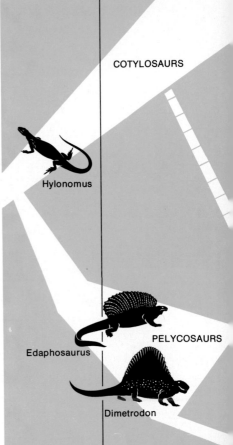

COTYLOSAURS

Hylonomus

PELYCOSAURS

Edaphosaurus

Dimetrodon

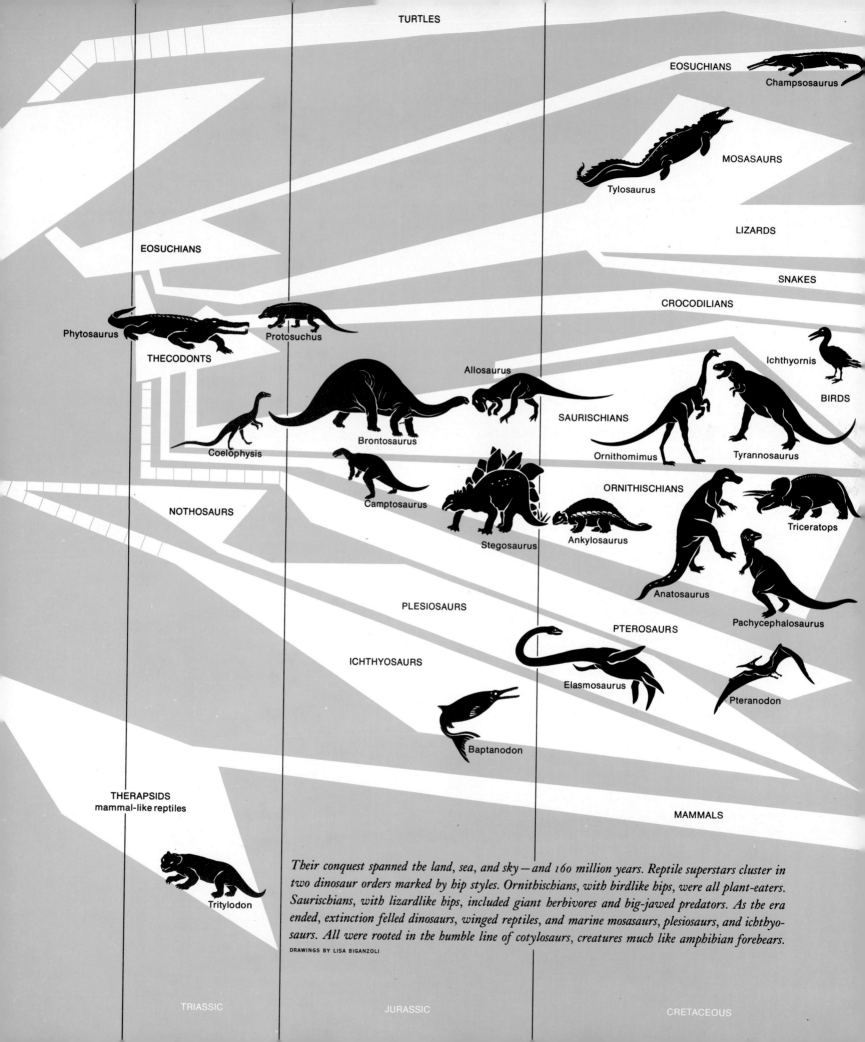

TURTLES

EOSUCHIANS

Champsosaurus

MOSASAURS

Tylosaurus

LIZARDS

SNAKES

CROCODILIANS

EOSUCHIANS

Ichthyornis

Phytosaurus

Protosuchus

BIRDS

THECODONTS

Allosaurus

SAURISCHIANS

Coelophysis

Brontosaurus

Ornithomimus

Tyrannosaurus

Camptosaurus

ORNITHISCHIANS

NOTHOSAURS

Stegosaurus

Ankylosaurus

Triceratops

Anatosaurus

Pachycephalosaurus

PLESIOSAURS

PTEROSAURS

Elasmosaurus

ICHTHYOSAURS

Pteranodon

Baptanodon

THERAPSIDS
mammal-like reptiles

MAMMALS

Tritylodon

*Their conquest spanned the land, sea, and sky—and 160 million years. Reptile superstars cluster in two dinosaur orders marked by hip styles. Ornithischians, with birdlike hips, were all plant-eaters. Saurischians, with lizardlike hips, included giant herbivores and big-jawed predators. As the era ended, extinction felled dinosaurs, winged reptiles, and marine mosasaurs, plesiosaurs, and ichthyosaurs. All were rooted in the humble line of cotylosaurs, creatures much like amphibian forebears.*

DRAWINGS BY LISA BIGANZOLI

TRIASSIC

JURASSIC

CRETACEOUS

A century after Hitchcock, more than 2,000 tracks of Triassic dinosaurs were discovered on a construction project near Rocky Hill, Connecticut. The site, fortunately on public land, was immediately designated a state park. From the orientation of the footprints, Professor John H. Ostrom of Yale concluded that many of the dinosaurs were in herds—gregarious reptiles, traveling around together.

In the world of fossils, it seems that where we find footprints we seldom find bones, and vice versa. Thus bones are scarce in the Connecticut River Valley—so rare indeed that every one is a treasure. In 1884 news of a bone find sent Professor Othniel Charles Marsh, the eccentric and far-removed predecessor of Ostrom at Yale, scurrying to a brownstone quarry near Manchester, Connecticut. He recovered part of a small dinosaur named *Ammosaurus;* the rest was gone, encased in a bridge abutment nearby. In 1967 Ostrom learned of plans for a new highway through Manchester. He studied more than 60 bridges in the area, then zeroed in on a 40-foot span across a brook. When wreckers demolished it in 1969, a team of fossil hunters pored over hundreds of stones. In one, sure enough, there was half of a thigh bone to match the half Marsh had found 85 years before.

Unlike the drab brownstone of the East, Triassic rocks of the Southwest create landscapes of unbelievably brilliant hues—reds and browns, grays, yellows, creamy whites in banded exposures stretching through Arizona, New Mexico, and Utah. They yield footprints, too, but especially bones, sometimes in great numbers.

For two summers in the late 1940's, I led an expedition from the American Museum

*Footsteps echo across the ages to tell a story of hunter and prey in 120-million-year-old stone. In a stream bed near Glen Rose, Texas, yard-long pads—a man can sit in them—are those of a vegetarian brontosaur. In parallel is the birdlike tread of a huge hunting dinosaur. Where the prey veered, so did the stalker.*
ROLAND T. BIRD

*A spiked tail gave* Stegosaurus *(below) some protection, but back plates left lots of haunch exposed. New studies at Yale find that the upraised bony shields may have been more useful for heat control.* OVERLEAF: Diplodocus's *whippy tail could have guarded its flanks; the sinuous neck, like an elephant's trunk, could reach treetop browse. Longest of dinosaurs,* Diplodocus *stretched some 90 feet, tip to tip.*
PAINTING BY ZDENEK BURIAN (ALSO OVERLEAF)

Bending to graze, Triceratops deploys the armament that would meet an attacker: a buckler of bone up to eight feet long, horns over snout and eyes, strong legs and neck muscles to power a lunging drive. With Tyrannosaurus around, the horned grazers needed every resource. Herding would help. Threatened, adults could encircle the young and face outward. "Nothing less than a tank could have penetrated such a ring of horned and beaked faces without being impaled or bitten," wrote paleontologist Nicholas Hotton.

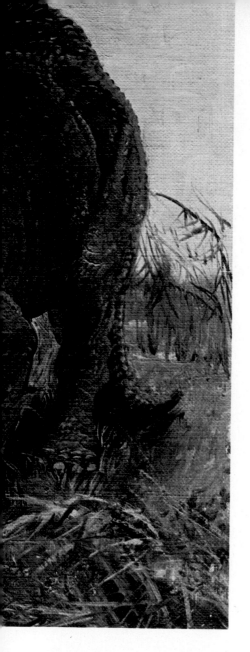

Triceratops *may also have locked horns in combat with its own kind. Evidence of social living among dinosaurs like these turned up in the celebrated Mongolian cache found by Roy Chapman Andrews in the 1920's. The remains of* Protoceratops, *a primitive horned dinosaur, included young and old, even unhatched eggs (left). Some nests looked as if females had turned to lay eggs in concentric circles. With up to 30 in a clutch, some scientists saw the possibility that more than one female shared a nest.*

of Natural History to the flaming red and yellow cliffs of northern New Mexico, near a delightful oasis known as Ghost Ranch. From scattered bones of this region Edward Drinker Cope, the paleontological rival of Marsh, had described a small, lightly boned dinosaur and called it *Coelophysis*—hollow nature. Our goal was to increase our fragmentary knowledge of this period and its life. One day a colleague brought me a bit of bone he had found on a long talus slope. It was no bigger than a fingertip, but it was unmistakably a piece of claw belonging to one of the earliest and smallest dinosaurs. At that moment I knew the thrill of finding treasure in the earth.

We followed the dribble of talus upslope and by some judicious probing discovered a stratum literally packed with the bones of *Coelophysis*. Hard, tedious days were spent removing tons of overburden—but the results were more than gratifying. We uncovered scores of skeletons, many complete down to the tiniest bones, all packed and intertwined in the greatest possible profusion—and confusion. It was like untangling a mass of paleontological jackstraws.

Long and slender, its bones hollow and very delicate, *Coelophysis* was a lightweight. Fully grown, it measured perhaps eight or ten feet, yet it probably weighed no more than 50 or 75 pounds. It ran on birdlike hind limbs, hunted prey with clawed forelimbs. Its bladelike teeth were finely serrated, evidently an adaptation for slicing flesh—applied in our day by the makers of steak knives.

In the body cavities of two skeletons we found bones of very small animals of the same species. The victims of cannibalism? Very possibly; crocodilians today sometimes eat the young of their species. Or is it possible that *Coelophysis* bore live young, as the desert night lizard of the Southwest does today? Probably not. The bones found within would make an embryo too large for the opening in the pelvis of the larger animal. The opening appears more suited for the passage of eggs.

At a distance of 200 million years we can only guess how this mass of dinosaurs died in one spot. They lived in a tropical land, probably ranging the high ground between streams inhabited by amphibians and crocodile-like phytosaurs. Perhaps a herd of *Coelophysis* perished in quicksand or sticky mud at the edge of a waterway.

Half a century before our Ghost Ranch expedition, fossil collectors from the American Museum came upon a sheepherder's cabin in southeastern Wyoming. It was not much to look at, but when the paleontologists examined its walls, they found that the cabin had been built entirely of large dinosaur bones! Other dinosaur bones lay scattered on the ground all around the cabin. Eventually the "Bone Cabin" quarry yielded freight-car loads of fossils.

Bone Cabin stood only a few miles away from the equally famous Como Bluff site, where nearly a quarter of a century earlier Professor Marsh's diggers had removed great quantities of dinosaur remains. The quarries are in rocks of the Morrison Formation—a geological horizon of late Jurassic age that stretches far and wide across some of the Western States, notably Wyoming, Utah, Colorado, and New Mexico. Several other Morrison sites have enriched collections. One still does; inside the visitor center at Dinosaur National Monument, near Vernal, Utah, you can see dinosaur skeletons being exposed on the face of the rock. Dinosaurs closely related to, or even identical with, the Morrison dinosaurs are found on other continents—again an indication of the close connections that typified the ancient landmasses.

The Jurassic Period that began 190 million years ago was an age of giants, especially in its later stages when dinosaurs of the group we call sauropods grew to unprecedented size—long-tailed, long-necked creatures such as *Diplodocus, Brachiosaurus,* and *Apatosaurus* (better known as *Brontosaurus*), ranging in length up to 80 or 90 feet. *Apatosaurus* probably weighed some 30 tons, while *Brachiosaurus,* giant among giants, may have weighed more than 80 tons—the largest animal ever to walk on land.

Our modern blue whale outstrips them—but it has the buoyancy of the sea to help it contend with gravity. For the giants of the Jurassic, gravity was an overwhelming factor in their daily lives. A man can jump a stream or tumble down a gully several times his height without serious hurt. No giant sauropod could jump a log or fall even the length of its height without severe injury. In fact, it would never get all four feet off the ground at once. It may be that the sauropods had just about reached the limit of size for land animals. As an animal grows longer, its mass mushrooms much more rapidly—generally the increase in mass is the cube of the increase in length. The strength of supporting members increases as well, but not in proportion to the added

*Conifers crowded the forests as the reptile reign reached middle age, when behemoths of Jurassic time bestrode the earth. Here scraggly araucarian trees mingle with wedge-shaped ancestors of today's sequoias. Time and circumstance transmuted earlier araucarians of some 200 million years ago into the brilliant gems of Petrified Forest National Park (opposite). Water rich in silica and other dissolved minerals of volcanic ash perked slowly through buried wood, petrifying it. The form remained, the substance changed—to stone.*

*Araucarians still grow—in many areas as ornamentals, wild in the Southern Hemisphere. One is the monkey puzzle tree, its limbs a prickly maze for climbing animals.*

PAINTING BY ZDENEK BURIAN. OPPOSITE: JOSEF MUENCH

find familiar—the reptiles browsed among early magnolias and palms. Rich evidence of Cretaceous life is spread across North America (as well as other continents). In 1858, Dr. Joseph Leidy of the Philadelphia Academy of Natural Sciences described the first dinosaur skeleton from North America—a large duckbill unearthed in Haddonfield, New Jersey, just across the Delaware River from Philadelphia. But most of our dinosaur fossils of Cretaceous time have come from farther west—from the Rocky Mountain States, from Alberta, Canada, from northern Mexico.

One of the most prolific localities is along the Red Deer River of Alberta. Here, during the first two decades of this century, several expeditions worked long and successfully to amass the magnificent dinosaur displays seen in the Royal Ontario Museum in Toronto, the National Museum of Natural Sciences in Ottawa, and the American Museum of Natural History in New York. In those days, before modern highways, fossil hunters enjoyed a truly relaxed pace. They spent the summers quietly floating downstream on flatboats, scanning the bordering cliffs for signs of bones, tying up to the bank when there was a skeleton to be collected. Alas! The domineering internal combustion engine has destroyed many pleasant aspects of life.

The revolution in earth history marked by the arrival of flowering plants did more than merely beautify the landscape. It also made available a new food supply, and the dinosaurs responded handsomely; this was the time when the plant-eaters reached the culmination of their development. The sides of a duckbill's jaws were "paved" with tightly packed rows of grinding teeth; beneath them other rows stood ready to push into place as soon as the teeth in use wore down. Thus a grinding mechanism with as many as 700 teeth might be available, sufficient to last the lifetime of the animal. Duck-billed dinosaurs lived close to rivers and lakes; evidently the broad, flat bill was used to probe and shovel in the muddy bottoms.

Of the other plant-eating groups, the dome-headed and the armored dinosaurs frequented the uplands, and throughout the west the ceratopsians with their stunning display of horns and frills wandered in great numbers. Hungry predators fed on these hosts of plant-eaters—*Gorgosaurus* and its even more terrifying relative *Tyrannosaurus*. Measuring up to 50 feet in length, the tyrant of the Cretaceous ranks as the largest land-living carnivore that ever existed.

These were the years when gigantic reptiles also ruled the seas, including the shallow seaway that cut through the continent. So it is in the chalky Niobrara Formation of Kansas that we find remains of long-necked plesiosaurs that sculled slowly along the surface with long strokes of their oarlike limbs, their heads darting from side to side to seize fishes; someone once described a plesiosaur as "a snake strung through the body of a turtle." Here, too, swam the marine lizards called mosasaurs; and the streamlined, fishlike ichthyosaurs, pursuing a way of life like that of modern porpoises; and turtles with shells ten feet or more in length. Hovering above the inland seaway and dipping down to partake of the bounteous supply of fishes were the pterosaurs, soaring on leathery wings. By this time bird life had become established

## The Strange Skulls of the Hadrosaurs

*From the neck down there was not much to tell them apart: bipedal vegetarians, good swimmers, about 30 feet long, drifting across the land in vast herds as the time of the dinosaurs was running out. But from the neck up the hadrosaurs, or duckbills, sported a wondrous assortment of skull shapes, source of endless debate and fanciful comparison. There was Kritosaurus with its Roman nose, Lambeosaurus and its hatchet, Corythosaurus with its cockscomb or Greek warrior's helmet, Parasaurolophus with its sweptback tube.*

*The uses of the crests? Educated guesses abound: for snorkeling, for butting, for resonating sounds, for sexual or species recognition. One widely held theory notes that long nasal passages meandering the hollow crests could improve the sense of smell—providing an early warning against predators.*

DRAWINGS BY JAY H. MATTERNES

Leaping lizards defend their fishing
grounds in the Niobrara Sea, where
the dry plains of Kansas lie today.
Its tail a powerful sculling oar,
the mosasaur called Tylosaurus
grew to 30 feet, could gulp a
600-pound fish. The seagoing
lizard closely resembled today's
Old World monitors. Its aerial rival
Pteranodon lifted a turkey-size
body on long, thin wings. Flying
reptiles, or pterosaurs, were the
largest creatures ever to take to
the air. The wings of one found in
Texas spanned 51 feet. Such giants
probably glided most of the time;
smaller pterosaurs would have
been more active fliers.

The old sea sliced the continent
north and south. When it retreated,
limy beds hardened to chalk,
burying bones that guide us to
the world of 70 million years ago.

PAINTING BY ZDENEK BURIAN

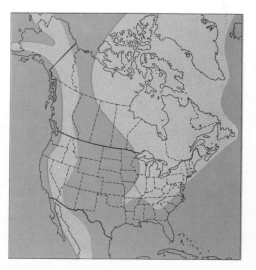

throughout the world; their bones turn up in the chalk beds of Kansas, where they lived on the sea, and shared the air with the flying reptiles. Mammals were numerous but still small, only minor players in the Cretaceous panorama.

Dinosaurs filled the land. In the Lance Formation of Wyoming and Montana, the uppermost and last of the Cretaceous deposits, the bones of horned dinosaurs abound. By all available criteria they were indeed living a successful life.

And then there were none. Suddenly, dinosaur bones disappear from the sediments of the earth, to be replaced in the Cenozoic Era that began 65 million years ago by the bones of the burgeoning mammals. Not only did the dinosaurs vanish, but also the flying reptiles along with them. So, too, the plesiosaurs and mosasaurs and ichthyosaurs. Almost the only reptiles to survive this great extinction were those familiar to us today—the turtles, crocodilians, lizards and snakes, and the strange tuatara of New Zealand, scarcely changed since the Age of Reptiles.

Why did the dinosaurs become extinct? The question has plagued many people for decades. Scientists and laymen have proposed theories by the score, all of them inadequate in one way or another. The question remains unanswered.

Some have suggested "racial senescence" as the cause; dinosaurs had simply run their course in the history of life and died out. But from the fossil record they seem quite vigorous right up to the end of their time. Did small mammals prey on their eggs and thus hasten their demise? Modern reptiles such as marine turtles and crocodilians suffer heavy egg predation, but they carry on. One theory holds that cooling climate caused by continental drift and mountain uplift was too much for the supposed cold-blooded dinosaurs. Fossil plants indicate some cooling at the end of Cretaceous time, but it does not seem drastic enough to have wiped out the dinosaurs. Moreover there are those crocodilians that survived in spite of any climatic variations.

Deadly epidemics have been offered as a cause. But epidemics are usually rather specific. Would any epidemic wipe out such a great variety of species? Perhaps, another interesting theory suggests, the eggs of the most recent dinosaurs were not viable. Dinosaur eggs with very thin shells have been found in Cretaceous beds in southern France. Were they affected in some manner parallel to the effects of DDT on the eggs of modern birds? So it goes. The ideas multiply; so do the questions.

The question has even been raised as to whether the dinosaurs are gone. It seems that the birds, which delight us with their variety and bright color and song, are descendants of some early dinosaurs. So in a sense we may wish to look at birds as feathered dinosaurs living on. It remains true, nonetheless, that with the end of Cretaceous history, the years when reptiles ruled the earth had come to an end.

---

*Crocodiles soak up Florida sunshine, curios in a tourist park—and in the history of life. The last of the ruling reptiles, crocodilians—alligators, crocodiles, and gavials, numbering about 20 species—forge a living link to days when the earth belonged to them and their kin, the dinosaurs. Then, mammals scurried from their path; now, in many places, they live on at the mercy of a mammal called man.*

ED COOPER

96

# ...And Birds Took Wing

George E. Watson

Thousands of hungry gulls, albatrosses, and shearwaters mobbed our small charter boat 65 miles off the Pacific coast. As we tossed chunks of suet overboard, our wake boiled with wheeling, screaming birds fighting over the morsels. For the seabird specialists aboard, taking a bird-watching break from a meeting in Seattle, the scene was unforgettable—a perfect busman's holiday.

As awesome as the sight of these birds was the manner of their coming. Their nesting chores done, they had gathered from the corners of the Pacific: sooty and flesh-footed shearwaters from New Zealand, pink-footed shearwaters from Chile, black-footed albatrosses from Hawaii, western and glaucous-winged gulls commuting from the Washington coast . . . soaring on ocean winds, flocking to spots like this one where food fishes concentrate, skimming the waves for hours on end. Flying.

I watched the heavy-bodied shearwaters running rapidly over the water with slender wings outstretched and motionless, planing into the breeze. As long as the leading edges of the wings were canted upward, the birds had lift, were weightless on the water, were flying. When the angle of attack was lowered, they plunged beneath the waves like feathered submarines. "We got plenty of flying fever from watching the birds," wrote Orville Wright, "but we got nothing about their secret of balance." How did birds begin to fly? I think there is a clue in those planing shearwaters.

Nature had evolved the mechanism of flight 150 million years before the emergence of birds. Giant insects, some with two-foot wingspreads, flitted through Carboniferous forests of the Paleozoic Era. Much later, reptiles took to the air; but the larger pterosaurs probably could only ride the currents like gliders—and how expertly the smaller ones flew is still an open question among scientists. So also with the oldest bird we know of, *Archaeopteryx*, the "ancient winged one." At best *Archaeopteryx* was not much of a flier, and it may not have gotten off the ground at all.

This primitive creature, dating from the time when the biggest of all dinosaurs roamed the earth, may have lived in North America or in other parts of the world, but its bones have been found only in one region of southern Germany. In 1861 workmen quarrying the fine-grained Solnhofen limestone used in high-quality lithographic printing found the fossil of an animal about as big as a crow with feather impressions surrounding the skeleton. Four more feathered specimens have since turned up in the 140-million-year-old rock. No other bird remains have been identified from the Jurassic Period anywhere else in the world.

Without the clear engraving of feathers in the superfine limestone, *Archaeopteryx* could easily have passed for a two-legged dinosaur similar to its contemporary, *Ornitholestes*. When the latter was discovered, it was seen as a hunter of birds—hence its name, which means "bird robber." More likely, *Ornitholestes* made its living chasing lizards or small mammals. Modern scientific theory traces the ancestry of birds to fast-running early dinosaurs of the Triassic Period.

The remains of *Archaeopteryx* show the typical birdlike wishbone—familiar to all chicken eaters—but there was no sign of a breastbone or other bony structure that could have anchored the strong muscles and shoulder girdle of a flying bird. Some

*Rosy reflections of a remote past, flamingos probe a Florida lagoon, sifting for food with bills inverted. Today the exotic beauties may straggle to the United States, or grace a pond as captives; 70 million years ago their ancestors waded the shallows of present-day Wyoming. Flamingos look like storks and herons, yet share some traits with ducks and avocets. Feather lice, of a kind that evolved along with their host birds, add an intriguing clue to lineage. The lice that parasitize the flamingo and duck families infest no other species.*

experts hold that the bird was arboreal, climbing trees with its claws, then gliding or flapping weakly from limb to limb. I favor a new theory advanced by Professor John Ostrom, who believes this early bird was a flightless runner that chased large flying insects along coastal mud flats, using its incipient wings like a butterfly net. According to Ostrom, feathers may already have evolved in certain small dinosaurs to minimize heat loss. In time forearm feathers grew longer until the wings could serve as a weapon. Anyone who has ever been attacked by angry mute swans or whacked by a penguin's flippers knows that wings need not function merely for flying. But did violent flailing lead to flight? I rather think it was something like the planing of those shearwaters—a primitive bird racing along with wings widespread, a sudden lightness developing as lift matched the burden of weight. With evolutionary changes in bone and muscle, birds could eventually defy gravity with powered flight.

Not until the late Cretaceous, some 50 million years after *Archaeopteryx*, do birds appear in the fossil record in North America. The gap seems illogical. The sudden burst of a diverse bird life, including some species remarkably close to modern families, implies the presence of earlier, more primitive birds, but they left no fossil trace. Perhaps we have found their bones and didn't recognize them—as might have been the case with *Archaeopteryx* without those crucial feather impressions. Bird bones, especially those of small species, make poor fossils in any event. Hollow and fragile, they are likely to be crushed, deformed, or eroded. Predators and scavengers may feast on dead birds, leaving the bone fragments scattered and broken. The best preservation occurs when mud covers the carcass soon after death, and most early remains are of large aquatic species.

Some 88 million years ago, 11 kinds of water birds fished the Cretaceous sea of inland North America. By then birds had mastered the art of flying—and some had already lost it. Flightless *Hesperornis* was an excellent diver, but legs set far back for swimming made it clumsy on land. One of its contemporary relatives, *Ichthyornis*, a good flier, ranged as far south as Texas. Just after their time, a tiny ibis, *Plegadornis*, waded saltwater mud flats in Alabama. And as the sea retreated in the last stages of the Cretaceous, we find another evolutionary flurry. From New Jersey came the first cormorant species, three rails, and five sandpipers. In Wyoming two loons, a flamingo, and five shorebirds lived among the last dinosaurs. From Baja California came the only known land bird of the Cretaceous,

*"Evolution caught in the act"*— Archaeopteryx, *the earliest bird known, shows links to dinosaur ancestors and to modern birds. In this crow-size creature of 140 million years ago, wings and plumage combined with a reptile's long, bony tail and jaws armed with sharp teeth. For flying, its wings stirred only a small flap; it lacked the muscle to take off. Clawed wings may have seized prey, as did the arms of the small dinosaur* Ornitholestes *(below). In time, beating wings lifted birds to mastery of the skies.*

PAINTING BY ZDENEK BURIAN.
DRAWING BY JAY H. MATTERNES

*Winged fishers throng rocky isles near the shores of the continent's Cretaceous sea. Ichthyornis (above), about the size of a stout tern, coursed the skies on strong wings, probably snatched fish from the water like a gull. The stunted wings of Hesperornis (opposite) were useless for flight, but the six-foot-long diver swam with power and agility. Among living kinds, only loons resemble it slightly. Both of these ancient toothed birds died out with the flying and marine reptiles that fished the same sea.*

*The fossil history of their time records a variety of water birds in North America, but only one land species, from Baja California— the first one found on the continent.*

*Alexornis.* It bears some resemblance to the living motmots and puffbirds of the tropics and may belong to an extinct family ancestral to the kingfishers and woodpeckers.

"Scarce as hen's teeth"—the old adage dies hard among ornithologists. Teeth and the strong jaws to support them are heavy, and birds needed to reduce weight for efficient flying. Ever since 1880—when Professor O. C. Marsh reported that *Hesperornis* and *Ichthyornis* "possessed teeth, a character hitherto unknown in the class of Birds"—ornithologists have found it hard to accept the fact. They were relieved in 1952 when the alleged jaws of *Ichthyornis* were attributed to a marine reptile. But new specimens prove that Marsh was right: Primitive birds had true teeth.

Eventually birds rid themselves of the weight penalty imposed by teeth, and found other ways of holding, tearing, and grinding food. Some fish-eaters such as mergansers have serrated bills for capturing slippery prey, but their jawbones are smooth. Hawks and owls grip prey with claws and either swallow it whole or tear it into mouth-size portions with sharp, hooked bills. Seed-eaters such as quails and pigeons swallow grit that functions like teeth to grind food in the muscular gizzard.

A scant fossil record tells little of how these adaptive changes came about, yet it does reveal that in the first 30 million years after the passing of the great reptiles all but 6 of the 27 living orders of birds existed somewhere in the world. Ducks, cranes,

primitive auks and owls, and the first North American heron made their debut by the Eocene. Among the first to appear as the Age of Reptiles ended was the flightless giant *Diatryma*. Because of its size and fierce-looking bill, it has been almost universally regarded as a meat-eater, perhaps the dominant land carnivore in North America until the predatory mammals appeared. But the bird lacks a hawk-like hook at the end of its bill. I think *Diatryma* was a peaceful grazer, using its massive bill to scythe coarse vegetation—somewhat like *Notornis*, largest of living rails and a voracious cropper of New Zealand's remote grasslands.

Among birds well-adapted for flight, vultures have few peers. Magnificent soaring scavengers with keen eyesight that might be compared to the vision of a man using binoculars, they patrol the skies hour upon hour, searching for carcasses across many square miles. When one sights a kill, others gather to share it. They comprise an ancient clan of immense size; one shadowed Ice Age landscapes with wings spanning nearly 17 feet—probably the largest flying bird that ever lived.

In the swamps of Wyoming 50 million years ago lived a forerunner, *Neocathartes*. It had the bare head of modern vultures, useful in probing messy food. But this bird was no marvel of soaring prowess. With its long legs and short wings, *Neocathartes* must have been a ground vulture, a solitary scavenger perhaps locating carrion by smell—as today's turkey vultures do. Engineers have seen turkey vultures circling spots where pipes are buried, apparently drawn by the smell of leaking gas.

For more than half a century Dr. Alexander Wetmore has enriched our knowledge of the history of bird life. He has named scores of genera and families and inspired many younger scientists to the work of completing the picture of the past. To the dean of avian paleontologists, the ancient ground vulture is the strangest of the more than 80 fossil birds he has described. Without a fossil record, who could have conjured up a ground vulture, or a monster such as *Diatryma?*

As the epochs succeeded one another, climates and landforms changed, and new birds evolved. Among them were quails and cuckoos and songbirds in the Oligocene; albatrosses, grebes, shearwaters, storm petrels, ospreys, falcons, prairie chickens, godwits, gulls, and parakeets—all with a modern look—in the Miocene; woodpeckers and doves in the Pliocene, last epoch before the Ice Age.

And bird life evolved the remarkable flying machine that has awed man through the ages. Hollow, thin-walled bones, reinforced with struts in larger species, shape a light yet strong frame. The skeleton of a frigatebird with a seven-foot wingspread weighs only four ounces—less than the plumage. Powerful wingbeats depend on two sets of flight muscles attached to the deep keel of the breastbone. The larger set produces the

*Graceful riders of the wind, common and roseate terns erupt from a Cape Cod marsh. Their tribe boasts the champion of commuters, the Arctic tern, which wings from one polar region to the other and back again each year—at a cruising speed of 30 mph. This migrant breaks its journey with rest stops on the sea, but another ocean tern, the sooty—a non-swimmer—may spend months aloft, coming ashore only to breed.*
HOPE ALEXANDER

down beat—the power stroke; the other operates over a pulley to power the up beat, or recovery stroke. Strong, flexible feathers overlap like roof shingles to make a smooth, impervious surface. Flying requires the consumption of large quantities of energy-rich foods. Yet birds apparently find flying worthwhile, for it gives them the ability to exploit food sources unavailable to most mammals and reptiles, and the means to escape land predators and harsh winters.

In February, 1964, I watched Arctic terns completing their "spring" molt in the long daylight of Antarctic summer. Years later I saw the same species raising young in August on barrier islands of Prudhoe Bay, Alaska. Why do some Arctic terns travel as much as 22,000 miles each year? Why do some birds migrate north and south, others east and west, still others merely drift down to sheltered valleys? We know their routes, but we know little of how they navigate—though sun, star patterns, landmarks, day-lengths, natural rhythms, possibly even the earth's magnetic field, apparently play varying roles in triggering and guiding seasonal movements.

Most migratory patterns were established in the last 18,000 years, as receding glaciers of the Ice Age again allowed access to the north. Repeated Pleistocene glaciations and changes in sea level speeded evolutionary change; the average life of a species, Dr. Pierce Brodkorb estimates, shrank from three million to half a million years. Extinction was common, but most modern birds existed in recognizable form; for the first time, fossils of small songbirds appear in numbers.

The ice dipped farther south in eastern North America, and the Gulf of Mexico cut off the retreat of birds. In the west, ice-free land swept unbroken to Mexico. Today we see the result in much richer bird life west of the 100th meridian.

Bird distribution continues to change rapidly as species adjust to new conditions. As a boy in Connecticut in the 1930's, I never saw a turkey vulture, tufted titmouse, Carolina wren, mockingbird, or cardinal. Today these southern birds live year-round in New York and New England. They may have pushed northward with a warming trend; perhaps suburban feeders bulging with seeds or the carrion of road kills helped them survive winters north of their usual ranges. The popularity of refrigerators may have encouraged the northward spread of barn owls. I have seen the nests of these birds in old abandoned ice houses in New York State.

Clearly, our activities can benefit birds, the most conspicuous of all wildlife, living closest to man. But there is another, much sorrier side to the story. Fossil history tells us extinction is an integral part of the evolutionary process that has given earth a legacy of some 9,000 living bird species, more than 800 in North America. The coming of man to the continent has diminished that legacy. The face of the land has been changed, destroying habitats that sustained birds. Hunting for food or sport has wiped out whole populations. Gone are the great auk, the Eskimo curlew, the passenger pigeon, the Carolina parakeet, the heath hen, and the Labrador duck. Where is the ivory-billed woodpecker? And where will Bachman's warbler and Kirtland's warbler, the California condor, and the whooping crane be tomorrow?

*Big bird of the Eocene,* Diatryma *made its home on the range of western North America. With the dinosaurs gone and most mammals still small, there was little to challenge this flightless titan that stood seven feet tall. Often pictured as a predator (above),* Diatryma *has undergone a change of image; it may have lived like an elephant, endlessly stuffing its huge maw with grass. As the Eocene ended, extinction overtook this giant—the fate, by one estimate, of 99 per cent of the million bird species evolved since* Archaeopteryx.
PAINTING AND SKETCH BY ZDENEK BURIAN

# ...And Flowers Bloomed
Robert O. Petty

I am sitting outside on a balmy May evening as our curve of earth tilts south again. The days are growing longer. Welling up from the valley beyond the yard's edge is an ancient sensory tide: awakening sounds, aromas of new growth, and the vague darting shadows of the spring. In the fading light I can still see the silhouette of a magnolia tree, the spiral symmetry of its few remaining flowers peaked to white in the blur of distance. Suddenly, whirring out of the Indiana twilight, a small brown body hits the porch behind me, then drops to the damp brick. There is a grating sound of tiny legs and wings . . . beetles coming out of the darkness as they have for centuries. "June bugs," my youngest son says. "May beetles," my older boy counters. "Well, Coleoptera, for sure," I interject. "And you're both right." As the boys turn over some of the leaf-eating beetles to explore their miniature anatomy, I look again at the magnolia, then back at the scatter of beetles. I think of other beetles, other evenings ages before this one, of the intricate saga of insects and flowering plants, and the voyage into being which they made possible for mammals, including *Homo sapiens*.

To know, all in all, mused Tennyson, consider the flower. What, exactly, is a flower? Even for botanists, the more we know, the more elusive the definition seems. Simply, a flowering plant is a plant which produces a fruit. And the fruit grows from the female parts of the flower and contains the seed. Flowering plants are called angiosperms, which means "encased seeds." Some plants, such as pine trees and other conifers, produce seeds which lie exposed, often between the scales of a cone. These plants belong to a group called gymnosperms—naked seeds.

Earlier land plants reproduced by scattering cells called spores, as ferns and mosses do today. Over hundreds of millions of years, plants developed the structures we now know—stems, leaves, and root systems in which specialized cells transported sap. But what of the fruit and the flower? Flowers seem so at the heart of earth's vegetation that it is difficult to imagine a world without them. Yet, in the long chronology of life, the architecture of a flower is a relatively recent innovation—only some 130 million years old. Other plants existed for eons without flowers and many of them live on today. Why this amazing structure should have evolved at all is the essence of our story.

What was the first flower like, and from what plant group did it arise? How many winter nights around the world have botanists wondered, imagining such a form as it tumbled to the earth, there to be lost in the drifting sediments of some Mesozoic flood. Surely there could be no discovery more precious to paleobotany. Yet, to this day, the exact origin of the flowering plant remains much as Charles Darwin described it: "an abominable mystery."

Foremost reason for the mystery is the profound absence of early fossils. They may be lying somewhere, waiting to be found. But the lack of fossils in itself could be a kind of evidence, suggesting that the first flowers may have evolved in places where fossils did not form readily, or where they have since been lost to erosion. We do know that a significant diversity of angiosperms had already evolved by late-Cretaceous times. About 70 million years ago water lilies grew in Virginia, magnolias in Kansas, breadfruit in Colorado. The existing fossil record tells us this and suggests

*From its golden cup, a California poppy barters pollen for pollination. A tiny anther-borne meal rewards the collops beetle for its services: carrying grains to fertilize nearby flowers. Bright petals work, too. Their short life's purpose: to lure pollinators. That done, they may offer a meal to a freeloading moth larva. Pollen and petals contain carotenoids, which add color to the flower parts—and also provide a vitamin source which helps insects see their vivid floral targets.*

## A Single Cell

*Nestled in cases, ripe fern spores (opposite) await dry air to burst each helmet-shaped sphere, and a breeze to scatter the dustlike cells. Of millions set free, a few grow into the quarter-inch, heart-shaped gametophyte, carrier of sex cells. Here, freed by a vital film of water, a male cell swims to an egg, creating a sexless, sporebearing plant. With their leapfrogging life cycle, ferns are both land plants and heirs of the ancient water plants they overtook 300 million years ago.*

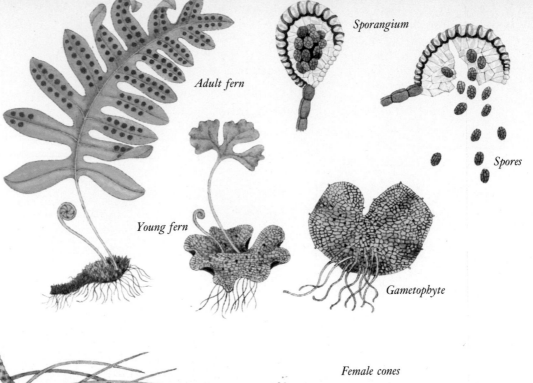

*Adult fern*

*Sporangium*

*Spores*

*Young fern*

*Gametophyte*

## The Naked Seed

*Pollen grains of conifer buoy up in lavish clouds at the whim of the wind. Some drift onto exposed ovules of female cones and—free of the need for access to water—begin the slow work of seed-making. Two years or more go by before warmth coaxes mature female cones to open, and reveals on their scales the naked seeds.*

*Early conifers grew in swamps, dominated landscapes 200 million years ago. Now the conifers are outnumbered by flowering trees.*

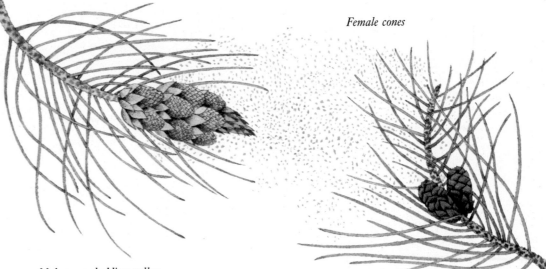

*Female cones*

*Male cones shedding pollen*

## Flowers and Fruits

*Innovative parenthood marks the flowering plant. Pollen finds its way, usually by wind or insect, from male anther to female stigma. Pollen tubes burrow through styles carrying a double charge—one sperm to create the infant plant, one to give the seed a unique food supply. Enclosing its embryos, the ovary matures to a fruit—orange, nut, peapod, seedcases of all kinds. Flowering plants shine as earth's youngest, largest plant group— up and coming for 130 million years.*

DIAGRAMS BY TONY CHEN

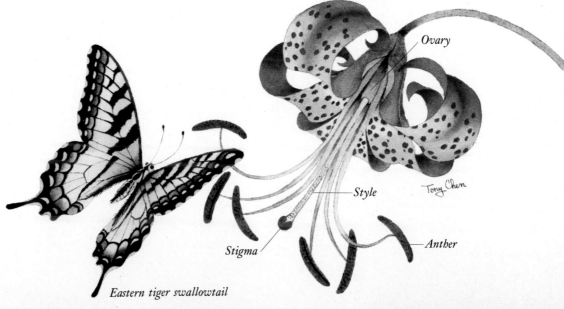

*Ovary*

*Style*

*Stigma*

*Anther*

Tony Chen

*Eastern tiger swallowtail*

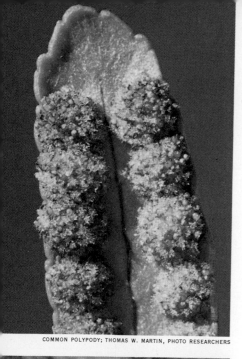

COMMON POLYPODY; THOMAS W. MARTIN, PHOTO RESEARCHERS

PIÑON PINE; DAVID CAVAGNARO

TURK'S-CAP LILY; WILLIAM D. GRIFFIN

an actual origin of angiosperm forerunners much earlier—some botanists believe as early as the Jurassic, more than 135 million years ago.

Of all fossil plant communities, we probably know best the "coal floras" of the late Paleozoic. During the time when this flora dominated the vast, moist continental lowlands, an almost inconspicuous assemblage of plants was casting new shadows in the drier, distant uplands. As the plates of earth's crust shifted, mountain masses arose. Rainfall diminished. These newer, diverse landscapes became increasingly important in the balance of survival. Wherever water tarried as it tumbled toward the sea or returned again to clouds—on the shaded slopes, in deep soils, here in a moisture seep, there a spring line—each niche offered a slight reprieve from a huge climatic fact emerging in the uplands and shaping all that sought to grow there. This new element was an increasing aridity which would stamp almost every major line of plants and animals as the "coal age" forests began to shrink more than 200 million years ago. Some plants were lifted out of an atmosphere rich in the vital carbon dioxide coming from damp, decaying swampland debris, into a new environment for photosynthesis—a thinner air but with a windfall of light energy.

From the fossil records of these older floras, fragment by fragment the changing pattern emerged. In the uplands new communities of conifers, seed ferns, and ginkgos—maidenhair trees—were finding their place in the sun. This rich subtropical vegetation of non-flowering plants spread across the Northern Hemisphere, in which North America and Eurasia were then combined as the single continent of Laurasia. Sea levels were much higher and climates more equable than now. In time the rising land masses and drifting continents ushered in broad climatic fluctuations—cyclic temperatures and rainfall, or what became the ecological challenge of sustained seasonal change.

In the Mesozoic, then, selective pressure was developing most intensely in those newly minted, semi-arid uplands where low moisture and higher light intensities required many new adaptations. In these regions plants came increasingly under a dual pressure, first from the physical stress of drought, and second from the energy loss to plant-eating animals, especially the primitive insects. But the abundance of mountain habitats provided a rich mosaic of environmental conditions, creating pockets of vegetation isolated from one another. Though all was still promise, still potential, the stage was set for the evolution of new, more adaptive plant forms. What follows is only a best guess, a consensus among botanists, and one which could change tomorrow, literally with the turning of a stone.

Most botanists agree that a progenitor group, something like the extinct seed-bearing ferns, led the way. Spore-producing leaves were steadily reduced and fused. Leaves producing male spores or pollen became the earliest stamens. Leaves bearing egg cups fused, and folded into carpels or pistils which would elaborate into fruits. As the stem axis shortened, cycles of outer leaves came together into disk-like whorls of many parts. In essence, what we call a "flower" emerged.

## Tides of Flowers, Waves of Grass

*Each beaked style of the wild filaree (opposite) will untwist into a barbed, seed-bearing pinwheel (left), five arms ripe to hitch a ride on passing fur, feather, or denim. Where they land, filaments respond to humidity— they swell and stretch, then shrink and curl (below), drilling into the earth the seeds of next spring's green growth and violet bloom.*

*Footloose baby plants in need of a home, seeds gambol—and gamble— in dispersal adaptations evolved through the ages. They twirl on wings, waft on parachutes. Ripened fruits squirt them, pressure-burst pods fling them beyond the shadow of the parent plant. Animals became fellow travelers—hungry birds discovered bright, tasty fruits. Some plants grew seed coats so tough that abrasion in an animal gut could do seeds no harm and even enhanced germination when they passed through to the ground. Grasses developed plumes and hairs, and the wind easily dispersed their seeds. By the Miocene Epoch, 26 million years ago, they skipped amidst the hoofs of grazing mammals on the spreading plains.*

OVERLEAF: *Exuberant wild bloom emblazons a springtime swell of Michigan meadow, evoking Emerson's words, "Earth laughs in flowers."*

Before the flowers appeared, cross-fertilization was accomplished mainly by the wind. Each plant had to produce large amounts of pollen—an effective, albeit expensive, way to maintain genetic variability. Variability is important, for natural selection depends on it. The precocious flowering plants were presented with an opportunity for genetic diversity without depending on the vagaries of the wind for pollination. Because at this time the energy-rich tissues of the flower were already being visited by voracious insects, especially beetles. Insects which ate the floral parts also inadvertently transported pollen. If a balance between the genetically controlled chemistry of attraction and that of protection could be achieved, if the pirating beetle could be bribed as a pollinator, then the uncertainty of wind pollination could be overcome with less pollen—a significant saving of energy. And so it was. The long drama of insects and flowering plants had begun.

Nectaries and a myriad of sugars which could selectively attract insects across miles and miles brought pollinators from one distant stand of plants to another. Some plants began turning out molecules simulating those produced in the insects themselves, such as the volatile sex scents. Exotic perfumes, a whole arsenal of olfactory messages, sent promises of food. Some species of one family, the Araceae, to which skunk cabbage and jack-in-the-pulpit belong, enticed flies as pollinators by mimicking the odor of decaying flesh. Similarly, compounds arose in certain vital tissues, such as immature seeds and seed coats, rendering them unpalatable and protecting them in a variety of other ways.

Food producing and conductive tissues became more efficient as did the entire process of reproduction. Angiosperms met the challenge of the seasons by developing dormancy—the ability to withstand periods of dryness and cold. They controlled rhythms of bud production and leaf fall. The protective fruit walls offered opportunities for new modes of dispersal, some exploiting wind and water again.

The long journey was underway that would lead to our most advanced plant families of today, such as the mints, sunflowers, orchids, and grasses. No other modern life form would prove more crucial than the grasses from which primitive man would select cereals—the storable fruits which have been prologue to every civilization.

All modern plants from their beginning have undergone change and, while perhaps no living family can be construed as most like the one from which the array of modern North American flowering plants arose, the magnolias are probably as representative of the ancestral type as any. A woody shrub or small tree bearing flowers whose parts are indefinite in number, petals and sepals appearing alike, leaf-like carpels—all its characters reflect that conjectured ancient form.

While the definitive character of the flowering plant is the seed encased in a fruit, this group has orchestrated an amazing variety of adaptations, which in concert created the most efficient and versatile plants that ever were. During the last 60 million years they have met virtually every conceivable environmental challenge, from tropics to tundra. Their success at being was prelude to our own.

# The Triumph
## of the Mammals

John H. Ostrom

Late April, 1878; cold and blustery with a raw hint of snow in the air. A solitary figure struggles along the steep slopes of Como Bluff some 50 miles northwest of Laramie, Wyoming. All winter long, William Reed has clambered over the harsh ridges on a fool's errand: to dig in the frozen ground for fossil bones. But winter work is hard to find in Wyoming Territory, so on he toils in his painstaking search for fossils—to send east to the professor at Yale College.

High on a ridge he picks up a rock with tiny bones in it. One is a jawbone only half an inch long, set with minute teeth—a far cry from the huge dinosaur bones he has been sending to Professor Othniel Charles Marsh since summer. Still, perhaps it will please the paleontologist. He carefully pockets the specimen and labors on, little realizing the importance of that small jaw. But Professor Marsh would recognize it as a breakthrough, the first discovery in the Western Hemisphere of a mammal fossil dating back to the heyday of the dinosaurs.

The little animal must have looked anything but triumphant. No bigger than a shrew, it was probably a voracious predator, confined by its size to darting furtively after insects in the shadow of the hulking dinosaurs. The great reptiles were lords of the Mesozoic Era, and in their midst an assortment of these small mammals led lives of "studied inconspicuousness." Yet from such inauspicious beginnings radiated the astonishing array of modern mammals, from shrews to the biggest animal that has ever lived—the 100-foot blue whale.

For millions of years the early mammals were no more imposing than today's mice, shrews, and chipmunks, and may well have looked like them. But they had new ways of doing things, radical innovations perhaps pioneered by the reptiles but later developed by the mammals as hallmarks of their kind. The mammals are warm-blooded; most wear a coat of hair or fur for insulation. Mothers incubate their young for long periods in a womb, then bear them alive and nurse them. This protects the newborn and allows a period for instruction; by contrast, most reptiles emerge from the egg into a world they must face alone. Mammals also developed better brains than their reptile predecessors, and thus a capacity for learning and applying that knowledge to life. When the dinosaurs died off, down from the trees and out of the underbrush crept a host of these small creatures to exploit the niches the reptiles had owned for more than 100 million years. The Cenozoic or "recent life" Era—the Age of Mammals —had begun. The time was 65 million years ago.

From the outset of the Cenozoic, the mammals showed a rapid, opportunistic expansion, a clear indication that they had already come a long way from the reptiles. But when had they broken away, and from which ancestors? The origins of major life forms are among the most intriguing of all evolutionary questions, and the search for the roots of the mammals has been especially intense. So when Professor Marsh got Bill Reed's precious jawbone he wired immediately for a thorough scouring of the area. Suddenly the big bones were eclipsed as Marsh's searchers crawled on hands and knees in a feverish new quest: Get the little bones! Others joined the search, but it took more than a year to find a second jaw—at a spot three miles away. The new site

*A hollow tree trunk for a nursery and a living fossil for a mother, young opossums add one more generation to a design virtually unchanged for 70 million years. One kit nurses, enacting anew the great leap of the mammals in the race with other life forms. Somehow the possum kept to an old life-style, remaining a marsupial that bears its young alive but shelters them long afterward in a pouch. Today its kind survives alone among North America's placentals, mammals whose newborn face the world more fully formed.*
ALLAN ROBERTS

# Survivors from the Cretaceous Begin Life in Peril

In the march of mammals, mother opossum plods to a different drum. No placenta nurtures her fetuses; in folds of uterine tissue they absorb nourishment for a scant 13 days, shortest known gestation of any mammal in the world. Born no bigger than a wasp, each naked mite will then drown in a fetal sac unless the mother licks it off. This done, it gets no help from her as it struggles through a forest of fur to a pouch opening (below, at right). For the perilous journey—some fall off, others miss the opening—it has but one asset; a pair of strong forelegs complete with tiny claws. Inside it finds some 13 teats, though rarely do all of them function. It must then clamp onto a good one or die if all are taken. There it develops as other mammals do in the womb. Hungry 2-month-olds still drop in for lunch (right), but when mother forages, they ride her back on nightly rounds.

Early in the Age of Mammals, placental animals began to outstrip marsupials. By then Australia was nearly isolated. Pouched mammals "Down Under" still muster some 170 species, winners by default in nature's quest for a better way.

LEONARD LEE RUE III, BRUCE COLEMAN INC.

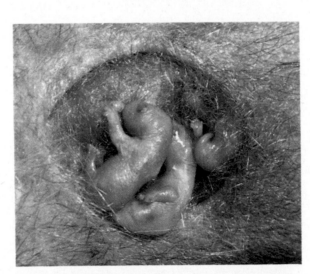

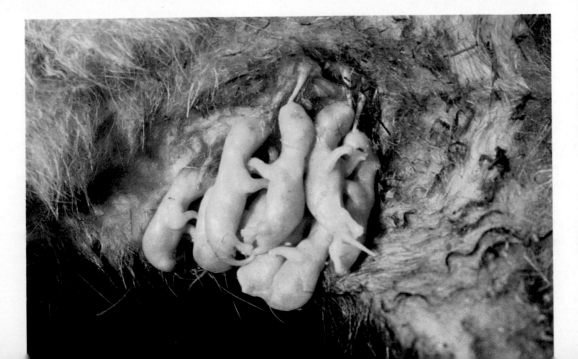

INSECTIVORES

Ictops

PRIMATES

Notharctus

EDENTATES

BATS

Icaronycteris

RODENTS

Steneofiber

Ischyrotomus

RABBITS

Moropus

PERISSODACTYLS

CONDYLARTHS

Phenacodus

Eohippus

ARTIODACTYLS

Archaeotherium

Syndyoceras

UINTATHERES

Uintatherium

PANTODONTS

Barylambda

ELEPHANTS
AND MASTODONS

Oxyaena

Hoplophoneus

Hemicyon

Eodelphis

Patriofelis

CREODONTS

Basilosaurus

WHALES

TRICONODONTS

Taeniolabis

MARSUPIALS

MULTITUBERCULATES

*Through the maze of Cenozoic time, mammals surged toward mastery of the land. When the dinosaurs fell 65 million years ago, creatures descended from tiny shrewlike ancestors quickly diversified into niches left empty. New groups arose, some to stay, others to fail—and still others, such as horses, rhinos, and primates, to die out here but flourish on other continents. Over the epochs and the coming Ice Age, "modern" mammals evolved—joined at last by a recent immigrant, Homo sapiens.*

DRAWINGS BY LISA BIGANZOLI

CRETACEOUS          PALEOCENE                    EOCENE                    OLIGOCENE                    MIOCENE

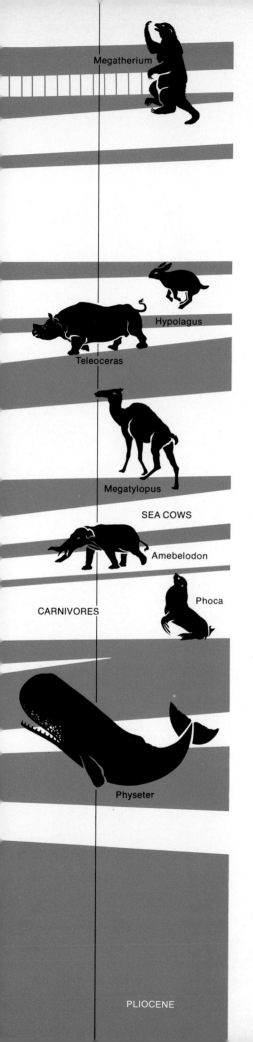

Megatherium

Hypolagus

Teleoceras

Megatylopus

SEA COWS

Amebelodon

CARNIVORES

Phoca

Physeter

became known as Quarry 9, the most important in the world for mammal fossils from the Jurassic Period, midpoint of the Age of Reptiles.

The Quarry 9 animals were small, probably furry creatures. Among them the shrewlike pantotheres seem the most likely ancestors of the two major mammal groups of today, the marsupial (or pouched) mammals and the placentals. But the creatures of Quarry 9 may not have borne live young; perhaps they were egg-layers like Australia's duck-billed platypus. Besides the pantotheres, we can recognize four other distinct, primitive orders; obviously the mammal threshold had been crossed long before the zenith of the dinosaurs. So the search for the earliest mammals has been pushed deeper into the past to the Triassic Period, which began more than 200 million years ago. Mammal fossils that old have been found on several continents, but not on North America. Here the quest continues, with good reason: The mammal saga began on Pangaea, the ancient sum of our modern continents. Life forms from this supercontinent are likely to be found on any of its pieces.

Teeth, because of their hardness, are the most lasting of fossils and thus the main basis for distinguishing these animals and their mammalian successors. The nipping incisors of many mammals are similar, but not the cheek teeth with their crown patterns of ridges and cone-like cusps. Among the Quarry 9 teeth the "triconodont" pattern has three main cusps in a line, the "symmetrodont" a wide symmetrical triangle, the "multituberculate" an array of points and ridges (or tubercles) in rows, and so on. All but the "multis" have sharp, high points for cutting and puncturing, much like the teeth of today's insect-eating shrews and moles, and suggesting a similar diet. Long, gnawing incisors and broad, grinding cheek teeth identify the multis as plant-eaters, apparently the first mammals to invade that niche.

To find teeth no bigger than large grains of sand, workers at Quarry 9 had to break up rock and examine the fragments with a magnifying glass, a slow, tedious job. But a later "tooth sleuth" found that fossil teeth which had weathered free were often picked up by ants and used along with sand in building anthills. So he shipped the hills to the professor—and even introduced new ant colonies so he could harvest their hills the following year! Today our ant assistants have been replaced by teams of students who wash the soil through special sieves in the field.

Why such concern over teeth? Mainly because we find so little else of these ancient animals. But perhaps after all they are the most revealing evidence we could want, for they show one experiment after another in tooth design to fit a variety of menus and life-styles—experiments in the critical job of getting and processing food.

As the mammals gathered strength toward the end of the Age of Reptiles, they left more than teeth. Our most exciting trove from Cretaceous times is an incredible 26,000 fossils from Montana's Bug Creek area: multis (as common, evidently, as mice today); marsupials, some probably ancestral to the opossum; and early placentals, including a sign of our own primate order: a single tooth from a mysterious animal named *Purgatorius*. At Bug Creek and other North American sites of this period, advanced opossum-like marsupials abound. Apparently the pouched mammals originated here, edged out the more primitive mammals (except the tenacious multis), and flourished until the placentals took over. The latter are named for the placenta, a membrane that nourishes the embryo in the womb; marsupials have an inefficient placenta or none at all. The placentals also have a better organized brain. In competition the placentals almost always won. But in Australia the marsupials were spared this unequal confrontation and have made a good showing. So it appears that the North American marsupials spread their progeny to other areas, then dwindled here to a single family, that of the slow-witted opossum. Why has this ancient beast survived among North America's competing placentals—and even extended its range in recent years? Perhaps because it will eat anything, live almost anywhere, multiply prolifically, and treat its young so casually that all but the fittest are weeded out.

Despite such primitive associates, we humans have little doubt that mammals are superior to other creatures. But perhaps we are all mammalian chauvinists. If other kinds of animals are less successful, why do they still exist? The point is that there is room for a variety of organisms, and there are many ways to make a living.

The mammalian way, for example, involves an unusually active life-style—probably the key to the mammals' success. Their high metabolism involves high body temperature, which is regulated internally at a nearly constant level. To help keep it constant,

## What Did It Look Like?

*At first, even the other searchers were skeptical. North American mammals of 100 million years ago were known from jaws and teeth, but no skeleton had ever been found. In 1974 Harvard's Dr. Farish A. Jenkins (below) led a National Geographic-sponsored expedition to Montana—and there in shale-and-sandstone badlands a co-worker, Charles R. Schaff, found the oldest fossil mammal skeleton ever unearthed in North America. A return trip in 1975 brought a twin to light. From them, artist and scientist flesh out an opossum-size meat-eater of the Cretaceous Period, similar*

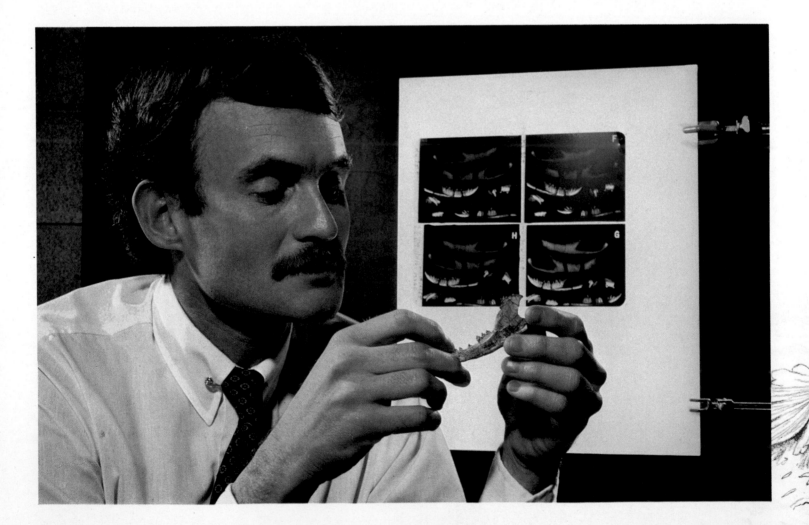

to the triconodonts of its day.

Rebuilding from the inside out, experts assembled the bones; by comparison with similar animals such as the opossum and tenrec of today, they judged posture and filled in missing parts. Artist Jay Matternes, renowned for such reconstructions, added the muscles this skeleton would need, again using living animals as guides. Fur clothes the mammals, but here guesswork supplies the pattern; stripes such as these would have helped this lowland forager hide. Amid litter of sequoia and ginkgo trees—also known from fossil evidence—the animal leaps at last to life, protecting from its own kin an investment in an ancient future.

VICTOR R. BOSWELL, JR., NATIONAL GEOGRAPHIC PHOTOGRAPHER. DRAWINGS BY JAY H. MATTERNES

Dr. Jenkins reconstructed a skeleton he calls "surprisingly large and robust."

Artist Matternes added musculature, drawing on experience in dissection.

Fat and fur round out the animal; missing bones leave its tail a mystery.

Were litters born or hatched, in nest or burrow? The artist makes this guess.

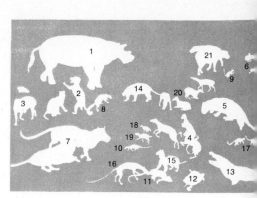

Animals of the Eocene answer
the artist's roll call in Wyoming's
Green River area. Fossils show plant
and animal types; studies of modern
creatures suggest color patterns.

Diversity keynotes the epoch.
Six-horned, saber-toothed, biggest
of land beasts, Uintatherium (1)
dines on greens. Trogosus (2)
gnaws bark as Hyrachyus (3),
a fleet-footed rhino, looks on.
A trio of Orohippus (4), an early
horse, lope by a log—and almost
into the jaws of Patriofelis (5)
whose splayed feet show the claws
most predators wore. Lemurlike
Smilodectes (6) was an early primate;
its order later quit the continent
and found homes elsewhere.

In many life-styles we see modern
counterparts: hyena in Mesonyx (7),
marmot in Ischyrotomus (8),
squirrel in Sciuravus (9), armadillo
in Metacheiromys (10)—and
near-twins to reptiles Saniwa
(11), Echmatemys (12), and toothy
Crocodilus (13). Stylinodon (14)
had gnawing teeth; Machaeroides
(15) was saber-toothed, unlike its
kin, archaic Sinopa (16). Hyopsodus
(17) had claws but ate plants.
Other vegetarians include hoofed,
even-toed Homacodon (18) and
Helohyus (19); the primitive tapir
Helaletes (20); and Palaeosyops
(21), a relative of the horses.

they can warm up by muscular activity such as shivering, and cool off by sweating or panting. Their nearest relatives, the reptiles, bask in the sun to get warm and scurry for shade to avert death from overheating. With the added advantage of fur or hair for insulation, most mammals need not depend on outside temperatures and can hunt for food even in the chill of night or the cold of winter.

That is essential, for they need much more food than their cold-blooded kin to fuel their higher metabolism. To use this fuel they also need to take in oxygen constantly. So mammals have developed a secondary palate that separates the nasal passages from the mouth and lets them chew and breathe at the same time. (Air breathed through a reptile's nostrils goes right into its mouth.) Thus the mammals can take time for chewing—and, over the centuries, for experimenting with better tooth designs—to speed digestion and make nutrients available more quickly. Reptiles usually gulp large chunks that digest very slowly, thereby limiting their activity.

Such differences give mammals another advantage: endurance. A lizard may run as fast as a cat, but after a short dash it seems to run out of gas. Actually it runs out of oxygen in its muscle tissues and falls into torpor until the debt is repaid, a slow process for the lizard, a brief pause for the cat. Even in the sprint the cat has an advantage, since the mammals have improved the primitive reptilian sprawl into a better running posture by drawing the legs in under the body.

With all these advantages, what took the mammals so long to rise? As the periods of the Mesozoic unfolded, each with its different array of life forms, the mammals stayed small and obscure. Perhaps the advantages of being a mammal had not yet been fully developed. Or maybe the dinosaurs simply monopolized all the large-animal slots.

In the dawntime of the mammals, Pangaea had begun to sunder. Now, as earth spun through Cenozoic time, the continents slid farther apart on their moving plates. The North Atlantic unzipped from south to north, keeping a tenuous link between North America and Europe for another 20 million years or so. Life forms had been fairly uniform across the supercontinent, but now each landmass was drifting through its own sequence of climatic and other circumstances, and thus developing its own peculiar roster of passengers—like Noah's arks, each voyaging the globe alone.

In North America the Rockies were rising; high plains were forming in the midlands. Forests waned before the spreading grasslands, which were born of the explosion of flowering plants in the previous Cretaceous Period. As new niches opened, new creatures arose to exploit them in a parade of evolutionary experiments. Many led nowhere; others led to today's vast array of mammal life.

In the ten million years of the Paleocene, opening epoch of the Age of Mammals,

*Big as a cow, an* Archaeotherium *duels a rival in an eroding savanna we now call the White River Badlands of South Dakota. These mammals of the Oligocene look like boars—and perhaps, as here, behaved like boars in battles for mates. But long legs and huge skulls set them apart from true pigs. The skull held only a puny brain and bulged with large cheek and jaw bumps whose purpose remains a mystery.*

*Trotting through time, the horse
has tailored foot and frame
to a changing American landscape.
Hyracotherium, its first known
ancestor, loomed no bigger than
a terrier. Often called Eohippus,
this "dawn horse" splayed four-toed
forefeet on the spongy forest floor
as it foraged 55 million years ago.
By Oligocene times, collie-size
Mesohippus browsed on three-toed
feet. As forests gave way to Miocene
grasslands, Merychippus stamped
only a middle toe into the sod—
and thus ran faster. First with only
one toe, Pliohippus foreshadowed
swift Equus, returned by Spaniards
to its homeland where thousands,
like these in the Pryor Mountains
of Montana and Wyoming,
again run wild in the grass.*

HOPE RYDEN. DIAGRAM BY LISA BIGANZOLI

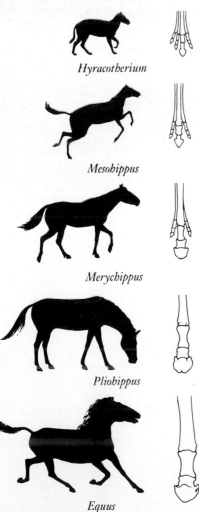

*Hyracotherium*

*Mesohippus*

*Merychippus*

*Pliohippus*

*Equus*

*Mammals of the Miocene draw life from the artist's brush. Four-toed* Merychyus *stares down a beaverlike* Steneofiber; *some scientists say this rodent dug the spiral burrows that later fossilized into "devil's corkscrews."* Merychyus *blended traits of sheep and pig in a "ruminating swine"—one of the oreodonts, gone now but dominant then. Hook and slingshot horns crown* Syndyoceras *(opposite). Like other two-toed runners, it arches its back to bound away. One-toed mammals, such as the horse, run with their backbones straight.*

PAINTINGS BY JAY H. MATTERNES; MUSEUM OF NATURAL HISTORY, SMITHSONIAN INSTITUTION

a variety of new orders arose as the mammals experimented explosively in every direction. Some of the results were grotesque; others might seem familiar today. Most of the early Paleocene mammals were dog-size or smaller, but as the pace picked up, so did size.

In the San Juan Basin of New Mexico, fossil evidence from 60 million years ago shows us an almost tropical Paleocene landscape. Lowlands burgeon with palms, cycads, and magnolias, together with willows and a variety of pines. Among them browse bizarre kinds of plant-eaters, the heavy-footed pantodonts. One of the biggest, the cow-size *Barylambda*, lumbers through the brush.

More diverse is a transitional group called the condylarths. *Phenacodus* supports a pig-size body on short, sturdy legs; five toes on each foot sprout wide claws that are beginning to look like the hoofs of later herbivores. But it has the big canine teeth of a meat-eater.

Fierce beasts leap from the underbrush to prey on the harmless vegetarians. Some are catlike ancestors of modern carnivores, but others—such as the small-brained creodonts—will become evolutionary dead ends. And perhaps high in the branches lurk the small heirs to the intriguing primate *Purgatorius* that left us that lone tooth at Bug Creek; by this time its line had expanded to four kinds of primates.

These same primate forms have been found in Europe, which in Paleocene times was still linked to North America. But none appeared in South America or Africa until much later. Thus, although the primates today are concentrated in the southern latitudes, the order may well have originated here or in Europe, where squirrel-like types gave way in the Eocene Epoch to agile creatures like the lemurs. With hands to grasp branches and long tails for balance, they clambered through a treetop world. But the final development of the primates was not to happen in North America. After 45 million years they died out here, returning late in the Ice Age in the form of man.

By the beginning of the Eocene Epoch, 55 million years ago, the world stage was being set for a new act and a new cast of players. North America's continental raft was pulling clear of Europe's. The growing Rockies spread sediment over the previous animal residents, leaving invaluable clues about early mammals in fossil boneyards of the Crazy Mountain area of Montana, the Bighorn Basin of Wyoming, and the Uinta Basin of Utah and Colorado.

Enormous lakes flooded the Green River Basin of what is now Colorado, Utah, and Wyoming, teeming with primitive perches, gars, and other forerunners of our modern freshwater fishes. In other basins roamed a curious mixture of the old Paleocene beasts and a variety of newcomers. Oaks, maples, hickories, and exotic breadfruit trees joined the rich forests of pines, palms, and cycads.

Primitive plant-eaters of the Paleocene were rare in the Eocene, the most successful group being the rhino-size *Uintatherium* family—grotesque, multihorned relatives of the once-dominant pantodonts. The largest stood seven feet at the shoulder, the giants of their day. Their skulls would one day be spectacular trophies to fossil hunters.

Meanwhile a great competition was brewing between two new vegetarian breeds, the forerunners of the modern hoofed mammals—the perissodactyls ("having an odd number of toes") and the artiodactyls ("having an even number of toes"). The ancestors of both groups picked their way across forest floors on five toes. But as the need to run increased on the opening savannas, they raised up on their central toes; side digits shrank to vestigial bone splints or disappeared entirely, leaving only a middle toe as in the horse family, or two middle toes as in the cloven-hoofed deer and its kin. Today the odd-toed tribe includes in its ranks the horses, rhinos, and tapirs, which have either three toes or a single large one on each foot. Their even-toed rivals are legion: Deer, cattle, pronghorns, pigs and peccaries, camels, hippos, musk oxen, goats, and sheep are the most familiar, with either two or four toes on each foot. It's not hard to judge who won the numbers game.

The Eocene Epoch was the heyday of the odd-toed hoofed mammals; 13 families arose. Most were dog- or pony-size—such as the little horse *Orohippus*. Later relatives grew to gigantic proportions. *Brontotherium*, the "thunder beast," was as big as an elephant, with a huge forked horn on its snout. Determined collectors pried loose its bones from near the Black Hills in the 1870's, under the noses of Sioux war parties who thought the fossil hunters were looking for gold.

By late Eocene times the ancient multituberculates had set an astonishing record for survival in the mammal world—some 100 million years. No mammal group we know of has topped that. But the rodents were finally nudging them out of their lucrative food niche and into oblivion. Being placentals, the rodents had an advantage. Today they are the most successful mammals; there are more species of rodents—squirrels, beavers, rats, mice, pocket gophers, guinea pigs, dozens more—than of any other order of mammals.

By the close of the Eocene some 38 million years ago, all the major mammal orders were well established. They had even invaded the sea and the air. A single incredibly delicate but perfect skeleton from the Green River lake beds of Wyoming shows that bats evolved very early and very quickly. Their origins are obscure, but their anatomy suggests they descended from tree dwellers that leaped after flying insects or netted them in large webbed hands.

The sea mammal story is no clearer. Primitive whale skeletons hint at ancestral carnivores that took to eating fish—but the largest of them, the 60-foot *Basilosaurus*, looks like a throwback to the days of the giant sea lizards.

Through the Oligocene Epoch, the long Miocene, and the

*Winners in the sprint for survival,
fleet-footed pronghorns graze in
South Dakota's Custer State Park,
a remnant of sprawling grasslands
that once fed these ruminants
by the million. Though named
Antilocapra, the "antelope-goat"
is actually neither. From small
deerlike mammals of the Miocene
Epoch its lineage fanned into
many variants. None emigrated
to other continents; none but
modern pronghorns survived the
great die-off of Pleistocene times.
Today's pronghorn, swiftest of our
mammals, can top 50 miles an hour.*

ENTHEOS

134

short Pliocene, the mammals continued to modernize. Among the holdovers were curious beasts such as ponderous, horselike *Moropus*. On into Miocene times these vegetarians dug up roots and tubers with the great claws on their long, powerful forelegs.

The climate cooled and temperatures showed greater fluctuation as the North American ark drifted northwestward. Grasslands spread, forests shrank—and with these changes, the fortunes of two groups in the horse family rose and fell. The large, fleet-footed grazers of the plains had high-crowned cheek teeth for chewing the abrasive, silica-rich grasses; their cousins had low-crowned teeth for browsing in the forests. The grazers flourished, but the browsers vanished before the onset of the Pliocene, last epoch before the Ice Age.

While great herds of vegetarians patrolled the plains and woodlands, a most impressive group of big plant-eaters lumbered onto the American scene: the mastodons, distant relatives of the elephants that would wander in during the Ice Age.

Driven south by cooling climates, the lowland-dwelling tapirs reached South America across the new land bridge that appeared a few million years before the Ice Age. The rhinos, too, dwindled in North America until the last survivor, squat *Teleoceras*, died out at the end of the Pliocene. Both families survived in the Old World, but in North America the horses were all that remained of the once-thriving perissodactyls. And they too would disappear.

During their rivals' steady decline, the even-toes proliferated exuberantly. As the Oligocene gave way to the Miocene some 26 million years ago, a varied family of "ruminating swine" about the size of sheep gained dominance—the oreodonts. This exclusively American group—among them the four-toed *Merychyus*—roamed the plains in what must have been millions. Their fossils are so numerous in the White River Badlands of South Dakota that some strata are called the "oreodont beds." With them flourished their relatives: the giant piglike *Archaeotherium* family, the earliest camels, and a strange, many-horned deerlike family that included *Syndyoceras*, a striking animal with a snout horn like a great slingshot.

It is hard to imagine what these sometimes wildly shaped horns were for. The beasts seem to have had more than enough for defense. Perhaps the elaborate projections were simply marks of sex distinction, or weapons wielded by males in mating battles. Or maybe they had other uses. It has been suggested that the ornate arrangements on some modern antelopes are tailored for use against the special attack technique of certain predators—or even as extra surface for temperature regulation.

Peccaries and pronghorns rounded out the roster of native American even-toes; *Merycodus* of the Pliocene is easily recognized as an ancestor of our pronghorns. The

*Even to the sea the mammals spread their kind. Here in the cradle of life a humpback whale glides out of a murky sunburst—and into oblivion's shadow as whalers hunt the ocean's titans to the brink of extinction. Out of murky beginnings swam whales of the Eocene Epoch, first with teeth, then others with plates of baleen for straining plankton from the water. Blue whales reach 135 tons, the largest mammals of all.*
WILLIAM R. CURTSINGER

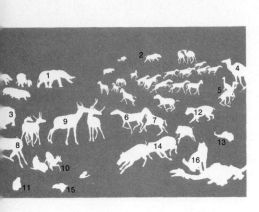

The end of Tertiary times approaches like a summer storm as mammals crowd a midwestern valley in the Pliocene Epoch. In grasslands that were forested before the Rockies rose, nature's balance tilts toward the hoofed herbivores. One newcomer lumbers into a sunny spotlight: the big, shovel-tusked Amebelodon *(1)*, kin to elephants. The burly rhinos Aphelops *(2)* and Teleoceras *(3)* share its valley—and its fate; each died out on this continent, though their families flourished in Eurasia. The same future awaits the 15-foot-tall camel Megatylopus *(4)*—whose dainty relative Procamelus *(5)* is also kin to llamas—and the one-toed horse Pliohippus *(6)*. Another horse, three-toed Neohipparion *(7)*, trots toward an evolutionary dead end.

Horns aplenty adorn the hoofed, even-toed Cranioceras *(8)* and Synthetoceras *(9)*, the pronghorn Merycodus *(10)*, even Epigaulus *(11)*, a burrowing rodent.

The bearlike dog Hemicyon *(12)* and the cat Pseudaelurus *(13)* turn hungry eyes to the peccary Prosthennops *(14)* and the rabbit Hypolagus *(15)*. The short-faced dog Osteoborus *(16)* watches them flee; there is plenty of food for predators in this grazers' Garden of Eden.

PAINTING BY JAY H. MATTERNES; MUSEUM OF
NATURAL HISTORY, SMITHSONIAN INSTITUTION

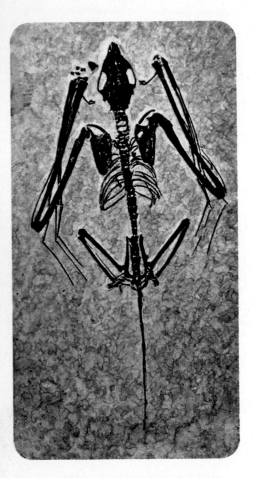

*They inherited the earth, spread to the sea—but of the many mammals, only the bats mastered the air. Yet they rank with some of the oldest land mammals living today. The big brown bat hanging from a branch (opposite) differs only a little from its earliest known ancestor,* Icaronycteris, *whose near-perfect fossil came to light in Wyoming deposits dating back some 50 million years. Unlike birds, many bats seem almost helpless on the ground—an irony of evolution, for on that firm footing the mammals have mastered the challenge of life.*

lineage of our modern deer developed in the Old World and eventually migrated from Asia, as did other modern even-toed groups including bison and ancestral cattle. Almost certainly these newcomers helped snuff out native horses and tapirs. The even-toed victory seems due to a combination of factors: superior limb construction for all-purpose bounding; adaptation to different foods (peccaries, for example, became omnivorous); and in some, perhaps the most important development: the ruminating stomach. This meant that they could graze quickly in the open, where the danger of exposure to predators was greatest, then retire to cover to chew the cud.

Plant-eaters were becoming faster, more alert, better equipped to elude predators. Meat-eaters had to keep pace or perish. The slow, dim-witted creodonts flunked the test, but the true carnivores—ancestral dogs and cats, raccoons and weasels—passed with flying colors. Their victorious tribe is called fissiped or "cloven foot" because the toes are separated all the way to the base. The fissipeds encompass both the "dog group" such as foxes, bears, raccoons, and otters, and the "cat group" that includes the hyenas and civets.

Early cats, stalking small horses or ponderous brontotheres across Oligocene savannas, came in two models: agile biting cats like our modern cougars and jaguars, and stabbing cats, the heavier sabertooths. The slashing sabers of *Hoplophoneus* could penetrate thick hides and leave deep wounds so the victim would bleed to death; such cats were ready and waiting to prey on young or sick stragglers when the tough-skinned elephants arrived. Biting cats such as *Pseudaelurus* of the Pliocene depended on a sudden pounce and quick bite into a vital organ. Most cats are not adapted to a lengthy chase, a tactic the dogs' ancestors have used since the Miocene.

From early doglike creatures dating back to the Eocene, 50 genera developed during the Age of Mammals. And diversity bred further experimentation. A huge Miocene "dog-bear" named *Hemicyon* foreshadowed the arrival of true bears. In the Ice Age its descendants switched from a carnivorous life-style and became omnivorous instead. And thereby hangs an attractive speculation.

In the seas along North American coasts range the flippered mammalian predators, the pinnipeds: seals, walruses, and sea lions. Suddenly appearing in the Miocene, they have no obvious ancestors, although it is thought that true seals may have had otter-like forebears. Walruses and sea lions, however, show some common resemblance to bears. Is it possible that some ancestral dog-bear waded into the water to catch fish, as modern bears still do? Might the experiment have become a habit—and the habit a beginning for whole new lines of creatures? Nature's process of evolution is always on the lookout for new opportunities.

As the ark "North America" drifted slowly across Cenozoic seas, floating farther from some of its sister arks and closer to others, the New World passengers evolved an increasingly distinctive and modern cast. But they were soon to be jolted out of their isolation. On the horizon ahead waited new links to other lands, the great threat of an Ice Age—and the era of man.

# Life in the Ice Age:
# Prelude to Today

Björn Kurtén

In slow and stately dance the ponderous plates of the earth's crust had been moving about, mountain chains rose and eroded, the waters laid down floodplains, always at their own serene rate. Gradually they had shaped landforms we recognize. In mammal life there came an undercurrent of quickening change. Perhaps in response to repeated pulses of cold as the Tertiary waned, the rate of evolution speeded up. Animals tended to grow larger; the world was becoming populated by giants. With the advent of the Ice Age, the tempo of change rose to a new crescendo. Animals were evolving in forms known today, mingling with the older, stranger forms of life.

At their greatest, ice fields up to two miles thick covered some six million square miles of North America, an awesome barrier from ocean to ocean. The glaciation influenced animal life of the Pleistocene Epoch in two important ways. First, the pressure of the ice and intense cold squeezed life zones southward into ever narrowing bands—the temperate zone with its deciduous forests, the subtropical and tropical zones. Second, the ice withheld water from the oceans, lowering the global sea level by as much as 400 feet. Where now the Bering Strait separates the New World from the Old, a broad land connection emerged. At the long-drowned Panamanian Isthmus, a bridge to South America had been upraised by plate movements. Animals could now migrate freely between the continents, adding variety to all.

Why did the Pleistocene ice fields develop? What is the machinery behind the Ice Age? The old Norse myths might explain the phenomenon as the chill breath of the Frost-giants blown over the land, while a monstrous wolf had swallowed the sun. The explanations of modern science, though more intricate and sophisticated, seem no less poetic, and no more certain.

Could it be that the sun did temporarily dim, either from its own internal processes or from an interstellar dust cloud rushing by? Does the solution lie in the processes that change the earth's surface, cause mountains to rise and seas to recede, and so affect the atmospheric circulation pattern and perhaps also the earth's retention of sunrays? Or in the slow wobble of the axis of the earth relative to its plane of orbit around the sun, causing sometimes cool summers and mild winters and at other times hot summers and cold winters? These and many other explanations have been advanced with excellent arguments, but none is universally accepted. Whatever the causes, the vast climatic changes had dramatic effects.

The history of Ice Age mammal life in North America may be told in three chapters, each named for a significant fossil site. It started some three million years ago with the Blancan, still essentially a Tertiary age; only toward its end did the cold winds of continental glaciation make themselves felt. Next came the Irvingtonian Age, beginning 1.8 million years ago; within it fell two great glaciations—the Nebraskan and the Kansan—and the warm intervals between. Finally, about half a million years ago the Rancholabrean Age commenced. It embraced the Illinoian and the Wisconsin glaciations, and ended about 10,000 years ago, when the modern epoch began.

The story is being pieced together, jigsaw fashion, from hundreds of fossil sites from Alaska to Mexico and Florida. Sometimes a single area reveals a long stretch of

*Massing a living fortress of flesh, shaggy hair, and thermal underwool, musk oxen meet the onslaught of arctic cold or carnivore as did their Ice Age ancestors. With such cold-adapted mammals as reindeer, woolly mammoth, bison, and wolf, they migrated from Eurasia across the Bering land bridge. Musk oxen made their move in the massive continent-to-continent exchange of animals 150,000 years ago, when sea level set an all-time low. Dying out in lands of origin, the musk ox makes its stand on tundra of Canada and Greenland.*
FRED BRUEMMER

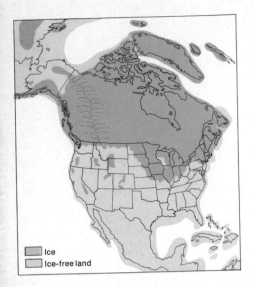

Ice
Ice-free land

White zenith: outer limits of
the ice that burdened
North America at least four times.
Earth's crust sagged. Seas shrank.
Land areas expanded. Over tongues
of land joining continents coursed
a two-way traffic in animals seeking
more congenial environments.
Separate ice fields, born in the east
and in the west, grew and finally
met, blocking entry from the north.
South of the frozen wasteland,
plant zones ranged from tundra
through coniferous forests to boreal
woods and bogs where the American
mastodon (opposite) roamed. This
elephant-like beast descended from
Old World forebears that entered
North America before the ice
spread over the land. Still here
as the ice melted—but now extinct—
it bore witness to an age.
PAINTING BY ZDENEK BURIAN

OVERLEAF: Subpolar glacier spills
over the lip of Greenland's icy
highland. This major remnant of
America's deep-frozen past, covering
80 percent of the island, forms an
invaluable Ice Age laboratory.
Antarctica and Greenland together
contain 99 percent of the world's
present-day glacial ice.
AUSTIN POST, U. S. GEOLOGICAL SURVEY

earth history—in the San Pedro Valley of Arizona, sectioned strata span two million years. At other points, the picture given may be a geological snapshot: a single fossil-bearing stratum in what remains of a transient river bed or in the recesses of a cave inhabited by animals or humans for only a few millenniums. From painstaking research—the identification and dating of innumerable fossil bones—emerges a very complex story. Before our eyes we can see the hordes of animals move across the continent, evolve, meet changes, do or die out. The mammals alone number some 500 species, ranging in size from tiny shrews to gigantic mammoths and ground sloths.

The Blancan Age took its name from Mount Blanco, Texas—a modest "White Mountain," closer to a molehill in size—where in 1891 men first dug up remains of its animal world. Now we know many areas where Blancans left their bones: Nebraska, Kansas, California, Florida. A site in Idaho yielded herds of fossil horses.

Horses made up a key group of Blancan old-timers, for their development centered in North America. Along their long evolutionary road trod ever more efficient variations on the horse theme until, about 3.2 million years ago, the one-toed modern genus *Equus* trotted in. But in Blancan times, a horse of another type still shared the scene: the three-toed, small and graceful *Nannippus*. These gazelle-horses died off gradually, region by region, until all had vanished; the one-toed types multiplied and came to reign supreme in the Ice Age. From North America they crossed the land bridges and reached nearly every corner of the inhabitable world.

Even more all-American than horses, camels until early Blancan times lived only on this continent. The many kinds varied from small, lightly built creatures to enormous animals with giraffe-like necks and legs. From them came the living llamas of South America and the camels of the Old World. Extinction, at the end of the Ice Age, robbed their home continent of both camels and horses. The pronghorn antelope is the sole surviving species of a third native North American group.

Horses, camels, and pronghorns all had particularly adapted to life on the open plain, and in Blancan times they ranged widely over the continent. Common forest dwellers included peccaries and a deer nearly identical with the living white-tail. A great variety of small animals—relatives and ancestors of pocket gophers, rats, mice, voles, shrews, and moles of today—filled in odd corners of the faunal portrait. We may certainly picture the Blancan as an age of plenty. Carnivores ranging from tiny weasels to hulking saber-toothed cats lived off the hordes of herbivores. One intriguing native was the bone-eating dog *Borophagus*. The size of a sheepdog, it had shorter legs, a massive head, and jaws armed with enormous bone-crushing teeth. *Borophagus* evolved in North America and has not been found elsewhere.

In addition to such old-line Americans, the continent nurtured members of clans that originated elsewhere in the world. Some also had a long history; for instance, mastodons—gigantic browsers that had reached America well back in the Tertiary, but had originated in Africa. Newer immigrants in the Blancan had arrived from South America by way of the recently emerged land connection. They came in

three principal guises: the big, hairy ground sloths; the tortoise-like giant glyptodonts; and the smaller, but still well-armored armadillos.

Among the immigrant carnivores from the Old World, perhaps the most surprising was a hyena, the only member of that family known to have reached the New World. Called *Chasmaporthetes*, it was a fast-running predator, probably making its living in about the same manner as the cheetah—catching its prey in a very swift dash. Scientists were understandably skeptical when in 1921 Oliver P. Hay of the Carnegie Institution made the first report of this unknown animal, based on a small fragment of jawbone found in Arizona. Seventeen years later a better-preserved jaw of the animal from a site in Texas confirmed Hay's bold deductions.

Soon afterward a fossil jaw and limb bones of a similar animal—called *Euryboas*—turned up in France. Since then I have had the thrill of identifying its remains in the most varied places—Moldavia, Transbaikalia, Mongolia, China, Africa.

Was *Chasmaporthetes* the same animal as *Euryboas?* In the spring of 1975 I saw the clinching evidence. At Inglis in Florida, Dr. S. David Webb and students turned up jaws and leg bones of *Chasmaporthetes*. Looking at those cheetah-like limb bones, I felt no doubt. The New World animal was the same kind of hunting hyena as the Old World one. In such tortuous ways we accumulate the evidence from fossil bones.

Slowly, during the Blancan, temperatures veered downward with many a stop and reversal. Far in the north, ice caps grew larger; winter snowfall outpaced summer melting. As water became locked into the land ice, the seas retreated, draining the flanks of continents and the inundated pathways between them. With the first great American glaciation, the Nebraskan—1.8 million years ago—the Irvingtonian Age started. The mammoth, herald of the new age, discovered America.

Mammoths, true elephants, had spread far and wide from their African home. Now they added another continent to their conquests. Their most striking difference from modern elephants lay in their huge tusks, quite extravagantly curved, growing to immense lengths. They may have used their tusks as snowplows to uncover grasses. Early mammoths in North America closely resembled their Eurasian ancestors. In the course of the Irvingtonian they grew still larger and their tusks more impressive. The immense imperial mammoths remained lords of the plains almost to the end of the Pleistocene. A few other species evolved, too—we are not sure how many.

Changing climates and environments had their effect on the old Blancan faunas, too. The time came when some old-timers vanished: gazelle-horses, bone-eating dogs, American hyenas. The normal flow of evolution decrees that some creatures go on and sire the life of the future, others drop out. The place of those that vanish is taken by others, some of which evolved on the spot, while others may have arrived by long routes from distant corners of the world.

The Irvingtonian Age, named for a site near San Francisco, is represented by fossil deposits from Cape Deceit in Alaska to the Anza-Borrego desert in California. Hay Springs in Nebraska, the river deposits in Meade County, Kansas, and in Inglis,

*From Florida's watery boneyard divers dredge up fossil treasure: 50,000-year-old mammoth bones. Paleontologist S. David Webb (above) raises a 3½-foot leg bone, darkened by long immersion in the mineral-laden river. A global shrinking of the sea during the Ice Age doubled the area of Florida, then as now a green haven from the cold. The Pleistocene winter crowd mixed northern exiles with such tropical types as the super sloth, Eremotherium, 20 feet long, able to sit on its haunches and munch greenery from the treetops.*

*Tooth-and-claw encounter: In a lava
fissure in New Mexico, a Shasta
ground sloth lay closeted 10,000
years. Dry, warm air mummified it,
preserving skin, muscles, claws,
as well as bones. How did it
get there? The artist envisioned
an attack by Smilodon, the sloth
backing off, tumbling into the cleft.
Clumsy, slow, and probably stupid,
the ground sloths ranged upward
in size from eight-foot-long Shastas
to the huge eremotheres; another,
Megalonyx jeffersonii, was among
the first fossil finds of Virginia,
described by Jefferson in 1797.
The sloth's long, unretractable
claws could be used in defense,
but the animal was no match for
the prey-stabbing sabertooth.
To clear the tips of its tusks,
Smilodon's lower jaw arced down
95° from the upper (a yawning
lion of today gapes only 65°).*

PAINTING BY ZDENEK BURIAN

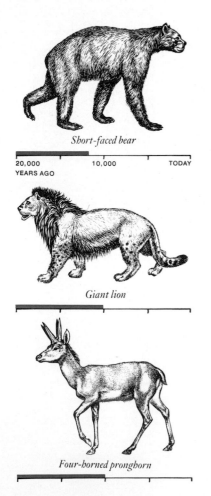

*Short-faced bear*

20,000  10,000  TODAY
YEARS AGO

*Giant lion*

*Four-horned pronghorn*

Florida (where *Chasmaporthetes* made its last stand), and caves such as one at Port Kennedy in Pennsylvania also contain fossils of Irvingtonian animals.

Nowhere is the story of the Irvingtonian Age more open to study than in the Great Plains, in an area from Nebraska southward into Texas. A long series of fossil-bearing strata gives us an insight into the gradual change and evolution of life. The Nebraskan Glaciation came and went, and animals spread northward during the warmer period. Then the climate became harsh again. A second great glaciation, the Kansan, gripped the land, and we find as evidence the shells and bones of northern life at Cudahy, Kansas. Comes another upswing in climate, and gigantic land tortoises live as far north as Kanopolis, Kansas. So the pendulum of climate swung in Irvingtonian times. And so it continued to swing afterward.

Bison spearheaded a new wave of migrants that enriched the North American living world once more. In the Old World, where bison evolved, we can trace their ancestry back through more slender cattle-like beasts to Tertiary antelopes. In America they seem to appear in a burst. Now we are in the early stages of another glaciation, the Illinoian. The Rancholabrean Age is beginning.

On the whole, the early bison in North America tended to immense size; they proliferated into many forms, undergoing a gradual diminution in stature and horn length in the course of the age. The greatest of all, *Bison latifrons*, had horn cores measuring seven feet from tip to tip (nearly three times that for a modern buffalo, which is certainly no baby). In life, the hornspan of *latifrons* was even greater, for the keratin sheath which makes up the outer part of the horn does not fossilize.

We tend to think of lions as tropical animals. But in the Ice Age they had spread north into the arctic life zone, crossed from Siberia into Alaska, then pressed southward when the climate became colder. The lion, extremely versatile, continued its southward trek, and toward the end of the Ice Age had reached Florida, California, even South America as far as Peru. At that time, at the peak of its success, it seems to have been the most widespread land mammal ever to exist except for man.

We have seen how living things evolved on the continent or made their way from distant parts of the world to form a community of exuberance and biological diversity in the late Ice Age. To them is finally added *man*, another immigrant from far-off lands. But first, let us glance at the continent as it existed before human beings came.

The northern part of the continent lay frozen in the grip of the Wisconsin ice from about 70,000 to 10,000 years ago. That ice field, perhaps the greatest ever on earth, included two systems. The largest, the Laurentide, grew from a nucleus near Hudson Bay to engulf nearly all of Canada and much of the northern United States. In the west another ice field developed on the cordillera and eventually coalesced with the Laurentide, forming an awesome highland up to 10,000 feet above sea level.

The northwestern tip of the continent stayed ice-free, but was isolated from the remainder by the frozen barrier. Instead, the area then joined Asia by the Bering land bridge. Across the treeless tundra moved great herds of hardy northern animals like the woolly mammoth, saiga antelope, Dall sheep, caribou, musk ox—all of Eurasian origin. Sparse woodlands and bogs formed a life zone for moose, wapiti (elk), wolverine, wolf, lion, and bear. Some native New World animals which had come north before the ice also were present: the short-faced bear, a ground sloth, and the American badger. Man was also present. In what guise we do not know, for we have remains of human handiwork only—tools made of bones and stone.

The southern edge of the ice wavered eastward through what is now Washington State and Montana, then looped southeast to Illinois and around to New Jersey. To the south, glaciers developed on mountains, tundra on lowland. Farther south the landscape changed to taiga—open coniferous woodlands. Study of the plant pollen and fossil animals in Pleistocene deposits tells us this was an "arctic" life zone—the collared lemming lived in southern Pennsylvania; the arctic shrew and caribou ranged the Appalachians as far south as Tennessee; northern birds like the ptarmigan and the spruce grouse ranged to Virginia and northern Georgia respectively.

In woods and bogs south of the ice browsed the American mastodon, one of the first Ice Age mammals to become known. In the late 18th century, learned men avidly discussed this animal, whose huge bones and teeth were plowed up in frontierlands of the young republic. Enterprising impresarios brought oddly mounted skeletons to the centers of the world: Paris and London savants marvelled at the remains of "Le grand mastodonte de l'Ohio" or the "Great Missourium." The mastodon roamed not only boreal forests and bogs; it was at home in the cypress swamps too.

In Florida, instead of plateaus and badlands as in the West, the paleontologist probes marshes, quarries, waterways. Regression of the seas brought Florida into close contact with tropical America. Ice Age immigrants from the south included not only animals now extinct but forms surviving today—not necessarily in Florida—like capybaras, vampire bats, ocelots, manatees, porcupines.

Peccaries must have been much in evidence, both in Florida and farther west. The long-nosed peccary apparently lived in the woods, the flat-headed in caves and on the plains. Bat Cave in Missouri yielded the remains of a hundred peccaries. Deposits on the plains dramatically reveal the destruction of small herds in dust storms; the dust that choked them also covered and preserved the bodies. The history of the flat-headed peccary recently has taken an unexpected happy turn—this is a case of a fossil coming back to life. In 1974 the flat-headed peccary, closely related to the vanished North American species, was seen alive in Paraguay.

West of the Great Plains, the Rockies harbored alpine animals: a small, short-legged mountain goat and a mountain deer related to the living Andean deer. The Great Basin: a surprise. Where we now see desert, a fertile lake district of Canadian aspect would have met the eye of a Pleistocene traveler. Beyond the Sierra Nevada, dazzling in its icy shroud, one of the most spectacular chapters of Ice Age life in North America was written. In the heart of Los Angeles is the former ranch that gave its name to the Rancholabrean Age. *(continued on page 159)*

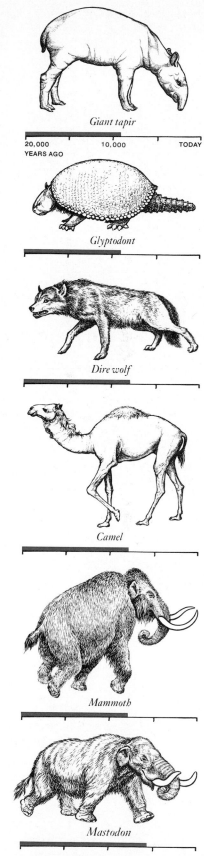

*Giant tapir*

20,000 YEARS AGO · 10,000 · TODAY

*Glyptodont*

*Dire wolf*

*Camel*

*Mammoth*

*Mastodon*

153

## The Survivors: Living Forms Linked to the Past

*Tale of longevity: The white flag upraised by a fleeing deer may signal "danger" to a fawn nearby and save a limb of the family tree. Fleet of foot and flexible of habit, white-tailed deer — born to be eaten — have endured a million years.*

*Big. Gregarious. Slow. The theme runs like a dirge through Ice Age obituaries. It would seem, says the author, "the bigger and more pretentious you are, the faster you may go out of business." Shrew, mouse, mole, squirrel, raccoon, coyote, fox, wolf, weasel — these dominate America's long-lived club, mammals whose lineages go back to the Pliocene. Small animals have scaled-down food and housing*

*needs and brief gestation periods, aids in outlasting hard times. But the fitness that spells survival takes myriad forms. Armor shields an armadillo (opposite, lower) threading a thicket; it digs into a burrow to elude coyotes — or cold. This tropical knight gets shivers at 72° F., may die of cold at 45°. Yet it flourishes in the Southwest.*

*The jaguar (right) in the south and wolverine, or glutton, in the north (opposite, upper), coped with vast climatic changes in their adopted land. Both face extinction as hunters take their pelts and encroaching man their wild habitat.*

WHITE-TAILED DEER; C. C. LOCKWOOD. JAGUAR;
TOM LARK, WESTERN WAYS FEATURES. WOLVERINE;
WILLIAM W. BACON III. ARMADILLO; BLAIR PITTMAN

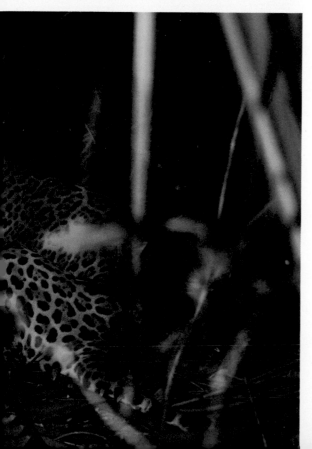

Belts of flora, like fauna, shifted
with the extent of the ice sheets
and climatic change. Taiga (left)
— moist forest of conifers such as
spruce, cedar, larch, jack pine —
fringed tundra abutting the ice.
Across the taiga strode the grandest
predator on the American Ice Age
stage. The short-faced bear, native
in origin, would dwarf Kodiak
bears of the present. More rangily
built, long and lithe of limb,
it likely was fast and ferocious.
The same stock also gave rise to
the Florida cave bear, a vegetarian,
heavily built and slow. It kept
to the south, Florida to Mexico,
while its short-faced kin claimed
the whole ice-free part of the
continent as a hunting ground.

PAINTING BY ZDENEK BURIAN

157

Here the remains of thousands of animals have been dug from the brea (asphalt). The pits, camouflaged by sheets of water, apparently acted as carnivore traps. Animals that came to drink got caught in the sticky mass. Their death struggles lured winged or four-footed predators and carrion feeders to a similar sticky end.

In the times of the Rancho La Brea fauna, the area was a rolling, open country with occasional stands of pine and cypress, and with juniper as the most common woody plant. With the sea in retreat, the maritime influence was less marked than at present. Grazing animals like bison, horses, and camels were more common than forest creatures. Although we find browsers such as the mastodon and *Megalonyx* sloth, the grazers—Columbian mammoth and *Glossotherium* sloth—dominate their groups.

Probably the most fascinating animal in the tar pits is the sabertooth, *Smilodon*. The big cat's remains pepper the continent south of the Wisconsin ice, but the occurrence at Rancho La Brea is unique in sheer numbers: well over 1,000 individuals. A larger descendant of the Blancan dirktooth, *Smilodon* attained the size of a big lion, and its upper canines enlarged into two great sabers with serrated edges. Heavily built and slow, it probably preyed on large, thick-skinned game. Many of the sabertooths flocking around the pits seeking easy prey were maimed, for the bones often reveal serious injuries. There are even cases where one or both sabers were broken off and the stumps worn down, showing the animal lived on afterward.

The most common mammal in the tar pits is the dire wolf, an extinct species heavier and with a more powerful dental battery than living wolves. Like the sabertooths and lions, dire wolves ranged widely, in the East as well as in South America. The giant lion visited the pits regularly, the mountain lion only rarely. Other entombed carnivores include coyotes, short-faced bear, black bear, skunks, and weasels.

Bird tallies at La Brea show a high percentage of flesh-eaters—more than half the total—including many eagles and vultures. The latter include the extinct *Teratornis* condor with a wingspan of more than 12 feet. Water birds like ducks, geese, herons, and plovers flocked to the pools. A ground fowl, the extinct turkey-like *Parapavo*, ranks among the commonest fossils. Pigeons, owls, and at least 36 perching species round off a remarkably full picture of Rancholabrean fauna.

Enter man. From where? Almost certainly he came to the New World across Beringia. In Thor Heyerdahl's words, the first man to die on American soil was Asian-born. People were present in Alaska and the Yukon well back in Wisconsin time. Carbon-14 dates on bone tools in this area range from 13,700 to 29,000 years ago. But during the maximum glaciation, ice blocked the road to the south. When humans first appeared south of the ice remains a hotly debated question.

---

*Ancient Americans and newcomers to the neighborhood meet at a spa near Las Vegas. Bones of extinct camels and horses and the tokens hunters left behind place* Homo sapiens *at Tule Springs 11,000 years ago. Said Charles Darwin, "What havoc the introduction of any new beast of prey must cause in a country, before the instincts of the indigenous inhabitants have become adapted to the stranger's craft or power."*
PAINTING BY JAY H. MATTERNES

159

A warmer interval, termed the Two Creeks Interstadial, heralded the final melting of the ice, beginning some 12,000 years ago. It opened up an ice-free corridor that men and animals could have traversed. Some evidence indicates that hunting bands, living off the land, did advance this way. The telltale fluted-point weapons so typical of early American cultures have been found at Engigstciak in the Yukon, at the very gate of the corridor. Another find from Edmonton, Alberta, might represent a later stage of the advance. Hemmed in on their right by the Cordilleran ice, on their left by the Laurentide, the invaders proceeded until ice-free country opened to the south.

Did the early settlers of Oregon and Idaho come this way? Cave sites in the area date back 11,580 to 13,200 years. Those dates crowd the beginning of the Two Creeks Interstadial somewhat too closely, presenting a puzzle as yet unsolved.

It does seem evident that well over 11,000 years ago the so-called Paleo-Indians had populated most of North America south of the ice. Their distinctive artifact is the Clovis point, named for the site in New Mexico. The leaf-shaped flint point had a "fluted" or hollowed-out base where it may have been attached to a split shaft. Such points have been found with mammoth remains, suggesting that these people specialized in hunting mammoths. They sometimes killed several at a time. At Lehner, Arizona, nine mammoths were found; at Dent, Colorado, at least 12 had been bagged. We know, too, that Paleo-Indians had dogs. Remains verify two distinct breeds: one a wolf-like dog not unlike the Eskimo dog, the other much smaller.

The Clovis tradition extended for a millennium. Then—perhaps because the mammoth herds were depleted—the hunters turned their interest to other prey, *Bison antiquus*, using the smaller and lighter Folsom projectile point. Still later, perhaps some 9,000 years ago, this big bison was supplanted by, or perhaps evolved into, the smaller *Bison occidentalis*. Hunters abandoned the fluting tradition for new types of weapons, exquisitely flaked points. At the Olsen-Chubbuck site in Colorado almost 200 *Bison occidentalis* were stampeded and killed by the late Paleo-Indians.

So far we are on reasonably safe ground. But in recent years, evidence of man's presence south of the ice, even in South America, at a much earlier date has been accumulating. At Taber, Alberta, fragments of a child's skull were found in a geological setting indicating an age well before the Wisconsin maximum; estimates range from 37,000 to 60,000 years. A series of potentially important human bone finds from California have been assigned dates from 17,150 to 48,000 years ago; dating methods include not only carbon 14 but also one which evaluates the change of amino acids in the collagen of bone. A skull from Ecuador was given the minimum age of 28,000 years by radiocarbon dating. The skull was assigned the same age by a study of the luminous properties, after gentle heating, of the calcium carbonate crystals that had formed inside it. Many other sites have yielded hearths with charcoal giving dates greatly exceeding the "accepted" 12,000-year limit, and assemblages of what apparently are primitive core tools may also point to the existence of vastly older cultural traditions than that of the Paleo-Indians.

*Linked in a Pleistocene food chain, thousands of animals met an early end in the ooze at Rancho La Brea in California. Herbivores such as the imperial mammoth came to drink from pools of water that veneered treacherous tar seeps. Trapped victims lured carnivores such as* Smilodon. *Predator and prey, mired down together, make a final feast for vultures. Called "death trap of the ages," La Brea's deadly glue garnered a bonanza for future bone sleuths. Analyzed and dated, its trove helps fill in the design and meaning of a fabulous yesterday.*

PAINTING BY ZDENEK BURIAN

If men did invade the continent at a much earlier time, what kind of people were they? Similar to present-day American Indians? Or of some earlier stock, perhaps with links to *Homo erectus* of Asia or Neanderthal man of Europe?

One thing seems clear: If there was a pre-Wisconsin invasion of human beings in America it had little or no effect on the animal life. The arrival of the Paleo-Indian, on the other hand, was soon followed by a dramatic demise of Pleistocene animals, particularly the large ones—the so-called megafauna. Within a few thousand years at most, they vanished: the mammoths and mastodons; the ground sloths, glyptodonts, and giant armadillos; the giant beavers and capybaras; the native horses and camels; many of the native deer, pronghorns, peccaries, and musk oxen; and carnivores like the sabertooths, the giant lions, the dire wolves, short-faced bears, and cave bears. In many parts of the continent, from Alaska to Florida, remains of megafauna have been found together with artifacts or bones of men. Is this coincidence? Or was it man the hunter who destroyed the megafauna?

According to one line of thought, persuasively argued by Paul S. Martin and others, man indeed devastated the wildlife of the continent in his advance across it. The big plant-feeders, which had not learned by experience the need to flee from human hunters, were easily butchered off. Large carnivores, deprived of prey, starved. Another, more conservative view points to the rapid change, and perhaps deterioration, of the environment at the end of the Pleistocene, depriving the megafauna of habitat. In this view, the effect of hunting man is incidental, or perhaps just the coup de grace.

The solution, if reached, may well turn out to be a compromise. In any case, there came a time, perhaps 8,000 years ago, when those great beasts were gone. A few, such as the mastodon, may have lingered; some dates suggest that it existed in the bogs and forests by the Great Lakes as recently as 6,000 years ago. We should not forget that many Ice Age species survive today, though most are significantly smaller now.

The end of the Pleistocene in North America is also the end of the huge mammals. Within a millennium or two, most of the great creatures that had played star parts on the stage of the Ice Age were gone; gone, too, the ice fields that had turned the northern lands into frozen waste for so long. One is tempted to think of the terrible Winter of Ragnarok in the old Norse mythology, of its doomed gods in a "world rushing to universal ruin." Yet Ragnarok was followed by a halcyon new era with the earth green and fertile once more; and the tremendous drama of the past vanished from the memory of humankind. Shaped by geological processes during time spans beyond our imagination, the continent lay ready to be settled by man, fulfilling in its beauty and diversity all the old prophecy of the *Voluspa* poetry.

*Now I see for a second time*
*Earth in fresh green rise from the sea;*
*The cataracts fall, the eagle flies....*

*Then once more will the wonderful*
*Golden tables be found in the grass,*
*Which once in old time the gods possessed.*

# The Living Land

## Edwin H. Colbert

We stood, my biologist friend and I, on a peak of the Front Range where it looms as an outpost bulwark of the Rocky Mountains in Colorado. The immense panorama absorbed us. We felt an integral part of the crinkled range stretching away to the north and south. In the fresh, invigorating air we seemed far removed from the hot plains that spread below us to the east, shimmering in the bright sunlight. Westward, we gazed at multiple ridges, and we could appreciate the foreboding of early pioneers as they faced the prospect of crossing the rugged land extending mile after mile to the shores of the Pacific Ocean.

Yet as we looked out across the vast landscape we saw it with very different eyes. For me, the geologist, the mountain on which we stood was not inert rock, but a dynamic thing, a great mass that had been lifted to its present height during millions of years of earth history. That upheaval stood dramatically apparent in the tilted sedimentary rocks along the eastern flank of the range—rocks that once were sandy plains where dinosaurs roamed. Intriguing tales and great spans of time lay recorded within the uplifted strata at my feet. And as I thought of the long succession of years represented by the mountains and plains within my gaze, the continent seemed to take on the attributes of something alive, a land ever moving and changing. It was a living land, extending far, far into the past.

To my companion, the biologist, the land also was alive, but in a different sense. He viewed the continent as the habitat for plants and animals—the place where trees and grasses, mammals and birds, reptiles and insects all live in complex relationships, not only with the rocks and soils beneath them, but also with each other. He was aware of the long ages that have made the land what it is today. Yet for him the past was a backdrop against which the drama of life takes place. His living land was here and now.

Had our vantage point been an orbiting satellite instead of a mountain peak, my friend and I actually could have seen the whole continent in all its ineffable grandeur. Still, we would have contemplated it with different eyes. To one of us there would have been the rocky expanse of the Canadian Shield in the northeast, the long folded ridges of the Appalachians, the great barriers of the Rockies and the Sierra Nevada, the plateaus and basins and coastal plains—all the physiographic divisions of the land. To the other, superimposed on the landforms there would have been the dark greens of tundra and coniferous forests, the variegated shades of deciduous woodlands, the emeralds and mustards of grassy prairies, the multitudinous plants and animals hidden in them—all the continent's biomes, its associations of living things.

Much like my friend and I, in this book thus far we have scanned North America from an encompassing view. We have surveyed it mainly through the eyes of geology and paleontology—the shaping of the continent and the progress of life as seen in fossil records. Now we turn to a closer approach, focusing on the continent through its regions, tying together its physiography and its biomes, linking the living land to the geological past.

I speak of tying together physiography and biomes with the realization that they don't necessarily package into the same neat categories. Geologists divide the United States and Canada into physical "provinces," each with distinctive characteristics. Plateaus, for example, cover about 15 percent of the continent, yet no two plateaus are identical. Some are semi-arid, some moist; some have been lifted higher than others by earth's thrusting. Rock formations vary. The kinds of life in them likewise differ. Consider also the Canadian Shield and the mighty Rockies; both are spread with coniferous forests, yet their animal inhabitants aren't alike. Too, mountains and rivers form barriers, but many plants and animals give little heed to them. Often enough the resemblances—or differences—in the life of the land have been determined by earth history rather than the present configuration of the continent.

The Ice Age most intimately imprints this heritage from the past. We live in the time of a glacial retreat. Only a few thousand years, a tiny fraction of a second on the geologic clock, have elapsed since the last great sheet melted. How adroitly life responded, inching northward to repopulate the thawing barrens as the ice ebbed. How marvelous the tradition of waterfowl migration then so precisely established—movements that spread stupendous numbers across the arctic nesting grounds each summer.

In the mid-1800's an ornithologist divided the world into realms based on the distribution of birds. Later, zoologists found that the scheme was applicable for all animals. Most of the North American continent falls into the Nearctic—new north—Zoogeographical Realm. It has many similarities to the Palaearctic—old north—of Europe and Asia. Plants and animals familiar to us are found in a broad northern band around the globe, but man's unprecedented slaughter here has accomplished in a few centuries what in the Old World took a thousand years or so. Virtual extinction of the bison is an example.

The Nearctic extends southward down the central spine of Mexico to the vicinity of Mexico City, where it meets the fringes of the Neotropical Realm of Central and South America. Let us turn now to look at this great Nearctic region through its physiographic provinces and its biomes. And though the two are contrasting approaches, which regard the continent from different viewpoints, nevertheless they see it as we shall: a living land—living through time, and living in the present.

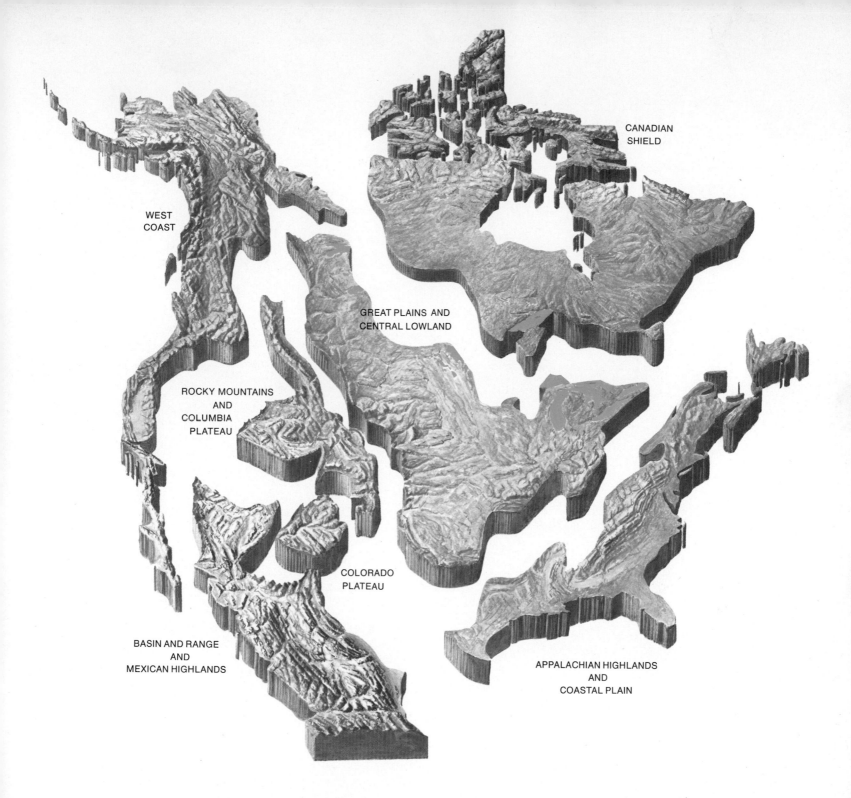

WEST
COAST

CANADIAN
SHIELD

GREAT PLAINS AND
CENTRAL LOWLAND

ROCKY MOUNTAINS
AND
COLUMBIA
PLATEAU

COLORADO
PLATEAU

BASIN AND RANGE
AND
MEXICAN HIGHLANDS

APPALACHIAN HIGHLANDS
AND
COASTAL PLAIN

# A Continental Mosaic

*That man of many accomplishments, soldier-explorer-scientist John Wesley Powell, was the first to attempt dividing the United States into geographic regions based on physical features. Today geologists delineate some 40 such "provinces" in the U. S. and Canada. Each has*

*a special character shaped by its geologic history, and each may also exhibit distinctive vegetation, soil, climate, and other factors. Sometimes, as Major Powell noted, boundary lines are "clearly drawn by nature"; sometimes they blend with one another. Provinces can be*

*grouped; the jigsaw arrangement adapted for this book links both comparable provinces—as in the Rocky Mountains—and dissimilar but related ones—the Appalachian highlands, adjoining piedmont, and coastal plain sweeping to the Gulf and to the Atlantic, for example.*

MAP BY TIBOR TOTH

# Canada's Ancient Shield

J. Tuzo Wilson

Hudson Bay and its surrounding lowlands lie like the hole in a broken doughnut, a hollow in a ring of vast wilderness broken only by Hudson Strait. No navigable rivers cross the immense spaces, nor do any fertile plains provide a highway. The summers are short and fly-infested, the winters long and bitter. In the north lies arctic waste. This jumble of rocks and cliffs, of lakes and swamps, of forest and tundra is a great shield of Precambrian rocks—some, at 3.6 billion years, almost as old as any on earth. All continents have ancient rock cores, called shields because of their shape and long stability. North America's core is the Canadian Shield, two million square miles of Canada and the United States, the frigid heart and solid foundation of the continent.

That few early explorers penetrated the boundless tracks of northern Canada is not surprising. More than 400 years ago Europeans entered the coastal bays and the Gulf of St. Lawrence, but most were content with what could be seen from the decks of their ships. Samuel de Champlain, in quest of furs, found a route up the St. Lawrence and Ottawa rivers. Henry Hudson, in 1610, adventuring on behalf of his native England, entered the great bay which bears his name, only to be cast adrift by mutineers. In the west the Danish navigator Vitus Bering had sighted through the Pacific mist a few mainland peaks, but he was unaware of their significance, for, as a contemporary chronicler wrote, "all beyond is uncertainty and conjecture."

In the 1670's the Hudson's Bay Company began to establish stockaded trading posts on the shores of the bay, to which Indians brought their furs. Curiosity and avarice spurred the traders on. They had heard stories from Mexico and Peru of treasure, of El Dorado, the fabled city of gold. Moreover, hope still lingered that a sea route might yet be found around the north of Canada or across the interior which would lead to the wondrous Orient. These hopes were encouraged by Indians who brought to the posts tales of a "Far-Away-Metal River" flowing through hills of gleaming copper rocks. Indeed, the Indians had copper nuggets to show, as well as necklaces, weapons, and tools fashioned from the bright metal. To find the source of the ore and to settle whether a Northwest Passage existed, the company in 1770 dispatched Samuel Hearne to the west. Hearne plodded with a party of Indians from Fort Prince of Wales, near present-day Churchill on the west coast of the bay, to the Arctic coast at the mouth of the Coppermine River and back—more than 2,000 miles.

Hearne's discoveries were unrewarding but important. He has left us a gripping journal and the first description of areas of the Canadian Shield not seen again by white men for more than a century. The importance for his own time was that he punctured a dream. There was no easy seaway to the Pacific. The Far-Away-Metal River—the Coppermine—also proved to have been a fantasy; in the "jumble of rocks and gravel" a four-hours' search turned up but one lump of copper "of any size."

The continent's great shield, exposed to view throughout the heart of Canada and,

*Eyes glittering pale as an Arctic sun, a female snowy owl homes into her nest on tundra less than two feet above soil frozen since the Ice Age. Only hunger drives this reluctant migrant south of its frigid realm.*
STEPHEN MASLOWSKI

in the United States, in the Adirondacks and parts of Michigan, Minnesota, and Wisconsin, underlies all the interior plains of North America. Deep erosion has exposed it in the Grand Canyon, in many of the Rocky Mountains, in the Llano uplift of Texas and along the Blue Ridge of the Appalachians.

The shield has played a fundamental role in Canadian history and economics. Its granite rocks produce a terrain that is rugged and infertile. Its harsh expanse divides Canada in two, rendering travel difficult between east and west. The effect is not altogether baneful, for the shield rocks are rich in minerals and the surface supports vast areas of commercial forests. For all of Canada from the Atlantic to Saskatchewan it provides a frontier. There Canadians can escape into a land of lakes and trees, usually less than a hundred miles from their homes. As the Yellowknife Indian Saltatha once asked about Heaven, "Is it more beautiful than the country of the musk-ox in summer, where sometimes the mist blows over the lakes, and sometimes the water is blue, and the loons cry very often? That is beautiful; and if Heaven is still more beautiful, my heart will be glad, and I shall be content to rest there till I am very old."

For a long time after Hearne's travels the shield remained a perplexity. Men thought of its hard and ancient rocks as granite, but that idea, like a fruitcake, hid a variety of details. The shield is so complex that even a century of careful study has revealed only the broad outlines of its nature. Pioneering geologists saw elsewhere, in the heart of mountain ranges, rocks like those exposed on the shield. These rocks suggested to them that shields are the roots of old mountains which have been worn down.

Consider how mountains are built. They form where two continental plates collide. The process is like the collision of two sheets of ice floating in a polar sea. The overlap pushes a ridge of ice into the air and forces a keel down into the water to form a root to the ridge. So it is with mountains. The process which forced up ranges like the Himalayas also pushed down a deep root of lighter crustal rock below the uplift. Just as ice floats in the sea with its ridges buoyed up by light roots of ice, so mountains are held in balance by their roots.

No part of the earth is subject to such rapid erosion as mountains. Rain and snow, freezing and thawing, torrents and glaciers reduce the mountaintops. As the mountains are lowered they become lighter, and the buoyant roots beneath slowly raise them up. This process—called isostasy—continues until all the roots have risen, the mountains are reduced to plains, and the crust is again of normal thickness. The result is the exposure of rocks which once were subject to the heat and high pressure that exist deep within mountain ranges. These are the shield rocks.

Today the Canadian Shield is a welter of granite knobs, deep gullies, swamp-filled hollows, and thickets of tangled shrubs and fallen trees. In every direction one's way is blocked by lakes and bogs and the wandering rivers that connect them. As a young geologist struggling through the woods, slipping on the rocks and clambering over cliffs, with a pack on my back or a canoe on my (continued on page 178)

# Canadian Shield

Begin with two million square miles
of Precambrian rock, faulted,
folded, altered, weathered. Belt it
with boreal forest; center it with
swamps; cap it with icy tundra.
Spangle it with lakes; net it with
rivers; rim it with mountains on
the east and plains on the west.
Result: the Canadian Shield.

Hardy plant pioneers of the shield
are the lichens (opposite). Part algae,
part fungi, lichens flourish,
encrusting bare rock. As ages pass,
their acids can break it down into
soils friendly to larger plants.

MAP BY TIBOR TOTH

Some arctic islands, of
younger rock, are not
part of the shield.

Queen
Elizabeth
Islands

Baffin Bay

Victoria
Island

Pond Inlet

• Coppermine

Coppermine
River

Great
Bear
Lake

NORTHWEST TERRITORIES

Back

Thelon

Baffin
Island

Foley
Island

Air
Force
Island

Prince
Charles
Island

Cape Dyer

Cumberland
Peninsula

Foxe Basin

Hudson
Strait

• Yellowknife

Great
Slave
Lake

Chesterfield
Inlet

ALBERTA

Lake
Athabasca

Seal

SASKATCHEWAN

Churchill

Hudson Bay

• Churchill

George

Baleine

NEWFOUNDLAND

LABRADOR

Nelson

• Thompson

MANITOBA

Churchill
• Churchill
Falls

James
Bay

QUEBEC

Gulf of
St. Lawrence

ONTARIO

CANADA

UNITED STATES

Lake
Superior

Timmins •
Kirkland Lake

Sudbury •
• Espanola

Ottawa

• Duluth

ADIRONDACK
MOUNTAINS

Lake Michigan

Lake Huron

Lake Erie

Lake
Ontario

| 0 | STATUTE MILES | 400 |
|---|---|---|

| 0 | KILOMETERS | 600 |
|---|---|---|

shoulders, sweat and flies blinding me, I was often reminded how hard a country it is. I spent many summers on the shield, flying into remote lakes by light planes which usually had a canoe lashed to the pontoons or under the wings. This load made takeoff so difficult that I frequently had to stand outside on the back of a pontoon to keep the weight aft until the pilot could get up speed. Then I could climb aboard through the spray before the plane became airborne.

From the air all the shield—except the mountains of Baffin Island and Labrador—is a level expanse so dotted with lakes that often a hundred are in sight at once. In summer the bare knobs of pink granite contrast with the green in the hollows and the dark swirls of the marshes. In winter the forests stand out as though sketched in charcoal; farther north the tundra is an abstract painting, white on white.

Between 3.6 and 2.5 billion years ago, the oldest shield rocks formed. They were once lavas and sedimentary rocks. Mountain-building so heated and squeezed them that they recrystallized completely. Between these granites of the oldest regions lie many narrow sinuous belts of greenstones, so called by early field geologists for their color. These were lavas evidently formed under water because they are structured in great blobs—pillows—like those which form when modern lavas erupt and cool on the ocean floor. The shield lavas may have erupted when the earth was hotter than today. They may be vestiges of ocean floors which closed to squeeze them between ancient, tiny continents. Their characteristic ore is gold. Greenstones weave across the shield north of Lake Superior, ringing Hudson Bay on the south and east and reaching into Minnesota and beneath the plains to the Rockies. North of Great Slave Lake and in Labrador are more of these ancient rocks. Younger granites which lack the belts of pillow lavas extend across most of the shield. Some, including those under the greater part of Samuel Hearne's route, are about 1.7 billion years old. Others, along the north shore of the St. Lawrence, in the Adirondacks, and in the Blue Ridge, are still younger—about 1.1 billion.

The last broad class of shield rock is sedimentary—little changed shales, sandstones, and limestones—resting upon older granites. One major north-south belt extends through central Labrador; it appears to have been laid down as coastal deposits upon the granites of western Labrador before another piece of continental crust collided with North America and added to its margin. Around Lake Superior and northeast of Lake Huron lie scattered areas of sedimentary rocks rich in copper, uranium, and silver. In the northwest shield, other large areas of similar rocks lie in and around the basins of Great Slave and Athabasca lakes and under much of the Arctic coast, extending up the Coppermine River.

I was at Coppermine in the winter of 1946 while commanding a Canadian military scientific expedition which I had named Exercise Musk-ox in honor of those rare animals of the region. They are not really oxen, but are related to sheep, a connection which shows in the skull-crashing battles of the rutting bulls. In summer musk oxen like to graze on grasses along river valleys and in moist meadows. In winter they shift to windswept hummocks and slopes where they paw through the snow to uncover willow shoots and frozen remnants of summer vegetation. Their strong sense of herd unity has often been their undoing. When approached they form a ring and stand their ground—a good defense against wolves but disastrous against hunters.

Our party, like Hearne's, set out from Churchill, leaving behind the great swag of boreal forest which arcs across the southern shield—the "spruce-moose biome," it's been called. We entered the "land of little sticks." Here the mossy tundra is patched with stunted spruce and willow which soon thin out to open windy prairies known as the Barren Grounds. Unlike Hearne, we traveled by large vehicles similar to light tanks. The expedition had split into two groups and in March I was waiting at Coppermine, our rendezvous. With me was Tom Manning, veteran Arctic explorer, geodetic scientist, biologist, and expert snowhouse builder.

Tom and I heard that some Tree River Eskimos had a sealing camp on an island 30 miles across the sea ice. We found a guide with a dog team and set out to pay a visit. The 30-below-zero night was dark except for a soft curtain of aurora borealis—not, that night, the magnificent display which the northern lights sometimes produce. In a zone radiating from the North Magnetic Pole charged electrons from the sun, guided by the earth's magnetic field, strike the upper atmosphere and cause it to glow like gas in a fluorescent tube. At times the whole sky is crossed by bands of swirling pastels, or shot with sudden rays of green, pink, purple, and yellow.

*At bay in a nook of orange star lichen, a collared lemming with its diet of vegetation anchors a food chain. It sustains larger creatures, from the snowy owl to the Arctic fox, even polar bears. For winter, this lemming grows a white coat, and unpigmented hair cells trap insulating air; claws thicken, the better to burrow in hard-packed snow. Frequent population peaks lead to hunger, stress, massive die-offs—and the cycle begins anew.*
TOM McHUGH, PHOTO RESEARCHERS

Despite our windproof parkas and pants, and the bulky mukluks on our feet, we got colder and colder. The dogs pulled on for three hours, the long, flat sled hissing and squeaking behind them. The sea ice was generally smooth but we took many a bumpy snowdrift. Partway we stopped by an upturned block of snow left by the Eskimos to mark a seal's breathing hole. Calculating—so it seemed to me— by the number of markers we had passed in the dark, our driver appraised that year's sealing as "good." A little farther on he spoke again: "See the lights." Soon a line of faint yellow glows appeared—the ice windows of an igloo village.

From the drifts around the igloos a swarm of barking dogs strained at their chains. Eskimos poured from the houses and small boys flocked to jump on top of us and ride the last few feet. Stiffly we rose from the sled and with great ceremony shook the hand of each villager. Even the infants stretched up till their heads popped out of the loose-fitting necks of their mothers' fur parkas; cheerfully they reached out tiny naked arms and hands to shake.

In one of the houses we were seated on the high snow bench, covered with caribou skins and blankets, that forms both bed and living place. The women had heated a great pot over a stone seal-oil lamp. We sat with the Eskimo men, who passed us bowls containing a two-course dinner: the first, seal soup ladled from the pot, and the second, boiled seal meat speared with a fork. The meat was delicious, sweet, not too tough, and floating in welcome fat. When our host asked if we would like to go to a dance, Tom eagerly accepted the chance to see a rare Eskimo drum dance. Inside the

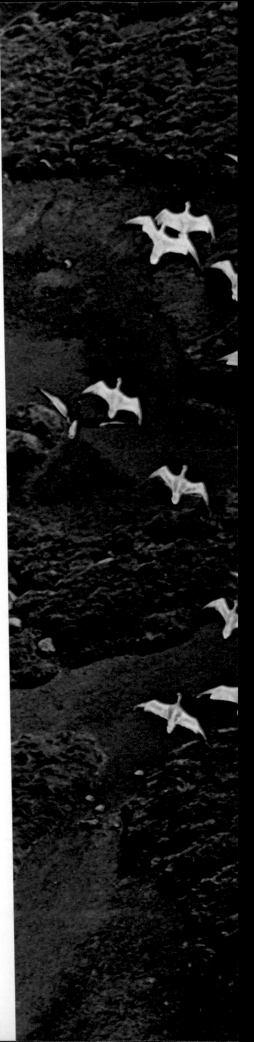

dance house—three igloos built together like coalesced soap bubbles—such a crowd milled about that the floor had turned to wet ice, and the snow roof was dripping. An Eskimo walked around blotting up the drips with snowballs.

One dancer performed at a time. Now a man, then a woman banged on the frame of a flat, caribou-skin drum almost a yard across, at the same time jumping, swaying, and singing. I recalled an account of one of these all-night festivities left by the Danish anthropologist, Knud Rasmussen. The songs he transcribed are hunting tales, love songs, hymns, and familiar stories of long-ago events. Listening to them, he said, was "like hearing breakers beating against rocky cliffs."

Although I was a stranger, I was not ignored. A woman said to me in broken English, "Have a fish"—and handed me a small char, raw and well aged. She then hospitably licked clean a glass for me and filled it with tea, lukewarm, sweet, and very good.

The next day in brilliant sunshine we returned to Coppermine and headed up the river valley in our "tanks." We saw in winter aspect the July scenery Hearne had described 175 years earlier—the barren hills and marshes near the seacoast, the gradual appearance of dwarfed pines and willows, the greenish tinges in the rock which he had taken to be a sign of the fabled copper deposits. We continued south, our vehicles bumping and rocking on their broad rubber tracks until we reached the smooth, snow-covered ice, several feet thick, on Great Bear Lake. We had crossed the tree line again. Two days out of Coppermine I drove the lead vehicle up the lakeshore to the Eldorado Mine. The buildings were perched on a cliff stained with the ores which had led to its discovery—yellow and light green oxides of uranium, red cobalt ore, green copper minerals, and native silver. Even then, in 1946, the mine was becoming depleted, but as the center of a wartime boomtown it had produced much of the uranium used in the first atomic bombs and piles.

Areas which are uniform in age, structure, and composition are called geological provinces. Between Great Bear and Great Slave lakes is a province of the most ancient rocks, probably a mosaic of still older continental fragments squeezed together when the earth was young. On either side of this Slave Province are younger granites; in one group, the Bear Province, lies the Eldorado Mine.

In 1939 I spent the summer mapping an area 150 miles south of Great Bear Lake. Plenty of cold, clear water to camp by and sparse woods not too hard to tramp through made our work pleasant, but a cloud of flies and mosquitos often trailed ten feet behind each of us like a fragile pennant. Aerial photographs guided us as we paddled or plodded. Today field workers use helicopters but we eschewed even outboard motors because it was too hard to backpack gasoline. We led a clean and peaceful life,

*Snow geese dapple the tundra on the west coast of Hudson Bay, goal of a 2,500-mile flight from winter grounds on the Gulf of Mexico. An abundant species, the geese settling to feed turn marshes to fields of snow; sometimes 1,200 pairs nest in a square mile. Timing is crucial in the short arctic summer. Mating often occurs on migration; eggs must be laid by mid-June for parents to rear goslings for August exodus.*
JEN AND DES BARTLETT

# The Arctic Loon: Great Diver of the Northland

On a mound of sticks and grass at the water's edge, the Arctic loon rears a family. Parents spell each other, turning eggs for even warmth (above) and brooding their young (opposite). A parent on guard feigns injury to decoy intruders (right, above). Precocious chicks swim with adults to learn the ways of life. Clumsy on land, Arctic loons breed near deep lakes; they herald plunging dives with doglike yelps. Though strong fliers, they can launch into the air only by a long, paddling scramble across the water. Some 30 million years of submarine specialization have shaped the loon to shoot through the water like a feathered fish.

JEN AND DES BARTLETT, BRUCE COLEMAN INC.

the air so quiet that if we stopped paddling I could hear the big dollar watch ticking in my companion's pocket at the other end of the canoe.

Our first attention was to the greenstone belts which we knew contained gold-bearing quartz veins. They proved easy to follow, but still we were puzzled. They all stopped abruptly along a great valley filled with lakes and swamps. On the other side there were no greenstones and the granite was more strongly banded, more variegated. We had discovered the boundary between the Slave and Bear provinces, but only years later did I recognize it as such.

Scattered in the woods were the winter huts of trappers. On portages we occasionally saw rotting birchbark canoes — a reminder of the old days. For the third summer running, I paddled up to a moose swimming in a lake. I was used to these large but shy creatures, and this time I grabbed the animal's antlers and jumped onto its back. The poor beast sank, but surfaced again with its head and antlers on one side of the canoe and me on the other. Since my companion sat helpless with laughter, I had no choice but to slide off and climb back on board.

Late in the summer the caribou herds returned to the woods from the Barren Grounds. Caribou are inquisitive, pugnacious, and more formidable than the larger moose. If we chased one, it was likely to turn and attack the canoe, and I never dared to swim with anything larger than a fawn. On land, if I stood still, caribou that perhaps had never seen a man would gingerly approach, sniffing the air and watching me intently. At night they regularly investigated our tent, stumbling and falling over the tent ropes. Black bears we saw less often. Occasionally a wolf appeared, or one of the smaller beasts — mink, porcupine, or beaver.

The habitat shared by these species gives them a good life in the summer, although life gets more exacting from south to north. The longer northern winter with its food shortages and extremes of cold makes special demands on animal life. Unlike migratory birds, mammals are year-round residents of the north and adapt to its hardships in various ways. On the shield some rodents hibernate. So do skunks. Lemmings winter in underground tunnels, insulated by a blanket of snow. Other animals — raccoons and bears, for instance — store up fat in the fall. They avoid the need to forage during the coldest months by falling into periods of dormancy but do not show the great decline in body temperature and metabolism which marks true hibernation. The moose often must forage all day long during the winter to find the leaves and twigs it eats at dawn and dusk in summer swamps. Moose range short distances seasonally, wintering in protected valleys. The caribou, on the other hand, is a nomad, in summer following changes in vegetation, in winter constantly seeking lichens under snow light enough to be pawed through. Moose are solitary animals, while caribou travel hundreds of miles in great herds from forested winter ranges to breed on the tundra.

In all the summers I spent on the shield I never carried a gun or saw an animal that was not more frightened of me than I was of it. Our main danger was drowning and, like Indians, we preferred to travel by the lakes rather than the rivers, even though, in

*Tundra trickery: Find the golden plover (opposite). Marathon flight from South America brings plovers to nest on a warm, ground-hugging camouflage of lichen and avens. To Eskimos, summer on the tundra is "the time of nesting birds." Noisy migrants teem, and white winter's silence bursts into sound and color.*

*Tracking the sun, an Arctic poppy (above) stores heat in its open bowl. Insects bask, sheltered from cool air and, as allies, pollinate when they move from flower to flower.*

FRED BRUEMMER. OPPOSITE: JEN AND DES BARTLETT, BRUCE COLEMAN INC.

*OVERLEAF: Barren-ground caribou flee deepening snow. Massively antlered bulls flank cows and a calf sporting nubs. On winter range, lichens make up half their forage.*

GEORGE W. CALEF

Banded iron formation

Uraninite

Silver

Chalcopyrite

Gold

one summer, we had to make 245 portages with packs and canoe. Most of the carries were short, however, and the smaller lakes were safe and pleasant.

Not so all the rivers. The most dangerous I encountered was the Taltson, which zigzags for 500 miles across the Churchill Province south of Great Slave Lake, surging over the rocks to many an angry stretch of white water. My respect for the Taltson was heightened after we met on its banks the only strangers we saw that summer.

In a half-hour's chat one evening we learned that the two, a chap named Christiansen and his Indian partner Ben Germain, were prospectors heading toward Tsu Lake where we later expected to meet our plane. We suggested another meeting there and went our separate ways. A week later, on approaching the rendezvous, we were alarmed to see flags of torn cloth fluttering on the trees and SOS messages scrawled on birchbark. One, which I kept, reads, "7 Aug 1938. Pardner drownded in the rapes. Im out on illent. Im going to try make that illent with sand on it till the plan com. Ben Germain." We found Ben and sent him out on our plane. The rapids at the Taltson's outlet from Tsu Lake we named after his late companion.

Naming the thousands of lakes and rivers was one of our diversions. Fred Jolliffe managed to get "Watta Lake" and "Quyta Lake" accepted. The Geographic Board of Canada felt that "Owattawetness Lake" was carrying the joke too far, but unaccountably accepted S.O.A.B. Creek for a particularly troublesome stream.

The Churchill Province extends from Great Slave Lake to northern Manitoba, where it was thrust against the Superior Province which underlies most of Ontario and Quebec. Today the railway from Winnipeg to Churchill follows this zone. Mines are worked in both provinces for gold, copper, lead, zinc, and iron. Along the east side of Superior Province, near Sudbury, Ontario, are the world's richest nickel deposits—the focus of a major geological controversy. The ores lie around the rim of a great oval ring of dark hills. Within this ring is a fertile basin, once a pine forest; its rocks are unlike those anywhere else in Canada.

Of the many theories about the origin of the Sudbury rocks and ores I favor the view that about 1.9 billion years ago a great meteorite fell, blasting a crater some 40 miles across. I believe that the impact blew the granite of the shield sky-high but that much of it then settled back into the hole. The force was enough to shatter the crust and lithosphere. Some of the melt from the mantle percolated up and was injected along the floor of the basin below the rock debris, melting and cooking up this fallen rock so that the lower part was again welded into granite and the remainder was left to form the unusual sedimentary rocks of the basin. As the whole slowly cooled further, solutions welled up like hot springs around the rim and deposited the rich ores of nickel, copper, platinum, and other metals.

In fact, about twenty meteor craters have now been recognized in Canada—near Ungava Bay, one forms a lake two miles across. That a quarter of the world's examples of these great circular scars are on the shield is a consequence of its age, for most large meteorites were gathered in by planets early in the life of the solar system.

Where a sapphire lake laps at roots
of ancient mountains in Ontario's
Killarney Provincial Park, shallow
Precambrian seas once spread,
compacting sand and silt in slowly
sinking beds. Cemented to rock, the
sediments buckled up. Mountains rose,
to be worn away by more than a
billion years of erosion to today's
stubs of quartzite and siltstone.
In soil pockets of bedrock crevices,
shallow-rooted white pine and black
spruce cling to a fragile foothold.
JOHN FOSTER

191

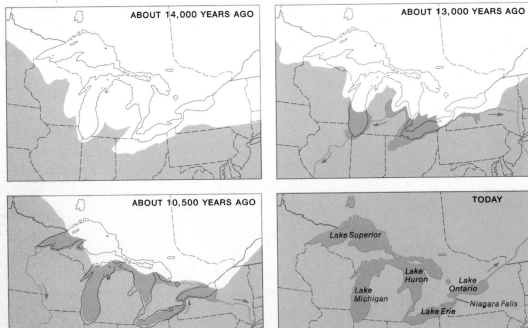

ABOUT 14,000 YEARS AGO

ABOUT 13,000 YEARS AGO

ABOUT 10,500 YEARS AGO

TODAY

Lake Superior

Lake Huron

Lake Michigan

Lake Ontario

Lake Erie

Niagara Falls

*Pounding for 10,000 years, waves have not erased glacial scars from Lake Superior's granite shoreline. From Precambrian times, water's ebb and flow across the heart of our land set the stage for the Great Lakes; eons of erosion carved valleys and basins. Then came the ice. Like a slow-motion yo-yo, it surged southward and melted back northward, scouring out hollows behind great ridges of debris.*

*Diagrams show some later stages. About 14,000 years ago, glaciers covered the area. When they began to melt, water ponded, filling the tip of Lake Michigan and parts of Huron and Erie.*

Modern mining techniques have varied greatly, but the simplest were used when I worked at Kirkland Lake and Timmins in Ontario. These mines exploited gold-bearing quartz veins a foot or two wide in the greenstone belts, veins which were vertical and easy to follow. Sinking a shaft a few thousand feet deep near each vein was a job for specialists. Other miners drove horizontal tunnels from the shafts to the veins. Rock was blasted down in excavations above the tunnels and dropped through chutes into ore cars which miners pushed to the shaft for hoisting to the surface. Gradually the miners worked their way upward from one level to the next.

I generally acted as helper to an experienced miner and the two of us were on our own, our world limited by pools of light cast from the acetylene lamps on our hard hats and by the walls of the damp, foggy caverns we created deep within the earth. The work was rugged, but we were independent, and even today, in highly mechanized mines, miners still share that fundamental feeling.

A few miles south of Sudbury lies yet another boundary. Here the granite belt of the Grenville Mountains was built against the more ancient Superior Province. Again the boundary is marked by old sedimentary rocks important for their ores—copper in Michigan, uranium and silver in Ontario. Along the north shore of Lake Huron these rocks, especially the pure white quartzites rising 1,000 feet in the La Cloche Hills, form country which hundreds of pleasure boats visit each summer. One beautiful spot is Dreamer's Rock on an Indian reservation near Espanola. Here a white pinnacle rises above a green sea of pine forest to an altar-like crest on which one can lie and gaze for miles to the shining lake and distant hills. One can indeed credit the story that this rock was the scene of Indian rites.

The great stretch of the Grenville Province from Lake Huron along the whole north shore of the St. Lawrence is splendid cottage country, close to eastern Canada's great cities, not too far from the United States. Three hours from city streets one can still drink water straight from the lake, still strip and swim in solitude, still feel a pioneer thrill as the boat heads through the waves driven by an autumn gale across a seventy-mile fetch of a great lake.

With luck one may see mink race over the rocks at the water's edge, hear splashing otter at play in a small lake, or come across a lumbering porcupine or skunk. Raccoons can be attracted to the cottage where they become tame enough to take from your hand the bread they love. In spring the females are thin, ragged, and ravenous. Later the reason appears—three or four fat, furry kits hanging back in the underbrush.

In the lake behind our cottage there is a beaver dam and sometimes we can see the sleek, blunt heads of the swimming beavers. We must be quiet or the most watchful will smack the water with its tail and the whole family will dive out of sight. Along the shores wild flowers grow. My favorites are the great white water lilies and the handsome scarlet cardinal flowers. Deep in moist spring woodlands you can find trillium and violets, and in glades among rocks and pines lady's-slipper orchids bloom yellow and pink. Midsummer brings Queen Anne's lace, and late summer, asters.

*The ancestral lakes of 13,000 years ago flowed mostly south, into the Mississippi. Back and forth the glacier seesawed, raising and lowering lake levels. Outlets waxed and waned. By 10,500 years ago major ice advances were past and the outlines we know today were emerging. Then the lakes drained both west into the Mississippi and east along the Mohawk Valley. Today the wayward waters all flow eastward into the St. Lawrence.*

*And still they change. Channels shift, mocking charts. Erie nibbles away its shoreline. Niagara Falls backs south some four feet a year as torrents wear its fragile shale.*
JOHN FOSTER

To me the most fascinating bird of our forest is the pileated woodpecker, red-crested and nearly as large as a raven. This grand creature hunts carpenter ants, and we can always tell that the birds are about by the long, rectangular holes they cut deep into dead or dying heartwood. We hear them hammering on the barren tops of tall trees—as well as on our tin stovepipe—and sometimes there comes back a distant answering tattoo. Bird watchers in Ontario forests claim that they can spot 60 or 70 species of birds on a June day—like the yellow-bellied sapsucker which makes rows of sapwells in a treetrunk, traps insects, and enjoys the combination snack; the ruby-throated hummingbird as it hovers over the wild honeysuckle or snatches insects flycatcher-style; or the tiny brown creeper with its nest under a loose strip of bark.

According to some ornithologists, warblers are our most characteristic bird, with 24 species breeding far from their winter homes in Latin America. Warblers, they say, are specialists in seeking nesting sites and in feeding; some divide the spruce woods into zones where the Cape May warbler flits about the very treetops while the Canada and the myrtle dart among the lowest branches—all in search of insects.

Not far north of the summer cottages, as Canadian distances are measured, is the area known as the Hudson Bay lowlands—the hole in the doughnut. Part is soggy black spruce and tamarack forest, part waterland, the "Great Muskeg." Grasses and rushes can grow if there is some drainage. If water stands still, sphagnum moss takes over and creates huge floating sponges of sod. My summer near James Bay struggling through the swamps in search of rock outcrops is one I shall never forget and do not want to repeat. Blackflies love this country. I don't. It does, however, challenge some geologists and prospectors. During the last century, some large diamonds have been picked up in soil and gravel south of the Great Lakes. It seems probable that the diamonds were carried there by glacial ice from Precambrian rocks lying to the north. Intriguing deposits of diamond-associated minerals have been found there, near the James Bay tamarack swamps, but—so far—no diamonds.

At the north end of Hudson Bay are low Arctic islands. Here, off the west coast of Baffin Island, are the last parts of North America to be discovered. In 1936 four young Englishmen fresh from Cambridge began a three-year exploration of the Foxe Basin region. They found a peninsula and two small barren islands which now, appropriately, bear the names Baird, Bray, and Rowley. The fourth man, Tom Manning, in typical self-effacing fashion, has no island. As a resourceful Arctic traveler, he has what he probably values more—the reputation of out-Eskimoing the Eskimo.

Some of us suspected that more islands might be hiding along that fog-shrouded coastline and in 1948 when the whole of Canada was photographed from the air, three

Nanook—*nomad, powerful amphibian, cunning stalker of seals*—*roams the Arctic trailed by the scavenging fox, shadowed by the carrion-loving raven. Polar bears winter near oceans and bays; often they drift on ice, even den up on floes, where puppy-size cubs are born. Spring breakup can carry bears far south into Hudson Bay; they summer inland, browsing on vegetation, at times blundering into settlements.*
H. P. L. KILIAAN

larger, low-lying islands far out in the basin appeared. The Canadian government sent Tom in a small boat to plant the flag on Foley, Air Force, and Prince Charles Islands. In one sense, that short voyage closed the exploration of North America. In another sense, of course, it goes on — by detail mapping of vast areas of the shield only reconnoitered by satellite surveillance and by prospectors drilling for ores.

Along the Labrador coast and on Baffin Island are mountains. I believe that the highlands here are part of the story of the formation of the Atlantic Ocean because the cliffs exactly match those of west Greenland. The clue that these shores were once united is the similarity of their Precambrian rocks, but the story of how and when they separated is told by a few small outcrops of lava atop the cliffs on either side. An ornithologist's photographs helped solve the mystery.

Along the jagged coastlines are enormous summer colonies of nesting sea birds. In 1950 a marine ornithologist, V. C. Wynne-Edwards, joined an expedition to the east coast of Baffin Island where, among polar bears, walrus, and harp seals, he found glaucous gulls, guillemots, murres, and a colony of fulmars numbering in the hundreds of thousands. The expedition saw fjords "with fantastic pinnacles and buttresses, all orange-red with the bird-cliff lichen," and birds swarming "like flies." Wynne-Edwards' photographs showed a cliff which seemed to be of lava. Three years later D. J. Kidd, a Toronto geologist, took a closer look. He found lavas. In 1963 I went with two students to see for myself.

We flew to Cape Dyer and walked to the edge of the 3,000-foot precipice overlooking the Atlantic. The lavas were there all right, and we camped in a July snowstorm. But most of the rocks we had come to study were inaccessible by land so we flew to Broughton Island to make arrangements to take to the water. Guided by two Eskimos in their large freight canoe, we headed back down the coast.

Navigation is high art in these fjord-indented, ice-plagued channels. The Eskimos have not lived so long off the sea, fishing and sealing so rugged a coast, without having become master pilots. Frequently we drew into crevices and inlets among the towering cliffs — harbors that no stranger would have noticed — where our guides scaled the heights to survey wind conditions and the ice floes and occasional icebergs drifting by, a menace to our boats. The ice sweeps south on currents, melting, turning, breaking, at the mercy of fierce Atlantic gales which sometimes pack it against the shore. When this happens Eskimos know that seals will be easy targets, and our journey halted often for our guides to take their prey. In summer the surface of the sea's pack ice melts to fresh water, so, as we maneuvered our canoe among the floes, now and then we scooped up water and boiled ourselves a pot of coffee.

Our study and mapping of the lavas showed us that about 80 million years ago there were great outpourings of molten rock into the 1.7-billion-year-old granites of this region and that, at the moment of this volcanic turmoil, Baffin Bay was opening to separate Greenland from Labrador and the Arctic islands. We had found another piece of the puzzle of continental drift and the spreading Atlantic Ocean.

## The Seafaring Saga of the Harp Seal

*In the glimmering under-ice world of the St. Lawrence Gulf, a harp seal attests to its scientific name,* Pagophilus groenlandicus — *ice-lover from Greenland. Gulf waters mark the seal herd's southernmost reach in an annual migration of some 2,000 miles. Despite their drive to reach whelping grounds, migrating seals seem a carefree troop, swimming on their backs, leaping, cavorting, and "standing up in the water," say observers, "so that they look like men."*
WILLIAM R. CURTSINGER

A nursing pup (above) balloons from a 15-pound newborn to some 100 pounds at 3 weeks. Adults fast while whelping, breeding, and molting; the mother converts her own blubber into the rich milk which fattens her offspring.

In twilight sociability, seals loll among the ice floes off their Magdalen Islands winter grounds. Here, in February and March, they bear young and mate. Hardy pups, on their own at 3 weeks, drift with the currents as hunger teaches them to find small crustaceans. All endure the annual molt — but growth of new coats coincides with the spring breakup of ice which turns the seal hordes north again.

By mid-June, with pups trailing, they reach southwest Greenland — a summer swim for a harp seal may be 700 miles above the Arctic Circle. By October, winter closes in the northern bays; November finds the herds once more streaming down the coasts on the southward-flowing Labrador Current, fattening on its cod and capelin.

Seals are pinnipeds — "fin-footed" mammals whose fossil record dates back to about 25 million years ago. Marine adaptation enables harp seals to dive 600 feet and to stay under a half hour. Their main predators are killer whales, polar bears, and man — whose commercial raids endanger the species itself.

WILLIAM R. CURTSINGER

The shores of Baffin fjords, as well as the low islands north of Hudson Bay, are ringed with gravel tiers—old beaches—showing that the land is rising from the sea. Radiocarbon dating of bones and wood, and measurement by tide gauges show that the land along the east side of Hudson Bay is rising by five feet a century. Most of Canada, in fact, is rising; sometimes the effects can be seen even in a short human life-span. Sandy Lunan, the Hudson's Bay Company trader at Baker Lake, told me in 1946 that since his arrival there 25 years earlier it had become harder to get small boats through shallow passages in Chesterfield Inlet.

We now know this uplift results from the melting of the last glaciers. Some two miles thick, the ice began melting—and lifting its load from the land—about 20,000 years ago and by 6,000 years ago had vanished from the continent, except for a few remnants which still cap the higher Arctic islands. The ice sheet was not static. It spread like syrup flowing off a pancake, until it broke off in icebergs in the ocean or melted in Kansas or Nebraska. It scoured the country, stirring and scattering the soil and rotted rock of millions of years. If much of the Canadian Shield is bare rock, it is because the glaciers carried far to the south and west the soil cover it once had. The meltwater changed it even more.

Several million cubic miles of ice turned to water, enlarging rivers like the Mississippi and the St. Lawrence to many times their present size. Potholes are scattered over the shield—circular depressions sometimes ten feet in diameter—where swirling currents drove water with its load of sand and gravel in a rotary motion. Smoothed channels mark where rivers flowed, forcing their way down through still-frozen portions of the glacier and along the ground beneath it. Many of these beds became clogged with gravel and remain as a network of ridges across the shield. I was fascinated, when aerial photographs became available, to trace the vanished rivers. Today these ridges, or eskers, as they are called, look like railway embankments, some of them hundreds of miles long, overgrown with trees in the woods, but conspicuous on treeless barrens—native hunters used them as lookouts. Their banks are scarred with the excavations of Arctic foxes and other small animals. Caribou and men alike follow age-old trails along the top, walking high and dry.

Almost exactly as Samuel Hearne saw it two centuries ago, the shield's wilderness remains intractable—Canada's everlasting frontier. It is at once the foundation upon which the North American continent rests and the mold in which the Canadian character is cast. The severity of the winters and the intransigence of the terrain have taught Canadians that without providence, affluence may be temporary. To survive in winter, preparations must be made in summer.

---

*Tiny human figures against an Arctic infinity, Eskimo children play ball on the sea ice of Baffin Island's Pond Inlet. For 4,000 years their ancestors preserved a harsh harmony with* nunassiaq, *the beautiful land. Now old ways are doomed. Settlements replace camp life, caribou parkas give way to store-bought clothes. But at Pond Inlet the sea's harvest still calls—each spring boys skip school to follow their fathers at sealing.*

JOHN DE VISSER

200

# Time-worn Highlands and Coastal Plain

Edward S. Deevey, Jr.

On a raft on a lake in the heart of the Berkshires, we spent a long hot day stabbing a tube into the water and hauling up core samples of mud. The worn old hills surrounded me with a familiar peace and beauty. Queechy Lake, about 35 miles from my birthplace in Albany, New York, had been my summer home since boyhood. But, as a scientist, I did not know enough about my lake. And that is why two students and I were on the raft. In that single day we spanned 12,000 years, back to the lake's birth. In a cylinder of fossil-rich ooze was a biography of Queechy, each layer of mud a chapter.

By the geological calendar, Queechy's story is very short. The lake's 50 feet of mud spans only the time since a glacier carved its basin and then withdrew. Nor is Queechy unique; glaciers are prodigious makers of lakes. And the lake itself is just a dimple in a vast realm of mountain and plain that courses from Newfoundland down the coast to Florida and around the Gulf of Mexico.

Queechy may have been chosen because I like the place so much. But the choice of a glacially created lake was not sentimental. I believe that the work of glaciers is the most important aspect of the natural history of the Appalachian highlands and the region they dominate. The area's vistas, products, and the ways its people make a living all trace directly to glacial landscaping. Also, we have to learn about life in an ice age. Though no one can be sure, I believe we are almost certainly entering an ice age and our descendants will almost certainly live in one.

There is no speed-reading method for deciphering a plug of mud. Those Queechy cores represented man-years of work. My two students are distinguished scientists now, but, after all their labors, they would admit there are unanswered questions in that mud. What are the questions we are trying to answer? Essentially, we want to learn the history of climates. We are trying to extend ecology from the present to the past so we can better understand the comings and goings of ice ages. By boring into the bottom of a glacial lake we can retrieve a time capsule. Plants can be identified from pollen encased in the mud, and climate can be inferred from the kinds of plants exporting pollen to each layer. A predominance of spruce pollen, for instance, indicates a cold climate; oak pollen, a warmer one.

To read Queechy's mud cores is to read the recent history of much of Appalachia. The lake, like the rest of the land that lay in the grip of glaciers, had little life when it started. Surrounded by tundra or rocky debris and fed by meltwater from masses of stagnant ice, the lake supported few algae and fewer fish. Its deepest deposit, viewed under a microscope, is an unrewarding paste of silty clay. The only fossils we see are wind-borne pollen grains of sedge and willow.

As we read higher up the core, we begin to find evidence of a changing climate, a time of glaciers becoming a time like our own—in the startlingly short span of about 1,000 years. Since then, environmental changes have been minor: slight swings from

---

*Gannets, descendants of marine birds that coursed Mesozoic skies, cruise the continent's eastern seaboard. These nest in spring on Canada's Bonaventure Island; they'll winter as far south as the Gulf of Mexico.*
JOHN LAUNOIS, BLACK STAR

HEPATICA AND FIDDLEHEAD FERN; WILLIAM A. BAKE

FIRE PINK; WILLIAM A. BAKE

BLADDERWORT; DAVID HISER

warmer to cooler, from relatively moist to relatively dry, in shifts signaled by increases in hickory pollen or decreases in hemlock pollen. In the last pages of the biography comes the denouement: farming, first by Indians, then by colonists. The clue: weeds, which favor land cleared of trees.

The first English settlers really had found a new world. What they looked upon—and, indeed, much of what we still look upon today—was incredibly youthful, the product of merely a few thousand years of postglacial climate. In fact, the traditional stepping-stone of the *Mayflower*'s passengers, Plymouth Rock, is a glacier's gift, a boulder called an erratic. An early theory held that icebergs, floating in the Biblical flood, dropped such boulders. Puzzling glacial deposits were called drift because it was thought that they had drifted in the ice of the Great Deluge.

Great ice sheets did, of course, haul rocks from one place and dump them in another, but even after science explained glaciation, geologists still continued to speak of drift. The colossal carrying power of glaciers can be gauged by the size of a granite erratic set down near Madison, New Hampshire. It weighs about 5,000 tons. Drift piled up as much as 400 feet in New England valleys; some valleys in New York's Finger Lakes region have 1,000-foot layers of drift.

As the glaciers ebbed and flowed, so did tropical and arctic animals and plants playing hide-and-seek with extinction. Caribou roamed Tennessee. Walruses lived along the coast of North Carolina. Woolly mammoths grazed on birch and willow six inches high in the tundra near Philadelphia—which at times had a climate like today's Churchill, Manitoba, on Hudson Bay, and at other times like that of Jacksonville, Florida. Between the glaciations, pawpaws and osage oranges grew at Toronto. Spruces and magnolias swapped places several times, as did armadillos and musk oxen. The north-south alignment of Appalachia's highlands paralleled the climate shifts. Broad, ice-free routes lay open to refuges in Florida for plants and animals driven south by the lash of arctic cold. (In Europe the Alps lay athwart escape routes, closing the Riviera to migrants. Such temperate types as hemlock, hickory, and hippopotamus became extinct in Europe.)

Wave after wave of ice, flowing from Labrador, covered all of eastern Canada and New England. The last sheet ended in a sinuous line that ran from Nantucket Shoals along Long Island to the outskirts of Philadelphia, then bent northward into lower New York State and curved southwestward to southern Illinois. In New England not only the Berkshires but also the lofty Presidential Range of the White Mountains were overtopped; the ice was at least half a mile thick. For about 30,000 years the only sign of life in northern Appalachia was probably an occasional snowy owl that alighted on top of the seemingly endless ice mountain.

When the last wave of ice began its slow retreat, change was imperceptible. Then, here and there a mountaintop emerged from the thinning ice. Great expanses of the glaciers began to melt. Masses of gravel and chunks of rock, suspended in the mile-high ice, jumbled together and finally dropped out. *(continued on page 212)*

# Appalachian Highlands and Coastal Plain

The Appalachian chain, whose rocky links began to take shape more than 400 million years ago, binds the birthlands of two nations. Stretching from Newfoundland's Long Range Mountains to slopes around Birmingham, Alabama, the Appalachians cover nearly half the north temperate zone's width.

To the highlands' weave of long ridges and valleys, the coastal plain adds a tracery of rivers and bay-scalloped shore. Seas cover half the plain, which forms the continental shelf; it drowned when glacial meltwater raised sea level. Between plain and mountain runs the piedmont, where waterpower generated cities. Strung now along the fall line, they create another kind of chain that binds the region.

Animals range habitats from the subarctic of bog lemming and caribou to the alligator-prowled bayous that fringe the Gulf of Mexico, whose surface waters reach 84°. Plants migrated here with people: forget-me-not, Queen Anne's lace, dandelion, spearmint. But bladderwort and most woodland flowers (opposite) are natives.

MAP BY TIBOR TOTH

STATUTE MILES 0–300

KILOMETERS 0–400

205

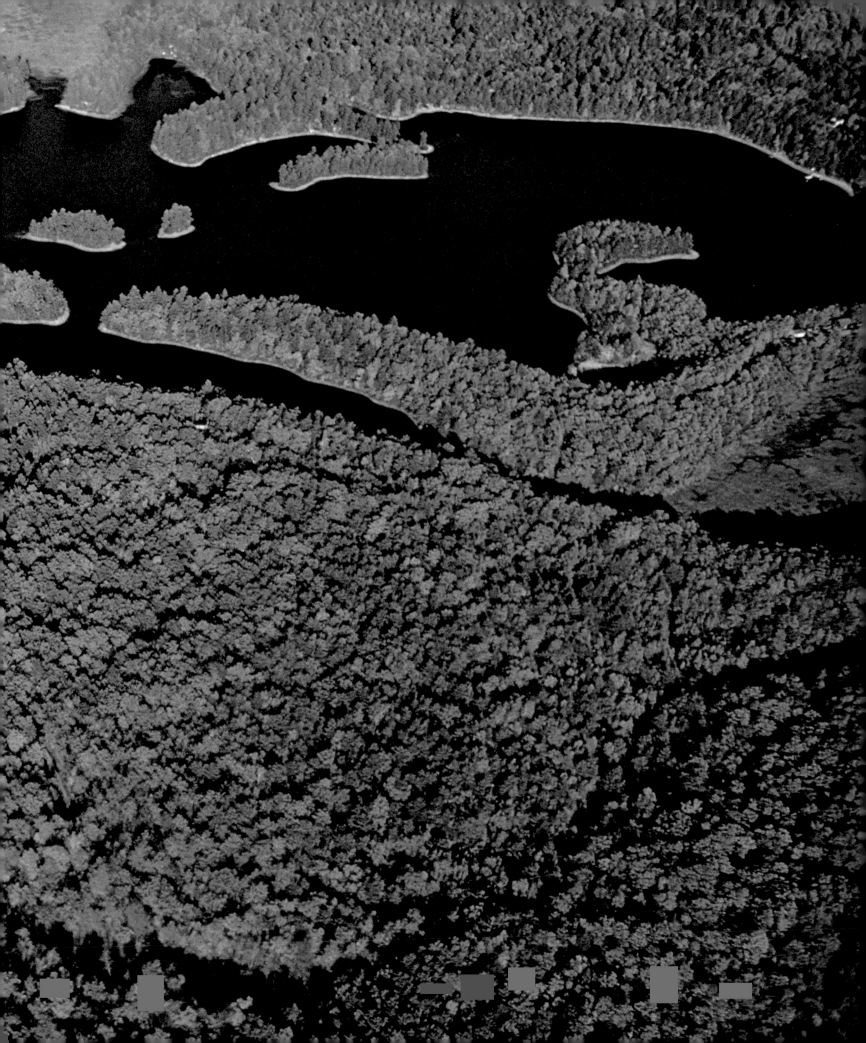

Piles of debris blocked valleys and created lake sites. Other piles, hauled along and then dumped, became hills called drumlins. (One is Bunker Hill.) Some strands of gravel became ridges, the "horsebacks" and "hogbacks" of Maine. Boulders, small rocks, and soil, scraped from Massachusetts, Vermont, and New Hampshire, were carried to Connecticut, whose own soil and rocks wound up on Long Island.

Blocks of ice broke off and embedded themselves in the sodden land. When the mammoth ice cubes melted, they left behind depressions called kettles. Sometimes the depressions filled with water. One such kettle pond is Henry Thoreau's Walden.

The withdrawal of the glacier is marked by a wide, thin sheet of "till," the boulders, gravel, sand, and clay that stayed when the melting ice pulled back. Where its edge was stable for some years, a thicker band, or end moraine, usually appears as a series of low hills. One forms the backbone of Cape Cod. Moraines course Long Island, whose principal highway routes thus were dictated by glaciers, not engineers. A moraine once spanned the Narrows between Brooklyn and Staten Island, sealing off the Hudson Valley and creating a titanic lake.

The last glaciation, which reached its maximum about 20,000 years ago, is the one most clearly recorded in the landscape of Appalachia because the erosive power of that ice sheet removed most traces of earlier ones. From other evidence, we know that several glaciations gripped northern Appalachia during the last short segment of earth's history we call the Pleistocene. For what happened long before that we must shift our view from the land we see to land that lies buried—or drowned. We must do this so that we can understand and appreciate the treasures locked in the rocks of Appalachia and beneath the waters off the seaboard.

Is such knowledge practical? Ask a seeker of coal, oil, or gas—the "fossil fuels" buried in Appalachia. Or ask any angler who tried to boil water at my cottage on Queechy Lake. The lake was scooped from limestone, which is softer than the rocks that stand as hills around such limestone basins. The lake water is "hard" and leaves a scaly deposit in teakettles; but it grows fine bass and perch. We always drive to the Massachusetts hills for our drinking water; the springs and lakes among those rocky hills offer soft water, free of limestone—and that's where the trout are. Such are the secrets of the rocks of Appalachia.

The sweep of the Appalachian highlands down the continent begins in the north with the Long Range Mountains, which rise about 2,600 feet above sea-girt Newfoundland. On the mainland the mountains continue with the Chic Chocs of the Gaspé Peninsula and the Notre Dame range east of Quebec. Mount Katahdin of Maine, northern end of the 2,015-mile Appalachian Trail, stands alone on a rumpled plain. So does another resister of erosion, Mount Monadnock of New Hampshire, which gave its name to the phenomenon of the solitary mountain. Both are part of the spine of the Appalachians, as are the White Mountains of New Hampshire, the Green Mountains of Vermont, the Berkshires, the Catskills, the Alleghenies, the Blue Ridge, and the Great Smokies, that fir-thatched roof of eastern America.

Eastward of the mountains, the land slopes to the piedmont, then to the coastal plain. Old, hard, metamorphic rock typically underlies the piedmont ("mountain feet"); soft, sedimentary rock blankets much of the coastal plain. The boundary between is the fall line: Rivers tumble over the hard rock of falls and rapids as the waters race down the slopes of the piedmont and reach the coastal plain. For cities built along the fall line, geology has been destiny.

South Carolina's history pivoted on the fall line, which separated the easygoing plantation life of the "Low Country" from the hills and small farms of the "Up Country." In 1790, in an attempt to foster unity between the regions, the capital was moved from Charleston of the coastal plain to Columbia of the piedmont. But the change hardly helped matters, for Columbia, being a fall-line city, was literally a source of power. Rushing water spun the wheels of grist and textile mills there, making their owners rich and politically potent. Hydroelectric plants later appeared on the sites where the mills had been.

On a night flight down the eastern edge of the continent—from, say, New Jersey to Virginia—you can see an electrical display of the fall line. A twinkling string links cities of the inner seaboard: Trenton, Philadelphia, Wilmington, Baltimore, Washington, Richmond, and Petersburg. More vividly than a mark on a map, that band of light shows the fall line. The founders of such cities picked a site where ships coming upriver on the tide could go no farther. At those sites the mill builders could tap the cheap power flowing by. And at the fall line a city could grow, for there the river could be crossed more easily; downstream, the river broadened, defying bridge builders. The Eastern Seaboard's earliest roads followed the fall line and connected the cities. So did railroads—and U. S. Interstate 95.

Many rivers, such as the Delaware, the Susquehanna, the Potomac, the James, the New, the French Broad, the Tombigbee, and the Tennessee, begin in the mountains and take wandering courses along valleys and then over ridges. Those rivers that crossed the coastal plain helped make it broad, for on their journeys through the mountains they carried a burden of silt which they dropped when, reaching the flatlands and spreading out, they lost momentum.

The coastal plain is broadest in the Carolinas and Georgia; the fall-line cities here include—besides Columbia—Augusta, Macon, and Columbus, Georgia. The plain bends around the southern flank of the Appalachians to Florida, Alabama, and Mississippi to merge with a similar plain that reverses the arc, beginning at the Mississippi Delta and nearly encircling the Gulf of Mexico.

In this region are the "youngest" city and state in the United States: New Orleans, its land built where the delta reached the sea around the time of William the Conqueror, and Florida, whose peninsula appeared out of the water about seven million years ago. For millions of years before that, marine shells, corals, and phosphatic mud landed on basement rocks of the drowned piedmont plateau, the seabed of Florida. Layer after layer built up in the seas until a 10,000-foot limestone mantle covered

*A water moccasin bares its fangs —and the white-lined "cottonmouth" that gives it another American name. The largest of three related species in North America, the viper can surpass five feet. Like many plants of Appalachia, it has an Asian twin. Predator in water and on land, it can outswim a fish or track down a small mammal. Though feared by people, the water moccasin usually lives where they don't. The copperhead, another member of the genus, often picks haunts near humans and inflicts far more surprise snakebites.*
ALAN BLANK, BRUCE COLEMAN INC.

213

the plateau. A slight arching of basement rock, the ebb and flow of Ice Age seas, some clay and sand from Georgia and Alabama—and the basic landscaping was done.

Like Florida, the coastal plain began as a sea bottom, and much of it still is. The visible portion, an expanse of low-lying land 100 to 200 miles wide, gives us thousands of miles of sandy beaches, including national seashores from Padre Island off Corpus Christi, Texas, to the dunes of Cape Cod and on to Sable Island, Nova Scotia. In its sweep along the gulf and up the Atlantic Seaboard the coastal plain provides the ground upon which 10 percent of the United States is built.

From Sandy Hook, New Jersey, to the rugged edge of New England and Canada's Maritimes, the coastal plain is mostly under water as the continental shelf. Its drowned plateaus are the fishing banks—from Grand off Newfoundland to Georges off New England—that for centuries have kept fishermen at work putting cod and other fish on European and American plates. No financier ever put a bank at a better location for maximum yield. Because the banks lie under only 100 to 200 feet of water, enough light, phosphate, and nitrate reach bottom to assure bountiful supplies of algae that sustain the banks' great schools of fish.

By a similarly fruitful union of geology and biology another feature of the plain—drowned river valleys—became bays rich in seafood. Such valleys underlie Long Island Sound as well as New York, Delaware, and Chesapeake bays. "Baltimore," wrote H. L. Mencken, "lay very near the immense protein factory of Chesapeake Bay, and out of the bay it ate divinely." Baltimore's seafood lives in a place of delicate balance: The bay's salinity ranges high enough to please oysters but low enough to discourage their predators, starfish and oyster-boring snails. Other bays, large and small, lured both marine and freshwater fishes, edible mollusks, great flocks of water birds—and in our early days explorers and colonists looking for food.

A 16th-century English mariner's complaint about Newfoundland turns out to be a fairly accurate description of the kind of place where the Appalachian mountain mass confronts the sea directly: an "uncomfortable coast, nothing appearing unto us but hideous rocks and mountains, bare of trees, and voide of any greene herbe." In a cleft along that treacherous coast, the craggy harbor of St. John's, Sir Humphrey Gilbert in 1583 claimed Newfoundland for England.

Explorers penetrated into the heart of the continent via the St. Lawrence River and the Great Lakes. The broad plain along the southern and gulf coasts invited other adventurers. Plantations spread, skirting the great marshes of Georgia and the Carolinas and following the gentle rises along the major rivers to soils so rich and easy to work that in some places a man could farm without a plow.

---

*Signature of New England, a stone fence embellishes a greening pasture near Norwich, Vermont. Glaciers buried the countryside here to a depth of some 2,000 feet, grinding mountains to nubbins and sowing the valleys with alien rock and rubble. Each spring the Yankee farmer harvests his crop of Ice Age souvenirs: cobbles and boulders thrust upward through the sod by the prying and lifting forces of winter frost.*
DEWITT JONES

Pincered gladiators clad in mottled
armor duel for territory in the
arena where life began. Spectators
include mussels, spiny sea urchins,
and stalked anemones—creatures
whose forebears lived in shallow seas
500 million years ago. Homarus
americanus, *the so-called "Maine
lobster," ranges the continental shelf
from Labrador to North Carolina.
It has a nearly identical European
kin. Fossil ancestors of these tasty
crustaceans have turned up
in Bavaria as well as Illinois.*

DAVID DOUBILET

217

Somewhere "lost behind the ranges" lay the country of the Apalachees, the Indian tribe after which the mountains were named. The land was not particularly formidable, but within its dense wilderness lurked Indians and strange animals. For two centuries after the first Spanish explorations in the southern tier and for a century after the establishment of flourishing agricultural colonies in Virginia and the Carolinas, the New World did not expand; the mountains remained a barrier across the westward course of empire.

The barrier is best viewed aloft. On a flight from Charleston across southern Appalachia, the coastal plain can be seen quickly giving way to the piedmont and the mountains around the high basin that is the site of Asheville, North Carolina. The terrain undulates in long folds of valleys and ridges that die away against the interior plateau, western counterpart of the piedmont. On the border of Kentucky, Tennessee, and Virginia, the ridgeline is cracked by the Cumberland Gap. Through this dip in the mountain wall passed the Wilderness Road, blazed by Daniel Boone in 1775. In the next 25 years some 300,000 pioneers took this way westward.

The valley-and-ridge pattern, 75 miles wide at its widest in Pennsylvania, stretches for more than 1,000 miles from Birmingham, Alabama, to Lake Champlain. Crumpled when Africa crashed into North America, the land then eroded for hundreds of millions of years. The folded landscape consists of hard rocks—the crests of ridges—and soft rocks, which floor the long valleys. Northward, even deeper erosion, of hard and soft rocks alike, has exposed the ancestral core of Appalachia, worn down to resemble the piedmont of the south. Much of the basic soil is the thin, stony stuff cursed by generations of New England farmers. Ice sheets contributed ground-up highland rocks, spread as gravel with silt in some of the deeper valleys.

The distribution of good soil has had much to do with the destiny of areas and people in Appalachia. Many of the migrants trekking through the Cumberland Gap sought not only more room but also better land. Why did some stay and some leave? A kind of answer echoes in the names of southern Appalachia's valleys, the vessels of the good soil and the bad. Place-names on a map tell how sedimentary rock rich in limestone and other fertilizing minerals has wound up in Rich Valley and Burke's Garden but somehow missed Poor Valley and Poverty Hollow.

Limestone caverns riddle the Shenandoah Valley, "breadbasket of the Confederacy" and apple basket of modern supermarkets. Limestone enriches the bluegrass of Kentucky, strengthening the bones of its thoroughbreds (and reputedly the mash of its bourbon). Far in the North, where the winters and the long summer days favor root crops rather than breadgrain, the limestone belt extends through Aroostook

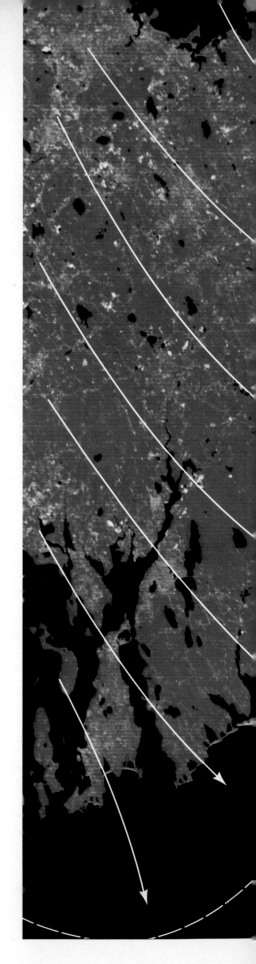

*Cape Cod, in a Space Age portrait from 570 miles up, flexes a fragile arm against ravages of tide and time. Ice sketched the outlines here, piling a ridge of debris that forms Nantucket and Martha's Vineyard. When the last glacier retreated 12,000 years ago, its scalloped lobes paused, creating the cape and its "forearm." The sea pounded the shorelines smooth—and will someday reclaim this land the Pilgrims knew.*
NASA (LANDSAT)

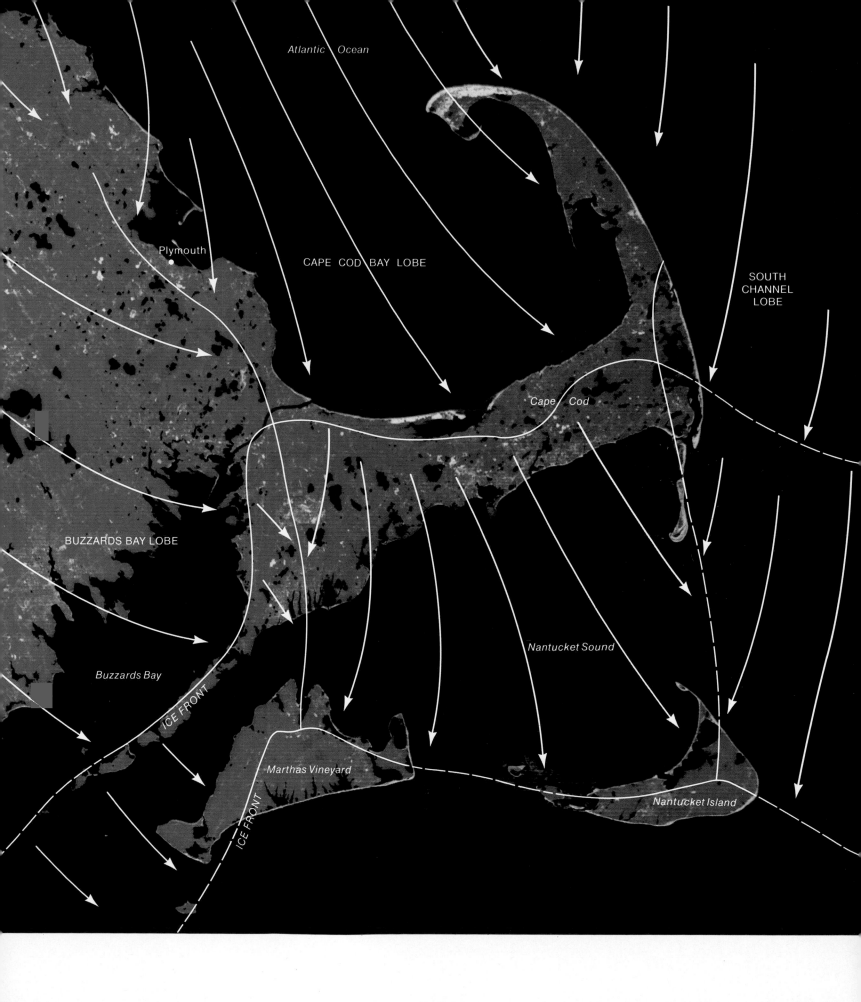

County in Maine to Prince Edward Island—making what has been dubbed a "spud-land" that produces much of the potato crop of the United States and Canada.

Other sedimentary rocks, known as Triassic red beds, form beneficial soils in a great belt that runs through much of the region. In Triassic time, from 225 to 190 million years ago, the core of Appalachia, already a high mountain mass, was wrenched and split from top to bottom. Gigantic rift valleys opened, and into these great troughs were dumped sandy deposits that later reddened to "rust" from oxidation of their iron.

At intervals enormous sheets of basaltic lava erupted from deep fissures and spread across the landscape. A westward-dipping lava sheet—called traprock from the Swedish *trapp* for "stairs"—exposes its edge as the towering Palisades along the western bank of the Hudson River, across from New York City. The softer red sandstone of the valley has been excavated by the river, which undermined but could not eat away the hard lava. Tilted to the east, the same lava sheet created the famous East Rock and West Rock at New Haven, Connecticut.

Iron supplies the distinctive color of the red beds' soil, but other minerals join to confer high fertility. As a bountiful belt it begins near the Bay of Fundy and underlies Nova Scotia's broad Annapolis Valley, a land of rolling farms and apple orchards. The belt swings southwest and follows virtually the entire length of the Connecticut Valley, a 410-mile-long corridor of New England agriculture and industry. The valley grows about 200 million pounds of potatoes a year, along with great quantities of other vegetables and the most valuable per-acre money crop produced in the United States: the shade-grown tobacco of Connecticut and Massachusetts. Yet in this cornucopia also sprout numerous factories and a network of hydroelectric dams, successors to the waterwheels that once tapped the river's power.

Red beds and trap sheets under much of New Jersey have helped make it "The Garden State" and have given the Carolinas their best agricultural soils. By contrast, piney woods cover much of the Carolinas' sandy coastal plain, where shortsighted, soil-depleting farming methods sapped the land in less than a century.

The giant we call Appalachia spans climatic and topographic extremes—its head brushing the harshest frigid wastes, its feet near the hot, moist tropics, its reach encompassing mountains, plains, and the sea. Upon its ancient rocks live wonders that flourished before the white man arrived and, with a few lamented exceptions, have endured despite his ever-growing presence. Some of the birds are gone forever. Except in scant remaining wilds, the woods no longer hear the timber wolf's howl or the bugling of the elk. But for the bird watcher or the plant seeker, this is a paradise.

The Great Smokies especially offer a garden of naturalists' splendors, from salamanders (about

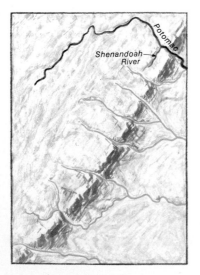

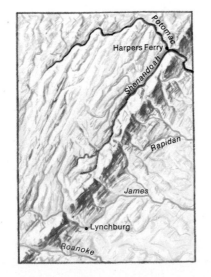

25 species) to flowering plants (nearly 1,400 varieties) to fungi (some 2,000). And southern Appalachia has some odd types, too.

I have three favorites: the Venus flytrap, an insect-eating plant of the Carolinas that Darwin called "one of the most wonderful in the world"; the anhinga, a fish-spearing bird of the wetlands of the Southeast; the bowfin, a fish that can live at least a full day out of water by using its air bladder as a lung. It is the only descendant of bony fishes with lungs that lived during the age of dinosaurs.

In a way, my favorites—along with many of the other plants and animals of the Appalachian highlands and the coastal plain—are descendants of a vanished world. A great gap exists between the ancient bedrock of the region and the soil that covers it. Some 200 million years of erosion has stripped relevant fossils from the highlands, effacing much of the history of the flora and fauna. The oldest fossils of this time span are buried deeply beneath the coastal plain sediments.

But scraps of the past can be found and read. From a bit of lignite, "brown coal," a paleobotanist can conjure up a forest and see it overwhelmed by migrating sand dunes or a shifting beach ridge. From lignite unearthed near Brandon, Vermont, he can picture a swamp forest resembling today's Okefenokee, a refuge for alligators and other wildlife in southeastern Georgia. Several million years ago black laurel, titi, and wild avocado (alligator pear) grew together in that Vermont swampland. All three plants still grow together in Georgia.

Analysis of plants in the lignite traced some to fruits of what Connecticut Yankees call sour gum or pepperidge and what the Creek Indians called tupelo. In its career as a plant and its afterlife as a peat-like fuel, the wood found its way into commerce, legitimate and otherwise. Its flames helped refine Jamaican sugar for making New England rum. Later, during a long coal-miners' strike, canny Vermonters used lignite as a household fuel and for the running of steam engines at iron mines. Phoenix-like, tupelo is consumed but resurrected in spirit, this time in southern Appalachia—as an abundant source of fuel for mountaineers' stills.

Tupelo also played a role in a botanical mystery that began in the 1840's, when a botanist named Asa Gray journeyed in southern Appalachia "through regions which abound with the choicest botanical treasures which the country affords." Dr. Gray, who would create the botany department at Harvard and become a confidant of Charles Darwin, was fascinated not only by the diversity of plants he collected in Appalachia but also by their kinship to Oriental specimens he later examined. (These included plants brought back from Commodore Matthew Perry's historic voyage to Japan in 1853.) Tupelo, wisteria, sassafras, hickory, magnolia, tulip tree, witch hazel, trailing arbutus, pachysandra—and such seeming all-Americans as Virginia creeper, Carolina jasmine, jack-in-the-pulpit, and skunk cabbage—all have Oriental twins. More than 50 genera among the region's native plants, though unknown in Europe or western North America, are found in eastern Asia.

Also similarly distributed are alligators, water moccasins, paddlefish, and a family

*Raccoons, notorious as panhandlers in parks and as trash-can raiders in suburbia, also snitch niches. With opossums, they have replaced the porcupine in a southern Appalachian niche it had pointedly occupied since the Pleistocene. Raccoons belong to a mammal family that began in North America about 35 million years ago. Species, varying from 5 to 30 pounds, range across the continent from southern Canada to northern South America.*
THASE DANIEL, BRUCE COLEMAN INC.

*Ribbons of light chase a rising
sun across the marshes of coastal
Georgia. Sheltered by offshore
barrier islands, some two million
acres of tidal wetlands like
this one south of Savannah fringe
the continent's eastern shore.
The daily ebb and flood of the sea
stirs a brackish brew of rotting
organic matter — the detritus that
nourishes and provides a nursery
for uncounted millions of creatures,
including the shellfish, finned
fish, and waterfowl savored by man.*

*Often disparaged as wasteland,
salt marshes grow edible plants
that feed a long chain of wildlife.
Acre for acre, marshes are four
times more productive than
the richest prairie cornfields.*

WILLIAM R. CURTSINGER

of giant salamanders—here, creatures about two feet long called hellbenders; in Asia, two species, including the Japanese giant salamander, at five feet the largest living amphibian in the world.

Most biological families, like people and their roses and rabbits, range all over the world. But Appalachia's Asiatic connection is not merely familial. Kinship is so recent and so close that virtually identical species appear in both places. Doubles can be found among varieties of ginseng, an herb the Chinese call *jen-shen,* "man-image." Mountain folk, who call the herb "sang," have been digging it up for the Oriental trade since the 18th century. The first American ship to reach Canton in 1784 carried a cargo of ginseng, prized as a panacea and aphrodisiac. Export dealers still range the mountains, paying up to $70 a pound for sang.

How did that herb manage to grow in two places so far apart? How can Asiatic and Appalachian forests resemble each other more than either one resembles the forests of Oregon or France? Similarity of climates and topography did not hold the answers to these questions asked by Asa Gray. Parallel evolution has made broadly similar types in similar environments: The trout in Appalachia's swift-running streams looks like the loach of Asia's swift-running streams; both rise to a dry fly. But similar shapes and habits do not prove common ancestry.

The answer lay not in what grows today but in what grew eons before—and in what happened to those ancestors. Early in the Cenozoic Era, some 60 million years ago, a mixed temperate forest of conifers and hardwoods girded the northern continents, which were still fused across the Atlantic. Most of the tropical plants, like the figs and palms once common as far north as Greenland and Alaska, were gradually withdrawing to the south, leaving only temperate types—oak, walnut, maple, tulip tree—that could stand cold winters. The deciduous habit, dropping the leaves in winter, had become the common adaptation of temperate trees.

A variety of animals found niches within the great northern forest. Hardy and adaptable, the plants and creatures of that global realm seemed indomitable. But many proved unable to withstand the colossal forces of geological change. On this continent, the upheaval of the Rockies and the Sierra Nevada formed a barrier against the rain-bearing Pacific winds, gradually transforming the climate of the interior, creating vast deserts and treeless grasslands.

The final blow to the temperate deciduous forest fell most heavily in Europe: Glaciation, grinding against a transverse mountain range, chilled the Riviera to a cold steppe and exterminated hundreds of plant and animal species. Fossil after fossil has turned up in Europe documenting the former wide distribution of hickory, hemlock, sassafras, magnolia—temperate species which in North America were able to move south ahead of the glaciers. You can get an idea of what was lost when you realize that in Great Smoky Mountains National Park alone there are nearly as many tree varieties as exist in all of Europe today.

But the geography of Asia, like that of North America, favored the migration of

## New Tourists Discover Florida

*In a growing community about 20 miles off Key West a magnificent frigatebird and her downy chick cross hook-tipped bills. Their X marks the spot of the only known nesting site of the species in the U. S. The chick was hatched on an islet of the Marquesas Keys, which curl beyond the Florida Keys. Mangrove mantles the uninhabited Marquesas, magnets of plant, marine, and bird life. Frigatebirds, soaring on seven-foot wings, range the Atlantic from the Bahamas to Brazil and the Cape Verde Islands. Their specialty is aerial robbery; on the wing they snatch fish caught by other seabirds. In the keys' refuges 185 bird species have been counted, including such rarities as the southern bald eagle, great white heron, osprey, and brown pelican.*

BIANCA LAVIES, NATIONAL GEOGRAPHIC PHOTOGRAPHER

Bits of limestone and coral barely above the sea, the Florida Keys trace a massive, 200-mile-long reef—which coral polyps still are building. Mangroves that fringe many keys also add territory, for these trees of land and water can create islands. The red mangrove (right) traps its fallen leaves and other debris within prop roots, making soil. Seedlings, retained until they grow on their own, root nearby or float off, able to live at sea for a year. Our mangroves may descend from African seedlings.

The tree's branches shelter birds and such wildlife as the anole (opposite), a quick color-change artist. Barnacles, which kick food into their mouths with feathery legs, become lifelong root tenants. Nearby are stables for sea horses and a lair for the oyster toadfish, a squat bottom dweller whose beauty is complemented by its typical nest—an old shoe or tin can.

BIANCA LAVIES, NATIONAL GEOGRAPHIC PHOTOGRAPHER

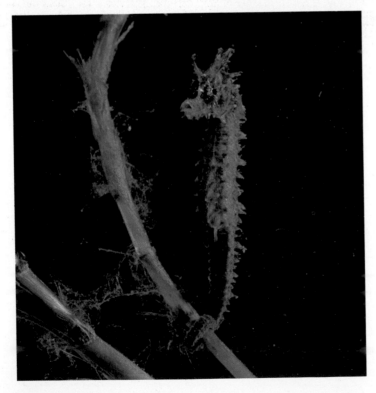

228

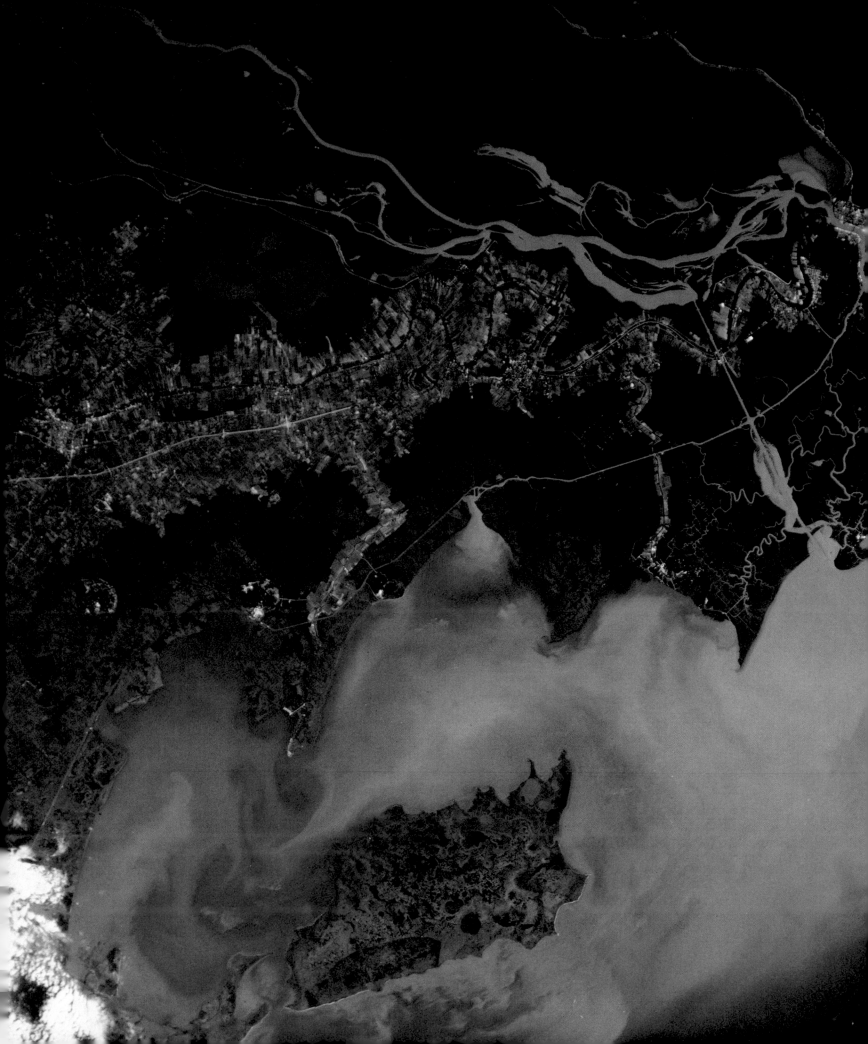

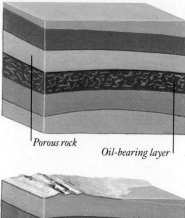

Porous rock    Oil-bearing layer

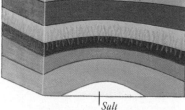

Salt

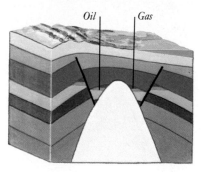

Oil    Gas

*Offshoot of the mighty Mississippi, the Atchafalaya River spreads a turbid plume of silt into the Gulf of Mexico. Each year the stream carries more than 130 million tons of sediment to sea — adding 300 yards to Louisiana's growing shore. Ancient seas covered the land here, leaving salt beds when they evaporated. Other deposits piled layers of sand, mud, and oozes rich in decaying organisms that turned into gas and oil (diagrams). Compression squeezed fossil fuels into adjacent porous rock. When rising salt domes skewed the layers, the fuels migrated upward. Trapped by impermeable walls, they lay in pools for lucky drillers to find.*

species driven south by the ice sheets. Across the vastness of eastern Asia a host of survivors spread and produced an amazing diversity. In any given plant group, for example, Asia usually has many more varieties than we find in Appalachia. Even such characteristic North American genera as magnolias, wisteria, and mayapples have twice as many species in China.

From the earliest days visitors to southern Appalachia were amazed by the endless assortment of woodland flowers, so many of which had never been seen in Europe. Naturalist John Bartram, who welcomed George Washington and Benjamin Franklin to his botanical garden near Philadelphia, trekked Appalachia and found a "variety of plants and flowers . . . beyond expression."

Species scorecards, however, ignore the majesty of the East's great forests and the life they shelter. Many of our most commonplace creatures, such as tree frogs and fireflies, seem exotic to visiting European naturalists, who can find only here — or in the lush and humid tropics — such an array of life. Much of the past, though, has faded away. The bison and the elk fled westward from the colonists as other beasts had once fled southward from the glaciers. Some birds — the passenger pigeon, the Carolina parakeet — vanished forever. The mountains of southern Appalachia, which naturalist Maurice Brooks once called "laboratories for the production of new races and species," became storehouses to be pried open for treasure.

At first just the trees had been for the taking. Out of the woods came naval stores, the tar and pitch for sailing ships, and the tall, straight white pines for masts. The king reserved the best trees for his Royal Navy. Defiantly, revolutionaries put the pine tree of freedom on their flags. For trees were part of life, and each had its role: black walnut, black cherry, sugar maple for the cabinetmakers; hickory for smoking country hams; oak for the charred whiskey casks; white-oak strips for the basket weavers; the trees that yielded nuts and fruits.

As the country grew and more houses and furnishings were needed, trees became raw material for an industry. And with industry came a new and lasting division of the region. The need not for arable land but for power lured money and factories to the area where waterpower could most easily be exploited: at the fall line. In southern Appalachia, an entrepreneur had to pass through tidewater and go upstream for many miles before encountering the break in slope that could power the waterwheels of mills. In New England and the Canadian Maritimes, the fast-running rivers almost invariably lay just behind the cities that already existed.

When industry demanded more power, Appalachia had a new source: coal, the legacy of immense swamps that, flourishing about 300 million years ago, deposited layer after layer of decaying vegetation. Unsqueezed, the stuff remained peat. Squeezed dry by continental upheavals and the pressure of accumulating sedimentary layers, it became lignite, and then soft coal. Compression of a 30-foot layer of mushy peat could make a foot-thick vein of coal. The more pressure, the higher the concentration of carbon and the harder the coal. Beneath what would become 11 states, geological forces were creating the future riches — and, ironically, the future poverty — of Appalachia. Soft bituminous coal lay in beds eight to ten feet thick under the plateaus. Harder anthracite coal seams coursed like black waves through the folded rocks of valleys and ridges. The coal could be mined by sinking deep shafts or by stripping off the land above the coal. The latter land-scarring technique accounts for the production of 48 percent of the coal mined in the United States.

Extraction of Appalachia's coal created an economic pattern that has much to do with scenery and the geology that underlies it. Valuable minerals are first discovered and then most easily removed where treasure-laden strata are exposed along river-banks or turned up on edge by a mountain-making process. (Some minerals buried under rich agricultural soil may not be as valuable as what is on top.) A mountain region, as a source of raw materials, almost invariably becomes dependent upon absentee investors, in this case people of the coastal plain and the port cities. This "client-dependency" relationship has had much to do with the depressed economy of central Appalachia and the Canadian Maritimes.

Economics linked to geology also can be seen in the development of the other fossil fuels discovered in Appalachia, petroleum and natural gas. They lie not in the mountains but beneath the central and western plateaus and the coastal plain. Oil can gush right in or around a city — Houston, for example — and make it rich. Since capital can exist near the gas and oil, local people can share in the treasures of their land. For ores and energy, as well as for crops and water, geology is destiny.

Much of Appalachia has disappeared under concrete. An urban network has made what seems to be a single city out of the Atlantic Seaboard from New England to Virginia. The highways do not meander the way the old roads did. When you drive you rarely can feel the roll and the curve of the land, the imperatives of geology. You have to climb above it all to get a sense of this once raw land, this place where Canada and the United States began.

"Great things are done when men and mountains meet," wrote William Blake, and so it has been with the people and the highlands of Appalachia. Stand on Mount Washington in the White Mountains, and the harsh, windswept beauty around you evokes the granite of the New England character, the hardscrabble tenacity of Down East. Atop Clingmans Dome in the Great Smokies you look out upon the beckoning of the American wilderness and the soul of the pioneer, the doer of great things.

As a scientist, I see something more: nature's selective artistry, the force that has shaped Appalachia since its upheaval, determining what would live there as plant and as animal. Through all this enormous reach of time the landscape has been alive. And it will remain alive during the eons to come, if we treat our land with respect.

Today we walk like giants — the first species since the rise of coral polyps that has the power to alter living landscapes. Here, in this place where so much has been altered, we cannot cease to be a technological society. But we can also be a moral society cherishing the land that sustains us all.

*"Under the sunset far into Vermont" — at a moment that Robert Frost inscribed — the Green Mountains roll through the fire and ice that end a New England winter's day. They are gentle now, the Verd-Mont that gave a state a name. But once they stood among the tallest peaks on earth. Born in the thrust that created the Appalachians, they hold marble and granite in their heart. Some rock is so compressed that quarried blocks spontaneously split or even explode, displaying the power that materialized in the great realm of the eastern mountains.*
DEWITT JONES

# The Grassy Heartland

Paul A. Johnsgard

The world is flat. As I stand in eastern North Dakota or western Minnesota, looking in all directions to a level horizon, that seems a reasonable assumption. Here on the dry bottom of a vanished Pleistocene lake we call Lake Agassiz, my eye finds no tall forests or deep river channels to soften the persistent flatness. In this part of the Central Lowland, even the deepest strata below my feet repeat the constant horizontals above.

Dull? Look again. The Great Plains and Central Lowland cover a fourth of the continent, extending all the way from Arctic tundra through the prairies to south Texas desert grassland. And they host a varied Noah's ark of animals amid a wide assortment of vegetation: caribou and armadillo, buffalo grass and balsam fir, the sandhill crane riding the chill north wind and the blind and pallid cavefish ghosting through the eternal midnight of an underground river.

Over this enormous expanse of forest and grassland, nature has worked on a grand scale. Ancient inland seas grew and waned across the continent's midsection, shaping the land's essential character as they deposited layer on layer of sediments. By the time the Rocky Mountains began to rise some 65 million years ago, the infant peaks looked eastward to flatlands covered with forests. When the Miocene Epoch dawned, the Rockies' great rain shadow was already blotting out the woodland. Desert plants moved in; grasses flourished in the cooler, drier climate. Grasshoppers, locusts, and beetles found a rich larder in the fast-growing grasses. So did some mammals; they relied more and more on grinding teeth, long legs, hoofed feet, and the chambered stomachs typical of ruminants—all useful adaptations in the new habitat. Small seed-eating birds such as the finches shifted easily from forest to grassland. Hemmed in on the west by the Rockies, on the east by the Appalachians, and on the south by deserts and the coastal plains of the Gulf of Mexico, many life forms spread northward to subarctic Canada, adapting as they went. In the process the Great Plains and Central Lowland became the climatic and biological barrier between east and west.

On this vast and stable platform, wind, water, and ice have scrawled unmistakable autographs. Streams tumbling out of the Rockies have spread silt over the plains in deep beds of sediment; half of the mountains' original mass now slumbers in this outwash apron. The boisterous streams of the Rockies and Appalachians contrast sharply with the sedate rivers of the flatlands—among them the James River, plodding some 700 miles through the Dakotas as it drops only five inches a mile. The "Jim" is probably the longest unnavigable river in the United States.

Millenniums ago, glaciers dumped rubble haphazardly on the prairie provinces and the Northern States. Meltwater gradually pooled up in sprawling lakes like Agassiz. Below the ground level, layers of limestone sediment that once formed the ancient seabeds have gradually been dissolved by subterranean seepage. Countless caves now perforate mid-America; the most famous is Mammoth Cave, a labyrinth of caverns

*Shaggy symbols of the prairie, bison in South Dakota's Wind Cave National Park roam a remnant of grasslands their forebears grazed in herds of a million and more. Pioneers decimated herds and habitat.*
ENTHEOS

SWITCH GRASS; ENTHEOS

SHOOTING STAR; PATRICIA CAULFIELD

SIDE OATS GRAMA; ENTHEOS

running like a colossal subway system under the hills of south central Kentucky.

What a difference between life in the sun and life in the endless night of such a cave! On the surface, sunlight fuels nature's engines, spurring the growth of green plants, the beginning of countless food chains. But in the cave a vital energy source is whatever happens to be brought in by animals or borne in by surface water. Now and then an animal or insect wanders in, gets lost, and dies; cave crickets and colonies of bats in some caves add both carrion and guano to the food supply. On these meager resources another link of a starkly simple food chain is anchored: the beetles, flatworms, and other invertebrates. In Mammoth Cave a pale and blind crayfish is the largest and most interesting of this group; it depends on keen smell and touch for finding its food. The last link in the chain at Mammoth Cave is a blind and nearly pigmentless fish endowed with highly sensitive vibration receptors. It also can detect odors and keep its equilibrium better than its nearest relatives outside caves. Thus it can navigate the Stygian waters without visual clues and seize even the smallest swimming prey.

Now come back to the mouth of Mammoth Cave and look around you. When your eyes have adjusted to the overwhelming sunlight, you will see a natural world that is mind-boggling in its richness and diversity compared to life in a cave. It is a green realm; the plants, from the tallest trees to the tiniest mosses and lichens, are arrayed so as to expose the greatest amount of chlorophyll to the sun. The 15 or 20 dominant tree species catch the light first with their broad, translucent leaves, passing a filtered and dappled pattern downward to 50-odd kinds of broad-leaved shrubs and understory trees and another dozen or so types of vines and evergreen shrubs. Finally, an even wider assortment of herbs covers the forest floor, living on the scraps of light that manage to escape through the shrubs and trees above.

Below, around, and above these many layers of plants are the animals, ranging from aphids to deer, that crop this plentiful food source. Each species in turn is cropped by predators. With a long, warm, and rather moist summer, spiders and insects are astonishingly abundant. Ten square miles may support 27 billion invertebrates during the two months of early summer—mostly insects and spiders evenly distributed among the trees, shrubs, herbs, litter, and soil. It is a banquet for birds: Nearly 16,000 small perching birds are likely to be breeding in this area, and during the two months they will consume some 386 million insects. The 750,000 trees will also support up to 50 predatory birds, such as owls and hawks, that prey largely on the abundant mice. Gray squirrels and flying squirrels may number from 20,000 to 40,000. The fox is a part of the natural community, as the wolf and mountain lion once were; under favorable conditions, ten square miles may harbor as many as 30 gray and red foxes.

The ancestral home of such forest communities was not the lowland but the Appalachians and the plateaus adjoining their western slopes. As ice sheets inched toward the present-day Ohio River, whole ecosystems were driven southward. Plants and animals found refuge in the mountains and farther south, beyond the ice. And when the last glaciers retreated, the forests advanced (continued on page 244)

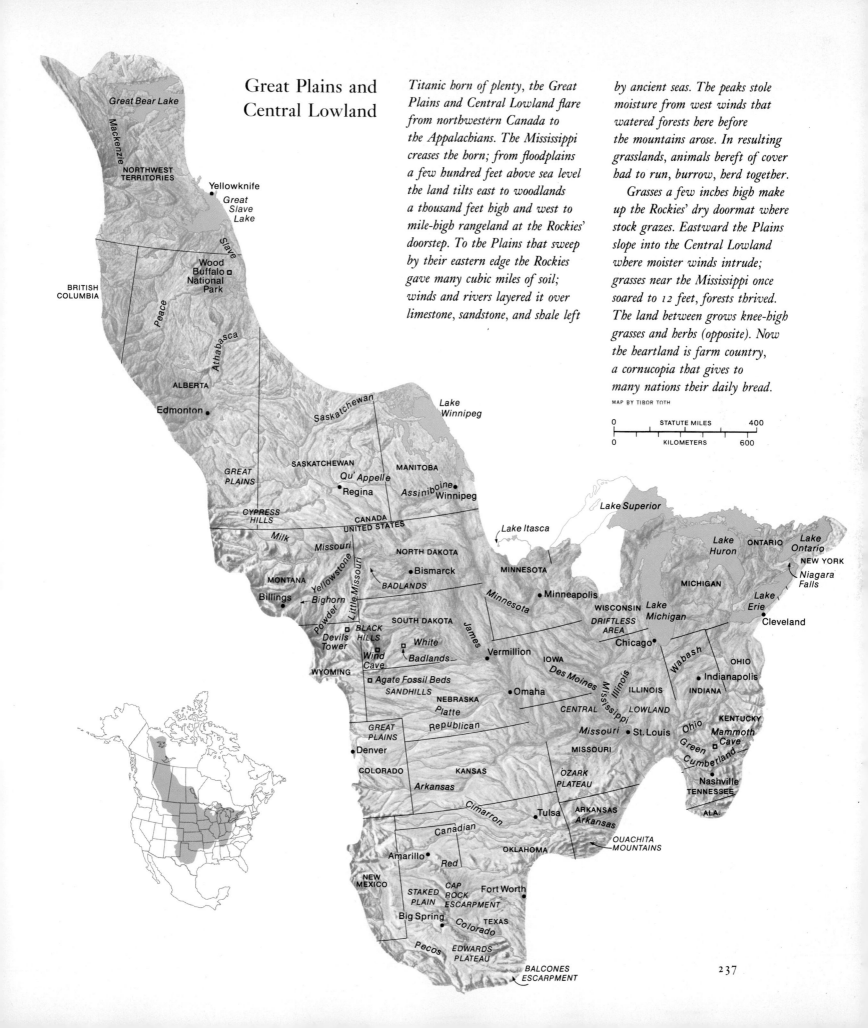

# Great Plains and Central Lowland

Titanic horn of plenty, the Great Plains and Central Lowland flare from northwestern Canada to the Appalachians. The Mississippi creases the horn; from floodplains a few hundred feet above sea level the land tilts east to woodlands a thousand feet high and west to mile-high rangeland at the Rockies' doorstep. To the Plains that sweep by their eastern edge the Rockies gave many cubic miles of soil; winds and rivers layered it over limestone, sandstone, and shale left by ancient seas. The peaks stole moisture from west winds that watered forests here before the mountains arose. In resulting grasslands, animals bereft of cover had to run, burrow, herd together.

Grasses a few inches high make up the Rockies' dry doormat where stock grazes. Eastward the Plains slope into the Central Lowland where moister winds intrude; grasses near the Mississippi once soared to 12 feet, forests thrived. The land between grows knee-high grasses and herbs (opposite). Now the heartland is farm country, a cornucopia that gives to many nations their daily bread.

MAP BY TIBOR TOTH

| 0 | STATUTE MILES | 400 |
| 0 | KILOMETERS | 600 |

Great Bear Lake

Mackenzie

NORTHWEST TERRITORIES

Yellowknife

Great Slave Lake

Slave

Wood Buffalo National Park

BRITISH COLUMBIA

Peace

Athabasca

ALBERTA

Edmonton

Saskatchewan

Lake Winnipeg

SASKATCHEWAN

MANITOBA

GREAT PLAINS

Qu' Appelle

Regina

Assiniboine

Winnipeg

CYPRESS HILLS

CANADA
UNITED STATES

Milk

Missouri

Lake Superior

Lake Itasca

Lake Huron

ONTARIO

Lake Ontario

NEW YORK

Niagara Falls

Yellowstone

NORTH DAKOTA

Bismarck

MINNESOTA

MONTANA

Billings

Bighorn

BADLANDS

Little Missouri

Minnesota

Minneapolis

MICHIGAN

Lake Erie

Cleveland

Powder

Devils Tower

BLACK HILLS

White

SOUTH DAKOTA

James

WISCONSIN

DRIFTLESS AREA

Lake Michigan

Wind Cave

Badlands

Vermillion

IOWA

Chicago

Wabash

OHIO

WYOMING

Agate Fossil Beds

SANDHILLS

Des Moines

Mississippi

Illinois

ILLINOIS

Indianapolis

INDIANA

Omaha

NEBRASKA

Platte

CENTRAL

LOWLAND

KENTUCKY

Mammoth Cave

GREAT PLAINS

Republican

Missouri

St. Louis

Ohio

Green

Denver

COLORADO

KANSAS

Arkansas

MISSOURI

OZARK PLATEAU

Cumberland

Nashville

TENNESSEE

Cimarron

ARKANSAS

Arkansas

ALA

Canadian

Tulsa

OUACHITA MOUNTAINS

Amarillo

Red

OKLAHOMA

NEW MEXICO

STAKED PLAIN

CAP ROCK ESCARPMENT

Fort Worth

Big Spring

Colorado

TEXAS

Pecos

EDWARDS PLATEAU

BALCONES ESCARPMENT

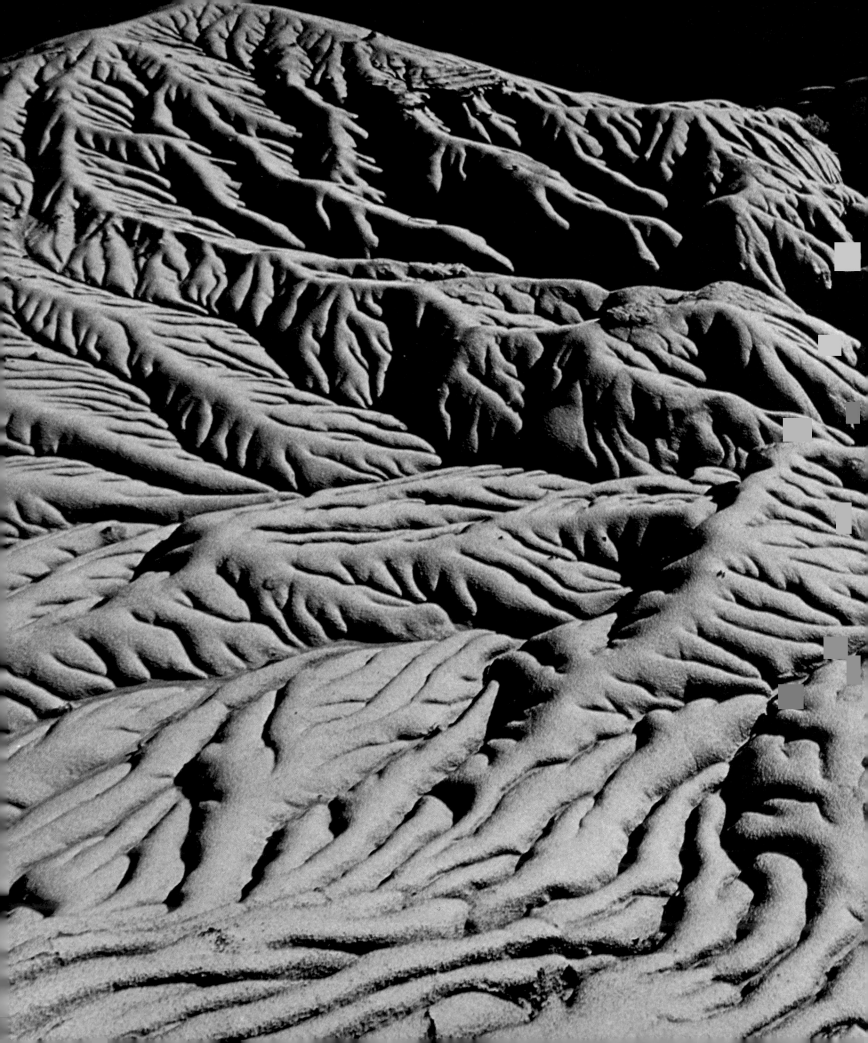

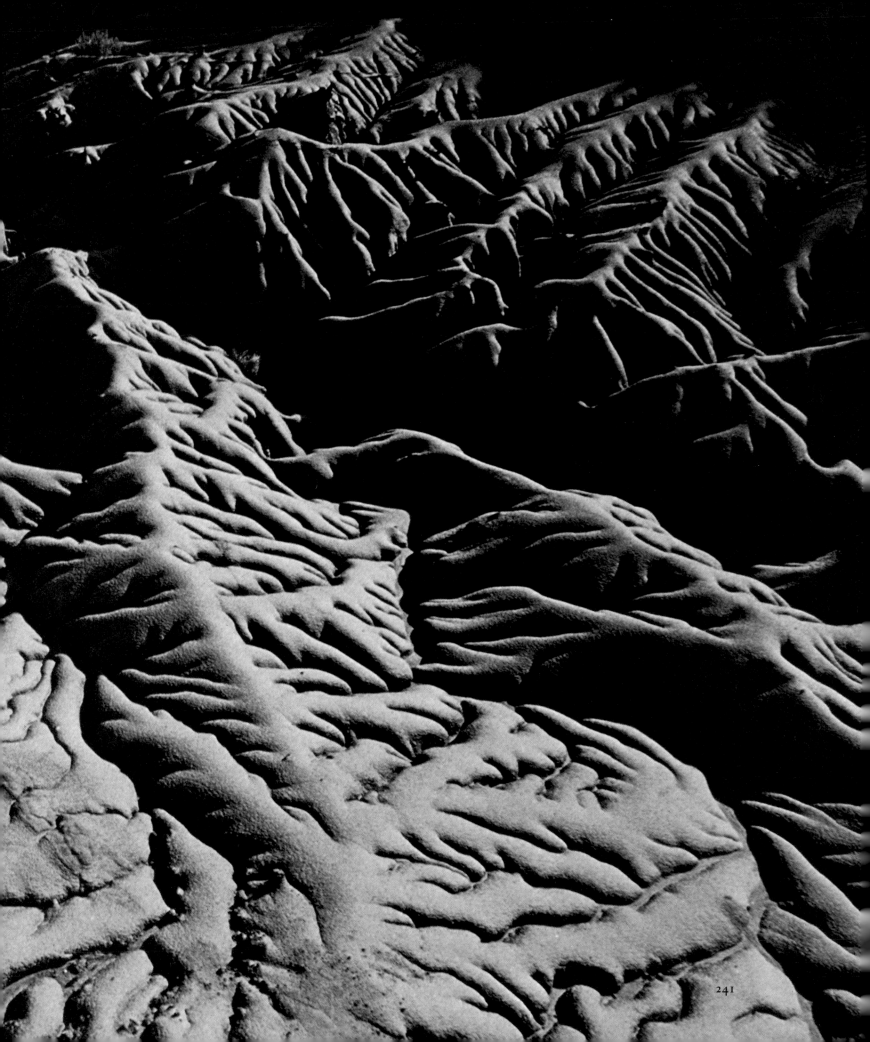

after them—westward along major river systems, where moist conditions reached well into the drier plains, and northward toward the ice itself, where cool summers slowed evaporation and thus compensated for light rainfall.

Moving northward, the broad-leaved trees advanced along with the cold-adapted evergreens, such as pines, spruces, and firs. We can still see the competitive mix in the deciduous-coniferous forests around the Great Lakes. In each locality the small differences in soil, precipitation, climate, and other conditions determine whether the conifers or the hardwoods dominate.

The forests that followed the rivers met a much harsher test: prairie fires that repeatedly roared into them from surrounding grasslands. Soon the more vulnerable species were burned out, leaving the rivers edged with fire-resistant trees such as the thick-barked oaks. But a river is a living, changing thing, and as it changes it alters the natural community around it. Follow the streams that dissect Nebraska from the semi-arid northwestern grasslands to the rich Missouri River bottomlands, and you can watch the cycle unfold. Near the headwaters only the wind-blown seeds of willows and occasional cottonwoods germinate; birds eat the fruits—and thus bring in the seeds—of shrubs and vines that gradually build up much of the understory. As the stream develops a floodplain, its shaded slopes and greater safety from prairie fires allow the elms, ashes, maples, and hackberries to survive. Swelled by tributaries, the stream cradles more and more of the life of the forest community; now you begin to see squirrels busily harvesting walnuts, hickory nuts, and acorns, thus spreading these trees as far upstream as they will grow.

As the great ice rearranged the forests, so it rerouted the streams. In its wake such watercourses as the Ohio River were born. Others, such as the once-mighty river we have posthumously named the Teays, fought a losing battle. For millions of years the Teays had worn a channel looping north, west, then south from the Appalachians of North Carolina to the Gulf of Mexico, which reached an arm up to present-day St. Louis. Then glaciers plugged its northernmost channel and turned miles of it into shimmering lakeland. When the ice backed off, much of the old channel was gone; a new one became the Ohio River, another the Kanawha River. The lower reaches of the Teays became the southern half of the Illinois River. One remnant of the original Teays River is the New River, born in western North Carolina, channeled through Virginia in a picturesque valley, and swallowed at last by the Kanawha in West Virginia. Ironically, the New River is probably one of the oldest rivers in North America.

Farther north the signs of glacial action are everywhere. Much of Minnesota, Wisconsin, and Michigan is underlain by a jumble of rock and gravel strewn by glaciers and meltwater streams. Sandy "beaches" tell of glacial lakes only recently drained. Streams meander down valleys far too big for them—valleys that once roared with torrents of meltwater. Undulating moraines mark the edges of the ponderous ice sheets. And yet, like a window in time, the Driftless Area—the southwestern fourth of Wisconsin and the adjoining 250 miles of the Mississippi Valley—shows

PAGES 238-239: *"Stinging air and moving cloud" herald a September thunderstorm on the featureless Wyoming plain. Gusty winds ripple unshorn fields until, as Willa Cather wrote, the whole country seems to be running. Spawned in early spring and summer, hailstones as large as potatoes destroy crops, split shingles, and kill birds.*
GALEN ROWELL

PAGES 240-241: *Mountains in miniature wrinkle a sandy mound near North Dakota's Little Missouri River. Weeds look like trees on the "horizon." Veins of lignite smolder beneath these badlands, baking clay into scoria. One early visitor called the badlands "hell with the fires out." But to varied forms of wildlife, this is home.*
ENTHEOS

PAGES 242-243: *Icy weathercock, a thistle points the way of howling winds that robed it in white. With little to slow them, blizzards can roar across the flatlands with killing fury. Settlers were often unready; the Massacre Winter of 1856-57 extinguished an entire frontier outpost. Drifts lingered in some sheltered ravines until June.*
ENTHEOS

us a face largely unscarred by glaciers. Here the traveler can marvel at rock towers, natural bridges, and graceful stone arches that a glacier would have pulverized without a pause. But as the ice dipped into the valleys that are now Lakes Superior and Michigan, it left the Driftless Area virtually untouched.

Around Minnesota's Lake Itasca, at the headwaters of the Mississippi, geological history and the competition of plant and animal species spring into sharp focus. Less than 50 miles to the west is the flat clay bed of Lake Agassiz; the gravelly hills that once marked its eastern shores are dotted with eastern forest hardwoods. But at Lake Itasca the hardwoods meet the northern coniferous forest. In a third of Itasca State Park—a 32,000-acre preserve of woodlands, lakes, and swamps—the conifers rule. Their needles and debris render the soil too acidic and nitrogen-poor for most of the hardwoods. In acidic pools and sphagnum bogs the sundew and pitcher plant make up for the lack of nitrogen by capturing and consuming insect prey. Fire once played a crucial role in Itasca's ecology, opening up clearings for seedlings that cannot tolerate the dense shade of their own parents. Without heat, the cones of the jack pine will not even open to release their seeds.

West of the Minnesota forests the grasslands come into their own, arcing across the continent from southern Alberta and Saskatchewan to central Texas. The great arc is the ancient home of the bison, pronghorn, prairie dog, and coyote. In parts it is a harsh environment, with temperatures as far below freezing in winter as above in summer. Breezes ripple the grasses, sometimes coalescing in tornadoes that can shriek with internal winds of 500 miles an hour. Yet during the summer a tremendous growth of forage nurtures animals that can adapt to the demanding climate.

Into such a setting, bison species now extinct emigrated from Asia. All but one of the several species that evolved in North America inexplicably disappeared, as did other large herbivores such as camels, horses, and mammoths. Thus, in contrast to Africa's grasslands, where many species evolved together and still coexist, the grasslands of North America developed incredible populations of a single animal, the bison, plus much smaller numbers of elk and deer. The plains also supported pronghorns—perhaps as many as 15 million of them—and innumerable jackrabbits, prairie dogs, and ground squirrels. Coyotes and wolves were the major predators, but the onslaught of hunters and the influx of settlers with their livestock eventually spelled disaster for both wild grazers and predators.

The pale plains race of the gray wolf has vanished. But the coyote has expanded its range into the forest of the Central Lowland and even the Eastern States. In the process it has angered poultry farmers and been accused of harassing deer. Yet its main diet continues to be what it catches best, the mice, ground squirrels, and rabbits that are so abundant almost everywhere the coyote roams.

At Wind Cave National Park in southwestern South Dakota, I recently renewed my respect for the lordly bison in an unforgettable way. I had come in October to study the rutting behavior of the park's small herd, and decided that a photo of a bull on a

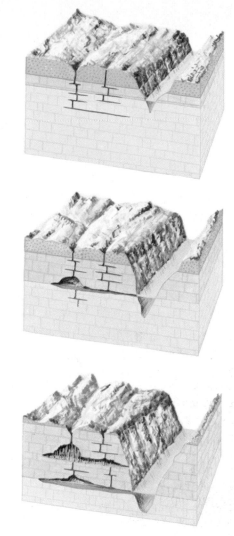

*Architect and decorator, water works thousands of years to carve a cave. Absorbing carbon dioxide from air and organic matter in the soil—thus forming weak acids—it seeps into cracks in the limestone, then follows the water table to a river (upper). Acids dissolve the stone, working deeper as the river lowers the water level (middle). Finally the cave is left high and dry, though another may form beneath (lower). Water drips from ceiling to floor; minerals in it build up as stalagmites, down as stalactites—a wonderland that surface erosion will later erase.*
DIAGRAMS BY TIBOR TOTH

## Life and Death in Nature's Murky Basement

*Once a colossal conduit, Dixon Cave echoes dryly to the tread of hikers. A cave-in severed it from Kentucky's Mammoth Cave, a vast labyrinth linked to Flint Ridge Cave in a system known to reach at least 180 miles.*

*A cave whose seepage runs dry is "dead." Mammoth is "alive," its walls shedding droplets into streams that emerge as springs to feed the nearby Green River. To cave creatures a river is a link to life; down into it from surface sinkholes come micro-organisms, forest litter, even dead animals,*

*first strands in a web of life that includes some 200 species.*

*About a fifth are "accidentals," surface dwellers tumbled in by a fall or flood. Another third are troglophiles, "cave lovers" that also are found in cool, dark crannies on the surface. From ancestral troglophiles, some of them probably refugees from the glaciers, descend the modern troglobites, true cave dwellers that cannot survive outside. A fifth of Mammoth's species dwell in this midnight world, needing no eyes or colors. Yet the finger-size cavefish glides*

*easily among the rocks, guided to openings—and prey—by sensors located on its lips and head. The four-inch crayfish monitors its surroundings with receptors in its antennae. Both creatures move slowly and stop often, lest they react to their own vibrations.*

*An eyeless millipede, short as a thumbnail, gropes for guano of the cave cricket. The cricket is a trogloxene; it feeds outside but comes in for shelter. Like the rivers, it provides manna from a world of dawns and seasons.*

THOMAS C. BARR, JR. (ALSO OPPOSITE).
CAVEFISH AND CRAYFISH: HOWARD N. SLOANE

hill against the setting sun would make a memorable scene. I worked around a small group until one bull was perfectly aligned with the reddening sun. As I snapped the shutter, he raised his head, looked at me—and charged! Too late I realized that the 50 yards separating us were far too few. I dropped my camera and fled down the hill. It was not an equal contest, and soon I could hear hoofs directly behind me. In desperation I threw myself to the side in a kicking, yelling somersault. The bull thundered past only a few feet away. I leaped up and ran to my car, and by the time he stopped and wheeled around, I was safely inside.

After dark I retrieved my camera; luckily it hadn't been trampled. I have since approached bison photography with greatly restrained enthusiasm. And with something else: a tiny hint of the literally earth-shaking power these animals must have wielded in days when they blanketed the plains in uncounted millions.

While the larger, darker wood bison roamed the northern forests and the Rockies, the plains bison ranged all the way to western New York and Pennsylvania. We will never know the exact populations the bison once attained; 19th-century gunners reduced the huge herds to a pitiful few score animals. One guess says there were 50 million bison in 1600! In such numbers they must have exerted an enormous influence on life throughout their range. Deep in the Rockies' rain shadow grow sagebrush and the perennial shortgrass species such as grama and buffalo grass; here we find elaborate anti-browsing adaptations such as spines and distasteful leaves. But farther east the moist winds from the Gulf and Great Lakes temper the dryness. The grasses become taller and more varied, and among the big and little bluestem, switch grass, and Indian grass, the broad-leaved herbs also thrive. Apparently the tall grasses, rather than ward off the grazers, have simply offset the effects of grazing; with more efficient root systems, they grow back more easily.

Only remnants of this tallgrass prairie are still intact, scattered here and there in parks and refuges. Studies of such areas have shown that the original prairie was a remarkably productive and diverse ecosystem, with few equals in the world. Homesteaders found the sod so dense it broke their plows. But in the plains farther west they encountered the "Great American Desert," an arid infinity with little wood or water. Here the sod gave many their only building material. With care, a house built of sod blocks could last a century.

The ability of grasses to bind soil together with their matted root systems is beautifully displayed in areas where the subsoil is little more than drifting sand dunes. In north central Nebraska, grass-covered dunes occupy more than 19,000 square miles, nearly a fourth of the state. Plants and animals face two special problems here: the instability of the sand and its inability to hold moisture at the surface. Plants risk either being covered by encroaching sand or having their roots exposed. So some rely on a taproot system. Many sandhill grasses also have spreading root systems near the surface, which not only assure maximum water-gathering ability but also bind the soil and reduce erosion. The bush morning-glory's roots may reach down 10 feet or more,

OVERLEAF: *Sun and cloud admire themselves in the Missouri's muddy mirror near Vermillion, South Dakota. Spawned by streams roiling out of the Montana Rockies, "Big Muddy" slows, broadens to a mile or more, and meanders down the flatlands, freighted with silt. Gravel washed from the mountains settles in the riverbed; in places the sediment lies 125 feet thick. Maps show the Missouri joining the Mississippi near St. Louis—but one theory says Big Muddy is the headstream of Old Man River and the upper Mississippi its tributary.*

DICK DURRANCE II, NATIONAL GEOGRAPHIC PHOTOGRAPHER

with laterals fanning out 15 to 25 feet in all directions. The grasses are indeed the glue that holds this fragile ecosystem together; remove them and you risk reactivating the dune in a process called "blowout."

An animal that is too heavy to walk on sand without sinking in may be unable to escape from its enemies. Further, the paucity of plant cover usually results in intense sunshine and heat, followed by rapid cooling at night and chilling temperatures by dawn. Kangaroo rats and jumping mice manage to move about by hopping, while the spotted lizard runs too rapidly to sink in. And in the chill of night or cold weather the lizard simply buries itself in the sand, thus also hiding from its enemies.

In such environments, ecological interactions are especially interesting. One late-winter weekend I drove to the eastern edge of the Nebraska Sandhills, one of the few places where the ranges of the sharp-tailed grouse and greater prairie chicken overlap. Though members of the same family, the sharptail is a bird of grassland and scattered scrub, while the prairie chicken favors a combination of grassland for breeding and small-grain cropland to help tide it over the winter. Few such areas remain, and so the prairie chicken's numbers are dwindling.

Grouse tracks peppered the snow of one sand dune area, and I knew this must be a display ground where the cocks battle for territories in which to "dance" and attract the hens. I set up my blind in late afternoon, hoping to see both species during the next morning's sunrise display. I entered it an hour or so before dawn and soon began to hear the aggressive *lock-a-lock* calls of male sharptails taking up their territorial positions. Occasionally the darkness reverberated with the *old-mul-doon* notes of a few prairie chicken cocks competing for space with the sharptails. But among the calls I could hear a strange *rin-so-white!*

As the darkness grudgingly gave way to a gray and overcast morning, I saw an odd bird trying to dance at the edge of the area. It was neither a prairie chicken nor a sharp-tailed grouse; I realized the intruder had to be a hybrid. Repeatedly the others chased it away, and the bird eventually gave up. In a real sense the hybrid reflected the recent history of the grasslands, so modified by man that some species have lost the struggle for existence, have been forced into habitats that suit them poorly, or have even begun to hybridize with their competing relatives.

Like islands in a sea of grass, the remains of old mountains — such as South Dakota's Black Hills — and other relicts of pre-Pleistocene times jut above the Great Plains. The Cypress Hills in southeastern Alberta and southwestern Saskatchewan

*By dark of night, masked bandits case a South Dakota prairie dog town. Mother ferret at left begins a night's hunt, leaving her twins at home in a burrow prairie dogs may have dug. By fall each young predator will hunt alone, sniffing out active prairie dog burrows, digging out the dirt the owners may plug them with each night, then slithering down to ferret out the roly-poly rodents. The ferret also has its foes — mainly man, who poisons prairie dogs lest they scar his fields. Today the ferret faces extinction.*
BILL RATCLIFFE

are the eroded remnant of a 35-million-year-old plateau that the glaciers bypassed. Their unique biota mixes grassland species—the kangaroo rat, sage grouse, sagebrush vole, and hog-nosed snake reach their northern limits here—with species more typical of the Rockies, such as the red crossbill, Audubon's warbler, and pine siskin. About 10 percent of the plants are mountain species. It all suggests that, about 10,000 to 12,000 years ago, a forest corridor linked the Cypress Hills and the Rockies.

The Black Hills are neither hills nor black. Robed in dark conifers, they are an isolated neighbor of the Rocky Mountains, untouched by glaciers but worn down by erosion. They too are a meeting ground of plant and animal communities: oak, ash, and elm like those in eastern woodlands, ponderosa pine and aspen as in the Rockies, spruce and birch reminiscent of Canada. More than 20 birds typical of the Rockies breed in the Black Hills, about half of them at the eastern edges of their ranges; they share the habitat with a dozen or so northern or high-mountain birds, plus several eastern species that are at or near their farthest reach west. In the meeting ground we find the eastern rose-breasted grosbeak hybridizing with the western black-headed grosbeak, the flickers, buntings, and woodpeckers of east and west blurring the genetic differences that have been developing between them since their ancestors were separated during Pleistocene times or before. And so the long-lost kin meet again on these Dakota slopes.

Where glaciers never reached, wind, water, and frost hold sway as sculptors of the land. Lacking a Pleistocene overburden, hills and outcrops expose older strata. One of the finest displays is the Agate Fossil Beds National Monument in Nebraska, where a Miocene stratum forms a high plateau rich in fossil mammals: horselike but clawed chalicotheres, three-toed horses, pony-size rhinoceroses by the thousand.

Close by, the White River begins its journey to the Missouri. Follow it northeast into South Dakota, and you travel even further back in time. Near what is now Badlands National Monument the White River rasped a channel through hills of soft rock; erosion then chipped away at the exposed bluffs until today they loom several miles back from the river in some places. Tributaries mimicked the process, resulting in the weird sculptures and tortuous canyons that fascinate visitors. World-famous fossil beds reach beyond Miocene times to the Oligocene Epoch to show us piglike entelodonts, saber-toothed cats, small dogs, tortoises, rabbits, and diminutive camels of some 35 million years ago. In these deposits we can not only glimpse ancient animal life but also watch it change through the Cenozoic Era.

Three unglaciated uplands sentinel the southern reaches of the plains and lowland: the Ozark Plateau and the Ouachita Mountains of southern Missouri, Arkansas, and

*Pot-bellied burgomasters peel a wary eye over their prairie dog town at Devils Tower National Monument, Wyoming. No dogs at all, these kin of the squirrels earn their name anew each time they spot a coyote, rattler, or owl: Their puplike bark warns all within earshot to take to the burrows. Once prairie dog towns peppered the plains; Texas claimed one of 25,000 square miles housing 400 million animals.*
ENTHEOS

## Urban Renewal on the Plains

*A patch of Wyoming goes to the dogs as the burrowing rodents build and rebuild the prairie dog town at Devils Tower National Monument, one of about a dozen protected from guns and poisons. Ranchers say their stock must have the grasses that are the prairie dog's staple diet; horsemen say their mounts break ankles in the burrow openings. But ecologists bemoan the loss of the energetic earthmovers whose tunneling plowed the plains and helped keep them grassy for thousands of years.*

*Upkeep and outreach keep each prairie dog town changing. Down goes a digger some 12 feet, carving corridors and rooms to serve as larder, guardhouse, latrine, and sleeping quarters. Dirt loosened by the animal's forepaws is kicked upstairs by the* back feet to ring the entry with a mound. It's all very tiring — but all worthwhile. The mound keeps out water runoff and serves as a watchtower. From it a lookout can sound an alarm that sends whole neighborhoods scurrying underground, and later rear up to signal the all-clear (opposite). Then the other residents emerge, nuzzling and even seeming to kiss each other in a recognition ritual that helps keep territorial lines drawn. A network of burrows houses a "coterie," usually one or two males, several females, and various juveniles.*

*As shapers of the landscape, prairie dogs at times rivaled even the bison hordes. Digging far deeper than any plow, these once-widespread rodents loosened soil, mixed top layers with subsoil, aerated it, and gave water a way to percolate downward. Lands they once tended now fall gradually to thistle, scrub, and mesquite.*

254

eastern Oklahoma, and the Edwards Plateau in south central Texas. The Ozarks and Ouachitas are separated only by the Arkansas River Valley, yet how different they are. In the Ozarks—not really mountains but a deeply eroded uplift—flat-lying beds of limestone and sandstone have been carved into a jumble of hills and valleys by the streams. Bluffs flank the sinuous valleys, ledgerock scars the slopes. The Ouachitas, by contrast, are deeply folded layers of sandstone, shales, and slates, marching in orderly ridges and valleys oriented east-and-west.

The Edwards Plateau begins at the ragged Balcones Escarpment, an eroded fault-line scarp where the Great Plains come to a halt above the coastal plains of the Gulf of Mexico. From there the plateau slopes gently northwestward to one of the most perfectly level areas on the North American continent: in Spanish, Llano Estacado; in English, the Staked Plain.

"A place where you saw a visitor coming at sunup and watched him all day, and then he didn't get to your place until half an hour late for supper"—that, to horse-and-buggy homesteaders, was the Staked Plain. To Spanish explorers it was a monotony of waist-high grass so devoid of landmarks that, it's said, they drove in stakes so they could find their trails. But the Staked Plain is not entirely featureless. Old bison trails still scribe the Cap Rock Escarpment that runs from near Big Spring to Amarillo, and dwindling flocks of lesser prairie chickens forage in sandy grass-lands dotted with alkaline lakes.

Not many forms of life can stand the salts of those lakes. But from October to winter's end they are the major refuge for North America's lesser sandhill cranes. And in the migration of the cranes we can trace the whole sweep of the plains.

In late February the birds flap northward in great flocks. In the Platte River Valley of Nebraska they spend most of March, commuting at dawn to stubble fields of wheat and corn, returning at dusk to roost in groups that sometimes muster more than 25,000 birds. On the river's sandbars and islands the cranes spend the night, safe from coyotes and other land predators. These great comings and goings are one of the least known and yet most impressive of all North American bird concentrations, a combination of sound and sight that can leave you breathless with awe.

About the first of April the cranes leave almost en masse and push as far north as weather permits. By mid-April most of them are at the northern edge of the grain belt, in southern Alberta and Saskatchewan. There they meet a broad sweep of aspens, the distinctive transition zone—or "ecotone"—between the prairies and the boreal forests of central Canada. The aspen "parkland" has its own special beauty—though that doesn't seem to slow the bulldozers or neutralize the plant-killing chemicals that are making inroads today, as the prairie fires made inroads before.

Unlike many North American trees, aspens are either male or female; a lone aspen cannot fertilize itself. Thus sexual reproduction by scattering seeds is generally less common than asexual reproduction by sending up root suckers. Many aspen groves are actually the outgrowth of a single tree. The aspen is a boon to wildlife; it grows

*Wreathed in juniper, a nesting golden-cheeked warbler haunts a virgin "cedar brake" on Texas' Edwards Plateau—the only place this rare bird breeds. Not so the orb weaver spiders; their webs snare dew and sun over much of the continent. Stringing non-sticky spokes, the spider adds a sticky spiral in a continuous sweep. One catch, and it may spin a new web.*
L. T. ADAMS. OPPOSITE: JAMES C. BONES

OVERLEAF: *Dawn veils the rocky Edwards Plateau; cedar elms and live oaks rise behind prickly-pear cactus. Narrow streams and steep canyons crisscross the limestone hills of this stock-raising region.*
JAMES C. BONES

257

# Dance of the Migrants

*Karoo, karoo — the bugling call of a lesser sandhill crane heralds the Nebraska dawn. Roosting on shoals and islets, the red-crowned birds cast a gauze of shadows across the "mile-wide, inch-deep" Platte River. In March some 200,000 cranes pause here on their annual journey north from winter quarters on the Staked Plain; some fly 600 miles nonstop. Gray-garbed sandhills feed, court, and loaf, marshalling in early April for their final passage into northern Canada and Alaska. Lusty beats of three-foot wings and a wild clamor of clucks punctuate elaborate courtship rites. Adults bow, parade, and flutter "like tipsy stilt-walkers trying to dance a minuet." Cranes also display when agitated, excited, or threatened.*

GEORGE SILK

back rapidly after a fire or other disturbance, it has abundant nutrients in its leaves, and it forms a canopy for other plants that are useful to animals. White-tailed deer, ruffed grouse, beavers, snowshoe hares, and a host of other creatures depend on the aspen in various latitudes throughout its range—from northern Mexico through the Rockies and Canadian parkland, and from east to west across the zone of northern or boreal coniferous forest.

This subarctic forest is dominated by only a few species of evergreens and deciduous trees, yet it blankets enormous areas of northern North America from western Alaska to the Atlantic coast. And it has a nearly identical counterpart in the forests of northern Europe and Asia. The Bering land bridge obviously allowed an interchange of plant as well as animal life during the Pleistocene Epoch, so that today the northernmost ecosystems of the three continents are much alike. The grasslands and the southern aridlands of the North American landmass also have counterparts across the oceans, but the similarities are not as striking between these ecosystems that have been evolving apart from each other for millions of years.

In northern Alberta and the District of Mackenzie, the Great Plains at their northern edge confront a realm of brief summers and hard winters, of permafrost, of subarctic woodland gradually blending into tundra. As the sandhill cranes straggle in during May, they join a transitional mix of wildlife. In Wood Buffalo National Park the wood bison and the somewhat smaller plains bison graze and hybridize in replenished herds, and a few woodland caribou wander the forests. Of more than 200 kinds of birds that have been found here, the majority are species we usually think of in connection with the eastern forests. The casual observer would hardly expect pelicans in such surroundings, yet the most northerly known nesting colony of white pelicans occurs 12 miles outside the park. Three species of grouse are common: the ruffed grouse of the aspen parkland and deciduous forest, the spruce grouse of the boreal forest, and the sharp-tailed grouse of the prairies and scrublands. And in 1954 the park was found to be the location of that most-searched-for nesting ground of one of the rarest of all American birds, the whooping crane.

The Canadian race of sandhill cranes breeds here, but the lesser sandhills don't nest with these slightly larger relatives. Far to the north the tundra calls, and so some of the cranes that left the Staked Plain of Texas and New Mexico in February find their way here by early May, rest awhile, and then push to the Arctic coastline hundreds of miles farther on. In so doing, they traverse the Great Plains from one end to the other, from semi-arid grassland to Arctic tundra—and from badly altered ecosystems to virgin wilderness where the hand of man is still absent.

---

*Soapweed blossoms spike the soft green folds of the Nebraska Sandhills, their roots helping hold together a fickle habitat. Here winds once romped in a sprawling sandbox, raising dunes grain by grain only to level them and build anew. Finally the grasses spread a stabilizing blanket. Now deer and cattle browse on hills called "choppies" as water birds nest in lake-studded meadows—a few of the gifts of the grass.*
PATRICIA CAULFIELD

# The Soaring
# Young Rockies

Charles B. Hunt

Early in the afternoon of November 15, 1806, a young Army officer rode to the top of a rise along the Arkansas River in what is now eastern Colorado. Gazing westward ahead of him across a vast expanse of arid, sage-covered plain, Capt. Zebulon Pike caught his first glimpse of the distant Rockies and the snow-clad peak looming above them that eventually would bear his name. To Pike and his men the mountains looked like "a small blue cloud." He reckoned their distance at 15 miles. But the clear, crisp air made distances deceptive. Actually the mountains were 120 miles away—a week's march in thin, threadbare summer uniforms. Later, Pike and three companions planned an afternoon's hike to the top of his "Grand Peak." After a six-day struggle, famished, exhausted, half frozen, the party stumbled back to camp, their attempt to reach the summit a resounding failure.

These were not the first white men to visit the Rockies. As early as 1540 a party of Coronado's scouts, marching north from Mexico in search of the fabled Seven Cities of Cíbola, had crossed a spur of the southern Rockies near present-day Santa Fe, New Mexico. And the year before Pike's journey, the Lewis and Clark expedition had threaded the maze of ranges in Montana and Idaho, hoping to find a navigable waterway to the Pacific. But aside from a few explorers—and a handful of French and English trappers who left scant record of their exploits—few whites had ever set eyes on these "shining mountains" of the West. To the world at large they remained a realm of the unknown distorted by faulty maps.

Pike's trek and the Lewis and Clark crossing changed all that. Their reports captured the nation's imagination and ushered in a golden age of Rocky Mountain exploration. By 1830 much of the magnificent chain stood revealed in all its grandeur —a tumult of ridges and soaring heights slashed by shadowed canyons and roaring rivers. First came trappers, traders, and mountain men in search of beaver pelts. In 1858 gold was found near present-day Denver and, in the fall of 1860, prospectors working Indian lands in central Idaho struck it rich in the rugged canyons of the Clearwater River near where it flows into the Snake. The stampede was on. Then, in the late 1860's, scientists such as John Wesley Powell and Ferdinand Hayden began systematic examinations of the region's geology and topography.

People unfamiliar with the Rockies tend to think of them as including every mountain from Denver west to the Pacific. Not so. The Rockies encompass only a relatively narrow, geologically distinct assemblage of 50 or more ranges bordering the Great Plains from northern New Mexico to the Liard River in northern British Columbia. They are part of a much larger mountain complex—a cordillera reaching 10,000 miles from Alaska to Patagonia that forms the backbone of two continents. Many peaks of the Rockies—at least 50 in Colorado—rise 14,000 feet above sea level, more than a mile and a half above the Great Plains to the east. Snow drapes their craggy summits for all but a few fleeting weeks of summer.

*Monarch of the wild, a bighorn ram surveys a wintry scene at Yellowstone National Park. Preserves like this give the mountain sheep room to roam; elsewhere man's encroachments steadily shrivel their range.*
HARRY ENGELS, VAN CLEVE PHOTOGRAPHY

QUAKING ASPEN; DAVID HISER

POLLEN CONES OF LODGEPOLE PINE; CY HAMPSON

WHITE PINE; ENTHEOS

A childhood spent in the avalanche-wracked mining hamlet of Telluride, high in the San Juan Mountains of southwestern Colorado, left author Theodora Kroeber with indelible memories: "In that thin, dry air life moved at a pace of almost terrible intensity. There were no neutral moments—the galloping brevity of spring and summer, the long months of winter with the threat of tragedy always hanging near. Colors were high—the reds in the soil, the fall gold of the aspens, the indescribable sky. Riding in summer and tobogganing in winter were fast and dangerous; the heights of the mountains and the depths of the canyons were beyond the norm.... God was a pagan god, in the air, over the mountains, in the waterfalls."

Others, too, have fallen under the Rockies' spell. Poets have hymned their enduring grace; Indians revered spirits that walked in the high places; and, today, visitors by the millions feast on the glory of mountain scenery preserved in swaths of wilderness and a dozen major parks scattered like diadems throughout this mountain system. And the Rockies provide more than solace and inspiration. Each year their forested slopes yield about an eighth of this nation's lumber supply, and miners extract from them about four billion dollars' worth of minerals. Brawling streams fed by melting snow contribute water to fully a third of the 48 contiguous states. The Continental Divide, the great watershed that separates eastward-flowing streams from those that run toward the Pacific, weaves a course of several thousand miles along the rims and ridges of the Rockies. In theory, at least, a hiker can walk the Divide through most of Canada and the United States without wetting his feet in a stream.

The Rockies are home to many a creature—from the tiniest shrews and voles scuttling about in dead leaves and meadow grasses to the great, dish-faced grizzly bear, at half a ton the largest land-dwelling carnivore this side of Alaska. In 1805 one of these huge beasts ran Meriwether Lewis into the Missouri River, evoking from him the comment that he would rather "fight two Indians than one bear." Today only a few hundred grizzlies are left in the Lower Forty-Eight, most of them in the wildest reaches of Yellowstone and Glacier national parks.

Cougars, coyotes, and bobcats roam the Rockies, as do a number of hoofed animals from nimble-footed bighorn sheep and mountain goats to lordly elk and moose. Mule deer wander the slopes and pronghorn antelope graze the lowland meadows at dusk and early in the morning. Woodland caribou range the forested highlands in Canada.

Few mammals live the entire year in the high alpine meadows above tree limit. With the onset of winter, the larger animals migrate downslope into sheltering forests and valleys. But a few small animals—pocket gophers, mice, pikas, marmots, and weasels—survive the winter in their storm-swept world by hibernating, by hunting incessantly, or by feeding on supplies stored during the summer.

Eagles, falcons, and hawks patrol the summer skies, soaring on updrafts and plummeting from the heights to pick off birds, small mammals, and other prey. Water pipits, horned larks, and rosy finches breed on the alpine tundra, but only one bird, the pullet-size ptarmigan, lives above tree *(continued on page 274)*

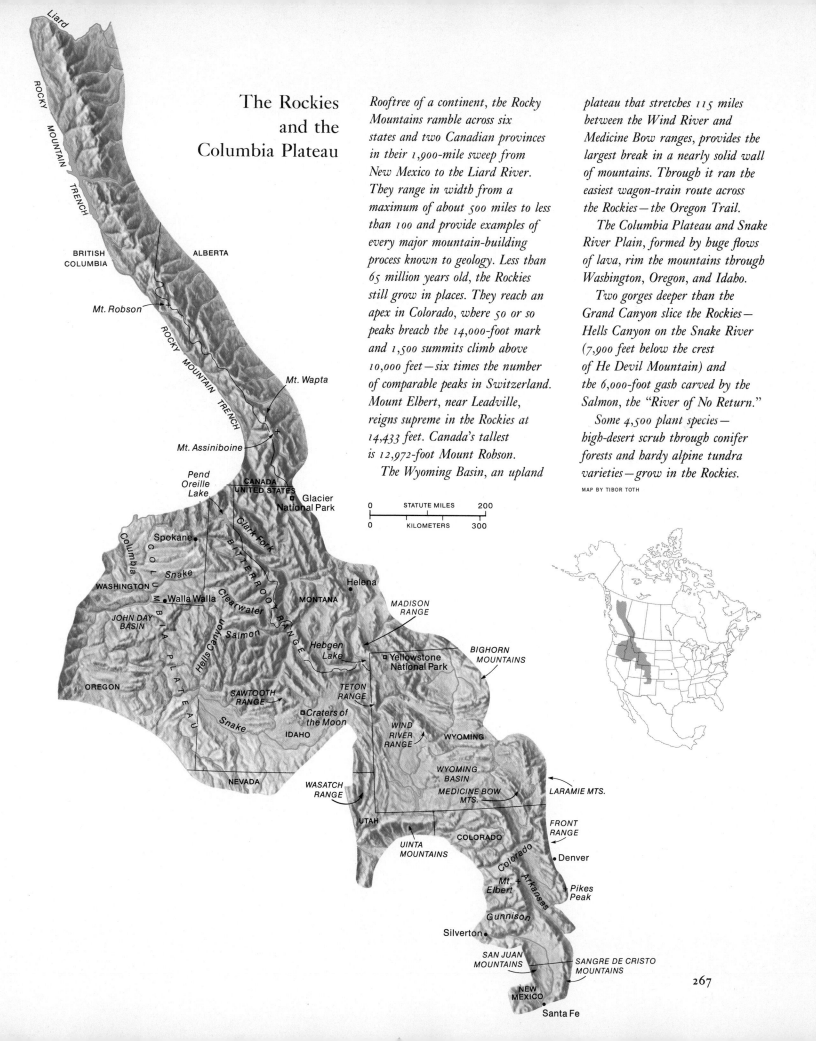

# The Rockies and the Columbia Plateau

*Rooftree of a continent, the Rocky Mountains ramble across six states and two Canadian provinces in their 1,900-mile sweep from New Mexico to the Liard River. They range in width from a maximum of about 500 miles to less than 100 and provide examples of every major mountain-building process known to geology. Less than 65 million years old, the Rockies still grow in places. They reach an apex in Colorado, where 50 or so peaks breach the 14,000-foot mark and 1,500 summits climb above 10,000 feet—six times the number of comparable peaks in Switzerland. Mount Elbert, near Leadville, reigns supreme in the Rockies at 14,433 feet. Canada's tallest is 12,972-foot Mount Robson.*

*The Wyoming Basin, an upland plateau that stretches 115 miles between the Wind River and Medicine Bow ranges, provides the largest break in a nearly solid wall of mountains. Through it ran the easiest wagon-train route across the Rockies—the Oregon Trail.*

*The Columbia Plateau and Snake River Plain, formed by huge flows of lava, rim the mountains through Washington, Oregon, and Idaho.*

*Two gorges deeper than the Grand Canyon slice the Rockies— Hells Canyon on the Snake River (7,900 feet below the crest of He Devil Mountain) and the 6,000-foot gash carved by the Salmon, the "River of No Return."*

*Some 4,500 plant species— high-desert scrub through conifer forests and hardy alpine tundra varieties—grow in the Rockies.*

MAP BY TIBOR TOTH

267

limit all year. The ptarmigan, a species of grouse, changes plumage to fit the season — mottled browns, blacks, and whites in summer and snowy white in winter. So effective is its camouflage that a 19th-century naturalist attempting to study these birds in the Colorado Rockies spotted two of them, then lost them. "Not locating either of the birds," he reported, "I returned to the spot where one had been. I had about decided to give up the search, when one of them commenced to peck my shoe."

Poets may sing about the ageless mountains — objects of wonder enduring through time. But, like everything else, mountains come and mountains go. Geologically speaking, the Rockies we know today are relatively young — a mere 65 million or so years old. And they are not the first mountains ever to cast their ragged shadows across these western lands. Long before the Rockies, other great ranges stood here and, assaulted by time and wind and water, they wore away to vast, nearly featureless plains. Ancient seas washed across the middle of the continent and a myriad of marine organisms — sponges, mollusks, jellyfish, and finned fishes long since extinct — swam where Rockies pinnacles now rise.

Many of these animals left evidence of their presence — fossil shells that may be seen throughout the Rockies wherever marine deposits, now turned to stone, have been uplifted. One of the most exciting paleontological events of modern times was the discovery of the Burgess Shale bed high on the slopes of Mount Wapta in the Canadian Rockies (page 58). Here, embedded in a thin gray band of sedimentary rock, scientists found perfectly preserved imprints of soft-bodied marine animals that had roamed the Cambrian sea more than 500 million years ago.

At the beginning of the Cretaceous Period some 135 million years ago, the opening act in the drama of the Rockies took place. Gradually the continental crust began to flex downward, creating an enormous crease, or trough, that ran the length of the area now occupied by these mountains. An immense seaway extending from the Arctic Ocean all the way to the Gulf of Mexico rolled in upon the land. At its widest — about a thousand miles — it spread across the midriff of the continent from Montana to Minnesota and Missouri (map, page 95). This Cretaceous sea was shallow, perhaps no more than a thousand feet at its deepest in northwestern Wyoming. West of the seaway, in what is now California, Nevada, Idaho, and parts of British Columbia, bulked an array of mountains known to geologists as the Mesocordilleran geanticline. From these highlands washed astonishing volumes of sediment — more than a million cubic miles of mud, sand, and stone that in Wyoming and other places covered the sagging seabed with deposits nearly four miles thick.

For 70 million years the great inland sea sparkled in the Cretaceous sun. Then, about 65 million years ago, the continental crust began to crack and buckle along the trough. Gradually the waters receded and the Rockies' peaks lifted skyward — much as pressure ridges form when ice floes collide on a storm-driven sea. The pressure continued intermittently for some 25 million years, folding and bending the bottom of the seaway, forming the basic pattern of the Rockies. The upfolds, called anticlines, became ridges and crests; the downfolds, or synclines, became structural valleys (as opposed to erosional valleys carved by running water). The Uinta Mountains of Utah and the Wind River and Bighorn ranges of Wyoming are examples of upfolded mountains.

In other places magma forced its way up through cracks in the tattered basement rock, forming huge granitic blisters in the overlying sediments. Wind and water eventually wore away the softer sedimentary layers, exposing the granite cores beneath.

Wherever the strain of folding proved too great, immense masses of rock fractured —or faulted. Some blocks then were thrust into the sky or tilted on their sides. The Madison and Gallatin ranges of southwestern Montana are examples of this type of activity, as are the Tetons in Wyoming and the Wasatch Range that looks out over Salt Lake City, Utah. Geologists call these structures fault-block mountains.

The Tetons themselves are among the younger mountains in the Rockies—at least in the shape we know them today. Much of their uplift has occurred in the last 10 million years or so along a 40-mile fracture known as the Teton Fault. The mountains are actually a slab of rock measuring 40 miles long by about 15 miles wide that has been forcibly injected with lava and pitched steeply upward along the fault. A few miles north of the Tetons some of this magma broke through the ground, creating the lava plateau that today forms a major part of Yellowstone National Park.

Farther north, in Montana's Glacier National Park area and extending into Canada, faulting and slipping took place on a phenomenal scale. Here, in a zone called the Lewis Overthrust, the entire mountain mass rode slowly up over the lip of the plains and slid eastward for a distance of about 35 miles.

The Canadian Rockies, regarded by many as the sublime expression of mountain majesty, are the result of yet another type of slippage—imbricated thrust faulting. This not-so-sublime geological expression describes, in effect, a stack of overlapping shingles thrust up onto the plains, steep side facing east.

Along the western flanks of the Canadian Rockies runs another unusual feature—a remarkably straight, steep-walled valley known as the Rocky Mountain Trench. Actually it may be a rift valley, a fissure that slices clear through the continental crust to the underlying part of the mantle. The trench, now largely filled with sediment, extends about 900 miles. It enters the United States only for a short distance before disappearing into the complexly deformed rocks of northern Montana.

Fire, too, played an important part in shaping the Rockies. At the southwest corner of Colorado, and bending southward into New Mexico, loom the San Juan Mountains, an enormous slag heap of volcanic material pierced by ragged spires of folded Precambrian rock. Here the 12,000- and 13,000-foot crests of the San Juan Needles and the Grenadiers create an impression of a wild and choppy sea.

Beginning about 35 million years ago and continuing on and off for at least 25 million years, the whole San Juan region was wracked by a series of explosions. Billions of tons of lava, ash, and other debris accumulated into a mile-high pile. Lighter particles, caught by winds aloft, spewed over tens of thousands of square miles in

*Haymaker of the heights, a pika suns itself between forays to gather the grasses it feeds on when winter grips its mountain home. The pika lives amid boulder fields at altitudes up to 12,000 feet, stowing its hay in bushel-size piles. Ancestors of this member of the hare family probably came here from Asia. Time and circumstance have adapted the pika to its harsh world: A compact body conserves heat; fur-clad soles provide traction on rocks. Pikas deposit their urine in nearly crystalline form—retaining body moisture in the dry air.*
BRUCE DALE, NATIONAL GEOGRAPHIC PHOTOGRAPHER

suffocating clouds of incandescent material. Magma chambers suddenly and violently ejecting their molten rock collapsed of their own weight, creating large, bowl-like calderas. One of them, at Silverton, Colorado, measures 10 to 15 miles in diameter. Subsequent outpourings of lava through the shattered caldera rims baked the surrounding rocks, altering them and forming many of the rich mineral deposits that eventually brought prospectors and miners into the San Juans.

Igneous activity also created the Colorado Mineral Belt, a 75-mile strip that cuts diagonally across the state from Leadville to near Boulder. But this was not the violent activity that built the San Juans. Instead, pillar-like injections of molten rock intruded the earth's crust much as a nail is driven into a board. Such intrusions, known as stocks, measure a mile or more in diameter and have proved to be valuable sources of gold, silver, lead, molybdenum, and other metals.

I n the northwest corner of Wyoming lies a land that has awed and intrigued man for thousands of years. Indians seldom visited this place, for the earth periodically trembled with the roars and fumings of malevolent spirits. Today Yellowstone National Park preserves one of the world's truly spectacular displays of igneous activity. Below much of the park, at a depth of several thousand feet, bulges the top of a magma dome. Measuring 30 miles across and descending at least 50 miles into the earth, this reservoir of molten rock provides heat that powers the park's thousands of geysers, boiling springs, and other thermal features. Strangely enough, the dome has also helped rescue the trumpeter swan from oblivion.

The story begins in 1933, when birdwatchers in the United States reported only 66 of these snow-white waterfowl winging southward on their annual migration from Canada. The skies once had resounded with the thunder of their wings and the clarion calls that reminded Canadian explorer Samuel Hearne of a French horn. But disaster stalked these largest of America's water birds. Nineteenth-century plume hunters slaughtered them, reducing the once-vast flocks to a few pitiable remnants. By 1900 the trumpeter was nearly extinct in the United States.

But partly as a result of the 1933 bird count, the alarm sounded and, four years later, Red Rock Lakes National Wildlife Refuge was established in a remote Montana valley 50 miles west of Yellowstone. Here the swans prospered. Today they number several hundred. One reason they have thrived is that they no longer migrate. Many of them spend the entire year in the shelter of the refuge—despite winters that are notoriously cold. The secret of their success involves a geological quirk: The Red Rock Lakes are fed by springs heated at Yellowstone's magma dome. Thus, even when the air temperature drops to 40 degrees below zero F., the water is at least partly ice free. The swans are able to feed and their survival in the United States now seems assured.

Still another kind of igneous activity is responsible for building some of the wildest, most remote country to be found in the lower 48 states—the Sawtooth and Bitterroot ranges of Idaho. Here, innumerable stocks of molten rock have punched up under the area's sedimentary blanket over a period of several million years. As the stocks

*Wild rock garden spangles a granite cranny on Mount Evans, part of Colorado's Front Range. The spring beauty plant earns its name, showy white blossoms fringing the red-piped rosette of leaves. A tough beauty as well, it thrusts a taproot down six feet to find nourishing soil and moisture. Yellow rockcress petals and cobalt hues of the alpine forget-me-not complete the bouquet.*

*Most alpine plants develop in cautious stages—some taking 15 years or more to mature and bloom. A fist-size clump of phlox may be more than a century old.*

DAVID MUENCH

277

## Battering Rams Duel for Ewes

*Crack! Brute strength collides head-on as bighorn rams battle for leadership of a flock in the Canadian Rockies. Again and again they lunge, squaring off for a fresh charge on their hind legs (above). Thus normally amiable males test their mettle during the fall mating season. Thick facial hides and porous, double-layered skulls cushion duelists whose horns may weigh as much as their entire skeletons. When they ram—at closing speeds of up to 45 mph—the blow can be heard a mile away. Spikehorned ewes drop their lambs in May or June.*

JAMES K. MORGAN

279

coalesced they formed an immense dome called a batholith. Erosion eventually wore away the overburden, exposing the granite core. One of the largest formations of its kind on the continent, the Idaho batholith sprawls across some 16,000 square miles. West of this high, rugged land runs the deepest chasm on the continent, the gorge cut by the Snake River as it churns through Hells Canyon.

Skirting the Bitterroot and Sawtooth ranges to the south and west spreads a landscape shaped by some of the most stupendous floods the world has ever known — floods of fire and floods of water. This is the Columbia Plateau and the Snake River Plain, contiguous regions that form a 700-mile-long crescent reaching from the Cascade Mountains of Washington and Oregon to Yellowstone Park — an area encompassing more than 100,000 square miles.

Visitors to the Columbia Plateau section of eastern Washington may notice something odd about the place: Here is a land of lava utterly without cones, craters, or any other volcanic landmark. The events that took place here *were* odd, and on a scale so colossal they are difficult to imagine.

During the Miocene, which began 26 million years ago, the plateau was torn into a crazy quilt of huge fissures, some of them many miles long. From these cracks gushed immense quantities of molten rock, inundating and obscuring evidence of earlier volcanic activity. This was thin, soupy, basaltic lava from deep within the earth, not the thick, more viscous kind that congeals into volcanic cones. Spreading almost as rapidly as water, the lava spilled across the basin floor, forming a huge lake of burning rock ringed by mountains. One flow in particular, the Roza Basalt Member, covered nearly 20,000 square miles to an average depth of 100 feet — seven times the volume of today's mighty Mount Rainier.

From time to time fresh outpourings of lava flooded much of the plateau, filling the deepest part of the basin, near Walla Walla, to a depth of more than a mile. Hundreds and even thousands of years passed between the cooling of one flow and the spreading of the next. Sometimes luxuriant forests took root in the rich volcanic soils that formed, only to be engulfed by the next flood of basaltic rock. Ginkgo Petrified Forest State Park, near the town of Vantage, Washington, today preserves several hundred plant species that were overwhelmed by the lava, including large trunks of the tree for which it was named.

Man was not here to witness these cataclysms, but other creatures were — including, perhaps, the famous "Blue Lake Rhino." In 1935 workers chanced upon a curiously shaped cavity at the base of a basalt cliff near Dry Falls in the lower section of the Grand Coulee. Poking around inside the hole, they found a few fossilized teeth and bones, all that remained of a small, extinct, rhinoceros called *Diceratherium*. Evidently the animal had been overtaken by lava in a small lake. The steaming, rapidly cooling basalt entombed the body, preserving its outline in a crude mold. What a jolt it must have been for the discoverer of the "cave" to learn that he had poked his head into a Miocene rhino — through its rump.

*Somber rock split by a blade of gleaming water marks the course of the Gunnison River as it slices through the Rockies of western Colorado. Here, at Black Canyon of the Gunnison National Monument, the river cleaves through more than 2,000 feet of some of the hardest rock known — granite-like gneisses and schists laced with veins of light, quartz-rich pegmatite. Only 40 feet wide across the bottom in some places, the canyon may have begun to form two million years ago. Since then the river has cut downward at a rate of about a foot every thousand years.*
DAVID MUENCH

281

## Yellowstone Winterland

Winter casts a pall of white across a land of fire. A bull elk pauses at Norris Geyser Basin in Yellowstone National Park to graze near "ghost trees" sheathed with rime ice by steaming vents. To avoid breaking through the ice and tumbling into hot springs, trappers of old followed tracks of the sure-footed elk whenever crossing such hazardous terrain.

Thermal cud weed (above), warmed and moistened by boiling water in the Fountain Paint Pot area, bravely blooms in January.

OVERLEAF: *A dormant hot spring, its waters drained away, keeps company with active pools in Yellowstone's Mammoth Terrace. Molten rock underground keeps the park's thermal system perking.*

ENTHEOS (ALSO OVERLEAF)

Swinging south and eastward into Oregon and Idaho, the traveler comes to the Snake River Plain, where astronauts trained briefly for their lunar visits. Much of this is stark, empty, forbidding country, a place where streams spilling from the mountains vanish into dark, porous lava. But even here life persists—rabbits and rodents and acres of greasewood and sage purpling into the sun-scorched distance.

The lavas that flowed here, great searing tongues up to 100 miles in length, are considerably younger than those of the Columbia Plateau—about three million years old. And they were less fluid. Cinder and lava cones pock the landscape, especially at Craters of the Moon National Monument in south central Idaho. Here, in a realm of blacks and browns and rusty reds, rivers of ebony rock twist past jagged spatter cones. Lava bombs—clots of molten rock hurled into the air high enough to partly solidify—litter the ground. Scientists estimate that lava flowed in the 83-square-mile monument as recently as 1,600 years ago. Some of it looks fresh enough to have flowed yesterday and, geologically speaking, that is not far from the truth.

Motorists driving west along Interstate 90 into Washington cross a rolling, fertile countryside, much of it sown with nodding stalks of wheat. Continuing westward, they come abruptly to a vastly different terrain—a land of black rock deeply scarred by labyrinthine canyons and washes, rock basins, buttes, and ripple marks so huge they resemble low, rolling ridges. The traveler has entered the northernmost reaches of the Columbia Plateau—the so-called Channeled Scablands of eastern Washington. Floods of molten lava shaped the scenery here, and so did some of the greatest floods of water ever recorded.

The story of these floods—the Spokane floods—took many years to piece together and was scoffed at as preposterously catastrophic when first proposed nearly half a century ago. But scientists studying relict beaches and "fossil" shorelines now believe the deluges were indeed catastrophic, and that the last and largest of them took place 18,000 to 20,000 years ago. But the story begins much earlier than that.

About ten million years ago the last lava flow overran the Columbia Plateau. Westerly winds in time blanketed the basin with silt and with volcanic ash from the Cascades. In places this loess, locally called Palouse soil, drifted to depths of 200 feet.

Then, about three million years ago, came the Ice Age and, eventually, a large tentacle of frozen water groped down the Purcell Trench into the northern Idaho panhandle. Slowly, inexorably, the ice advanced, crossing the Rathdrum Prairie, scouring out the basin of present-day Pend Oreille Lake, and, finally, grinding to a halt against the northern buttress of the Bitterroot Mountains. Where the ice stopped it formed a 2,000-foot-high dam across the canyon of the Clark Fork River. With nowhere to go, glacial meltwater backed up eastward into Montana, creating Pleistocene Lake Missoula. When full, the lake covered an area of 3,000 square miles and held 500 cubic miles of water—about half the volume of today's Lake Michigan.

Then one day the ice dam failed. With a heave and a roar, a wall of water choked with ice and boulders as big as a house churned down Clark Fork Canyon, spewed

## Watery World of the Beaver

*Powerful thrusts of its webbed hind feet propel a beaver into the murk of a mountain pond. As it dives, valve-like flaps of skin seal the animal's nostrils and ears; transparent membranes cover its eyes, protecting them and affording keen underwater vision. Oversize lungs and liver hold large amounts of air and oxygenated blood. The heart rate slows, stretching air supplies so that the beaver can remain submerged for as long as 15 minutes —or swim half a mile.*

*Man has long admired North America's largest rodent for its industry and feats of hydraulic engineering. (The longest dam known, near Berlin, New Hampshire, extended 4,000 feet and formed a pond ample for 40 beaver lodges.)*

WILLIAM R. CURTSINGER

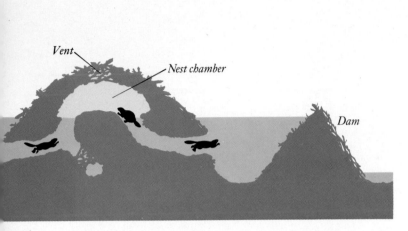

Vent · Nest chamber · Dam

A beaver builds dams to control water flow, and in the process creates a moat around its lodge (below and diagram). By raising water levels, the dam also brings food and building material within floating distance (opposite, upper). Mud daubed on the dwelling makes a fortress impregnable to most foes. Beavers usually mate for life. Kits are born in the spring, fully furred and open-eyed, and learn to swim within hours of birth.

From birth to death—about 12 years in the wild—a beaver never stops growing. Adults average about 50 pounds—a mere shadow of the bear-size ancestral beavers that roamed the Ice Age landscape.

Several Indian tribes believed that giant beavers built the continents, heaping mud and stone from the bottom of the primordial sea. And because the white man coveted its pelt, no other animal played such an important role in the exploration of North America.

JEN AND DES BARTLETT, BRUCE COLEMAN INC.
DIAGRAM BY LISA BIGANZOLI

*Perched on a bough, a spruce grouse fans the white-tipped feathers that distinguish it from four other Rockies grouse species. Sometimes called a "fool hen" because of its tameness around man, the bird moves grudgingly even when attacked with sticks or stones. Indian braves disdained such easy prey except in direst need.*

*A blue grouse cock (below) struts and displays his colorful throat sacs in a courtship rite designed to win a mate. The blue grouse, unlike most mountain birds, wanders upslope at summer's end to winter in the high spruce forest.*

CY HAMPSON

across the Idaho panhandle, and fanned out onto the Columbia Plateau beyond, where Spokane stands today. At maximum flow, nearly 400 million cubic feet of water a second erupted from the canyon mouth—ten times the combined flow of all the rivers on earth! In less than two weeks Pleistocene Lake Missoula lay drained and empty.

West of Spokane, meanwhile, the flood split into three great rivers and numerous interlacing channels. The rushing water stripped away the Palouse soil. It scoured out the Scablands and carved deep, wide, flat-bottomed washes in the underlying basalt. The largest of these, Grand Coulee, curves 50 miles between canyon walls up to 900 feet high. The torrents raged through the basin, filling much of it and backing up into a large lake before the water could escape to the Pacific through Wallula Gap and the Columbia River. All told, more than 30 such deluges may have swept through the Scablands at various times during the Ice Age.

Just as ice and water wrought their handiwork on the Columbia Plateau, so they put the finishing touches to the Rockies. Although the great continental ice sheets barely crossed the Canadian border in the western reaches of the continent, cold, wet weather spawned local glaciers that mantled the Rockies all the way to their southern tip. Wherever these alpine glaciers moved, they left their marks upon the land, rasping away at mountain flanks, grinding V-shaped valleys into U-shaped ones, quarrying bowl-like cirques, and strewing rubble along their lines of march. Countless tarns and alpine ponds fed by melting snow, their basins scooped by grinding ice, are a legacy of Ice Age glaciers. In Wyoming's Bighorn and Wind River ranges, and elsewhere, these lovely alpine pools stairstep down the mountains, linked to one another by a single strand of running water. Because of their fancied resemblance to beads on a rosary, such ponds sometimes are called paternoster lakes.

Difficult as it may be to picture today, the Rockies region once was cloaked with lush, almost tropical forests. Palms, fig trees, tropical ferns and other plants now found in Mexico and Central America flourished in the area about 55 million years ago, according to fossil evidence unearthed in the John Day Basin of eastern Oregon. When the ancestral Cascades began to rise some 40 million years ago, the climate gradually changed; redwoods and such hardwoods as walnut, oak, maple, and beech took over. Many of the hardwoods that grew in these Oligocene forests came originally from around Cook Inlet, Alaska, migrating southward as seeds or nuts buried and forgotten by squirrels and other rodents. One botanist estimates that such transport could have taken place at a rate of about a mile in a thousand years. The distances involved here, less than 2,000 miles, could easily have been managed at a rate very much slower than that—a good example of how slow processes accomplish great changes over the vastness of geologic time.

To climb in the Rockies today is to journey through several different life zones. With each thousand feet of altitude the average temperature drops 3.5 degrees, humidity in the air increases, and soils tend to become more acidic—changes that profoundly influence plant growth. In Colorado and Utah, forests of piñon and juniper or scrub oak cover the lower slopes while willows, alders, birches, cottonwoods, and other broadleafs nestle in the valley bottoms and along watercourses. Gradually, as you climb higher, these forests give way to stands of blue spruce and resin-scented groves of ponderosa pine. Here, too, grow the slender quaking aspens with leaves that shimmer and dance in the lightest breeze.

Above the ponderosas grow lodgepole pines, once used by Indians to make frameworks for lodges. Between 7,000 and 9,000 feet the stately Douglas fir predominates and, beyond that, various spruces and alpine firs take over, growing in cool, dense stands. Between 10,000 and 11,000 feet even the hardy Engelmann spruce begins to falter, twisting into gnarled, stunted forms as it approaches the upper limits of tree growth. Finally, beyond the tree line, grow flowering plants and grasses similar to those found on the Arctic tundra. Here, during the few short weeks of summer, spread alpine rock gardens of incredible beauty, strewing the crags and highland meadows with masses of color. Colorado alone has more than 300 alpine plant species, including phloxes and saxifrages, kobresia, arctic gentians, and sedges.

Resetting our geologic time clocks, we go back now 35 or 40 million years—around the beginning of the Oligocene—when the precursors of today's Cascades were rising and the San Juan eruptions were beginning to rock the Colorado countryside. By now the Rockies had achieved full growth relative to the Great Plains. The major ranges and valleys were in place much as they appear on modern maps. But the plains and the mountain bases were close to sea level. The site of Denver was nowhere near a mile high. Then, beginning 40 million years ago, much of western North America underwent a massive upward flexing that eventually would thrust the highest Rockies peaks to an altitude of 14,000 feet above sea level and turn the Great Plains into a giant ramp sloping downhill all the way to the Mississippi.

No one knows what caused this arching along the trough of the old Cretaceous seaway—or indeed what caused the Rockies to rumple in the first place. Theories that involve the shifting of continents and the overriding of oceanic plates ingeniously explain the rise of coastal mountains such as the Andes and the Cascades. But the Rockies lie as much as a thousand miles inland, a third of the way across the continent. It seems, therefore, that their formation and uplift is only indirectly a result of colliding crustal plates. Perhaps when the Pacific and North American plates first came into contact, the initial shock bent the crust downward where the granitic skin was thinnest, creating the Cretaceous trough. Subsequent compression of the continental granites as North America rode up over the Pacific plate may have buckled, warped, and fractured the crust. Or perhaps large convection cells welling up from deep inside the mantle created "hot spots" or "plumes" of superheated material that puckered and lifted the continent as it drifted along above them. Whatever the reason for the Rockies, one thing is certain—they did not spring up full blown in a single convulsive upheaval, or even in several upheavals, as geologists formerly believed.

A good, if somewhat violent, example of how the earth continually readjusts took

OVERLEAF: *The mighty Columbia rolls on to a rendezvous with the John Day River (foreground) in the flood-scarred Columbia Plateau borderlands between Oregon and Washington. Ice Age deluges rampaged through the area, sloshing across part of this tongue of land and carrying away much of its rich volcanic topsoil. The John Day, named for a young guide, cuts through fossil beds abounding in prehistoric plants and animals, including the remains of humpless camels and three-toed horses.*
WILLIAM A. GARNETT

291

place in the vicinity of Yellowstone National Park on the night of August 17, 1959. Here, at a few minutes before midnight, the earth's crust slipped at a point near man-made Hebgen Lake, just beyond the park's western boundary. Mountains shook. Dust boiled. Boulders fell rattling from the heights. The face of a mountain in the Madison Range suddenly broke loose, burying two dozen sleeping campers beneath 80 million tons of rock and rubble. Buoyed on a cushion of compressed air, the landslide tore across the valley of the Madison River, damming it and forming Earthquake Lake a few miles downstream from Hebgen Lake.

"It was horrible," recalled a survivor who, with his wife, was forced by rapidly rising water to scramble into a tree. "While we struggled to hold on, we could see the mountains sliding and falling every few minutes. There'd be a terrific roar, followed by more slides. I thought the world was coming to an end."

Inside the park, 20 miles to the east, buildings swayed and creaked. The massive stone chimney at Old Faithful Inn collapsed into an empty dining room. "The ground got right up and shook—like a horse galloping," one astonished visitor reported. Geysers went berserk. Some, long dormant, suddenly blew their tops. Others went into continuous "wild" phases, shrieking and hurling steam and water high into the air. Grand Geyser, a star performer for many years, suddenly quit. Old Faithful slowed its average 61-minute cycle to 65 minutes.

When the steam and dust had settled, fresh fault scarps 15 feet high and up to 20 miles long scarred the surrounding countryside. One fault slashed through the middle of a barn, lifting half of it 10 feet above the other half. The bottom of Hebgen Lake lay tilted at a new angle, submerging roads and houses along the northeast shore beneath 20 feet of water while, at the opposite side, stranding boats and docks 20 feet above the new lake level.

Though severe, the Hebgen jolt was only one of hundreds that have shaken the Rockies since July 4, 1805, when Lewis and Clark reported a quake near the Great Falls of the Missouri. A seismically active belt extends diagonally across the mountains from the Colorado Plateau to near Helena, Montana—a zone marked by the outpourings of dozens of hot springs. Every year the region quivers perceptibly with between 20 and 40 tremors, and about once a decade it experiences a severe wallop.

And so the Rockies grew—and still grow, inch by agonizing inch. And inch by inch they wear away, a grain, a pebble, a boulder at a time. The Rockies of today are not the Rockies of yesterday, nor will they be the Rockies of a thousand years from now. Millions of years are involved in the birth and growth and death of a major mountain system—spans of time as difficult to visualize as the public debt. But a foot of uplift in a thousand years is not hard to imagine. Many parts of the country, especially along the Pacific coast, bob around at rates much livelier than that. Continue the uplift for ten million years—not long geologically—and a 10,000-foot-high range becomes distinctly possible. Slow and easy does it. One thing is sure: Mountain-building takes a heap of time.

*Dwarf buckwheat, its silvery leaves topped by nodding blossoms, graces a cinder garden at Craters of the Moon National Monument in Idaho. In the distance rise the snow-wreathed Pioneer Mountains, site of famed Sun Valley ski trails. Though the plants stand less than six inches high, their roots sink 3 or 4 feet into the ground to soak up moisture before it can drain away through 2,000 feet of porous lava. East of the monument, Big Lost River and other streams disappear into the basalt, emerging again at Thousand Springs near Twin Falls—100 miles away.*

ENTHEOS

# Canyons of Wonder,
# Rivers of Time

William J. Breed

Many colorful characters have lived at the Grand Canyon, but few can compare with John Hance, pioneer, prospector, miner, and, before the turn of the century, builder of the first tourist facilities on the South Rim. An inveterate storyteller, he is remembered for his tall tales. One day a new arrival noticed that Hance's index finger was missing. "How did it happen?" asked the visitor. John grinned. "I plumb wore it off pointing at the scenery!"

If you could wear off your finger pointing at the scenery in Grand Canyon, you could wear off your arm pointing out the spectaculars of the whole Colorado Plateau. A circular platform of 130,000 square miles 5,000 to over 13,000 feet above sea level, it centers on the Four Corners where Utah, Colorado, Arizona, and New Mexico meet. Sparse rainfall gives much of the plateau a desertlike environment, making it a remote, rocky land of startling contrasts. Here changing life zones march up the sides of canyons with remarkable variety—from thirsty creosote bushes at the lowest levels, through stands of leafy hardwoods, to cool forests of spruce and fir on the heights. Coyotes patrol sagebrush flats for rabbits, cougars prowl piney woodlands for deer, and hawks scan craggy cliffs for rock squirrels.

But nature has worked her greatest contrasts in the landscaped rock. Everyone can admire these wonders—and the famous national parks and monuments that preserve them: Vishnu Temple in Grand Canyon, the Narrows and Great White Throne in Zion, the Grabens and Upheaval Dome in Canyonlands, the windows, spires, and pinnacles at Arches, the Castle at Capitol Reef, the Queen's Garden at Bryce . . . the list seems endless. But few people know how the wonders came to be. Even fewer realize that it took more than a billion years to form the rocks and carve them into the scenic masterpieces we know today.

Most of the Colorado Plateau is characterized by horizontal surfaces etched into mesas and buttes, stone bridges and arches, ridges and canyons, and colorful cliffs of every description. In these respects the plateau is strikingly different from its neighboring provinces. To the west it looks down on the north-south trending mountains and sediment-filled basins of the Basin and Range. To the east it looks up at the folded crystalline rocks and towering relief of the Rockies.

The Colorado Plateau itself has been uplifted, but the uplift was gentle and the layered sedimentary rocks have not been greatly disturbed by structural, or internal, change. Because these layers are so dramatically exposed by erosion, the plateau has long been a training ground for geologists. Earth history and the procession of life are revealed here like so many pages in a book.

I like to picture the Colorado Plateau—actually a broad shelf of many smaller plateaus—as a layer cake put together by a wild baker, with layers and icing of all different thicknesses and colors. Unlike tortured areas of the earth's surface where old rock layers have been folded and faulted and pushed on top of younger rock, here on the

*Lithesome cougar rests from the hunt near Zion National Park in Utah. In highland forests of the rimrock, the big cat stalks mule deer but also dines on smaller animals, including porcupines—quills and all.*

plateau the rock strata are usually still in place with the oldest on the bottom of our cake and the youngest layers at the top. The best place to study the oldest is at the bottom of the Grand Canyon, where the Colorado River has scoured its way into the earth's crust for what some scientists estimate to be ten million years.

You can reach the bottom of the Grand Canyon several ways: From the rim, walk (most intimate), or ride a mule (most interesting), or from Lees Ferry far upstream shoot the river rapids (most exciting). No matter how you get there, you find a deep black inner gorge walled with metamorphic rock—medium-grained schists and coarse-grained gneisses changed from their previous structure by heat and pressure 1.7 billion years ago during Precambrian times. Veins of pink granite lace the walls. Geologists call all these basement rocks the Vishnu Schist.

Because metamorphic rocks usually form deep down at the roots of mountains during crustal movement and folding, the presence of the Vishnu Schist indicates that mountains rose here in Arizona long ago. Wind and water and heat and frost wore away that earliest mountain range—perhaps 16,000 to 20,000 feet high—to a feature-less plain at sea level. The plain must have looked vastly different from any seen on earth today, for no known life existed then except algae and bacteria. Traces of these primitive organisms have been found in the Gunflint Iron Formation of the Canadian Shield (page 54), but any evidence of them here in the West probably was obliterated by the titanic, welding forces of metamorphism.

The oldest record of life on the plateau is found in the layers of rock immediately above the Vishnu Schist. Deposited to a thickness of more than two miles mainly by rivers and tidal waters, these beds record a period of half a billion years—beginning about a billion years ago—when complex forms of life struggled for a start. Paleontologists at first reported jellyfish and primitive clamlike mollusks from these strata, but it is now believed the jellyfish-like markings were created by gas escaping from the sediments. The only definitely known life forms are microscopic algal bodies in thin, limey deposits built up by algae.

During those half billion years the layers bowed up, then broke and slipped along fault lines, creating another range of mountains which in time eroded once again down to a plain. But this time nature was relatively gentle, and the sedimentary layers and their delicate fossils escaped the traumatic transformation into metamorphic rock. Geologists call these layers the Grand Canyon Series and the period that formed them the Grand Canyon Revolution. Their remnants now lie at tilted angles, buried under 3,500 feet of neatly layered horizontal rock of the Paleozoic Era.

It is these colored horizontal layers, magically changing hues in the changing light, that most people remember when they think of the Grand Canyon. The layers start at the bottom with the 100-to-300-foot-thick Tapeats Sandstone and rise like a ladder to the Kaibab Limestone at the top. For 300 million years after the mountains of the Grand Canyon Revolution disappeared—from 500 to 200 million years ago—seas and rivers and deserts alternately deposited the layers as (continued on page 308)

# The Colorado Plateau

This high tableland belongs to the Colorado River, master mover of rock. Fed by snowmelt from the Rockies and by sparse rainfall that nourishes a wide variety of plants (opposite), it carries away the wreckage of erosion. Some believe that long ago the Colorado flowed south along the course of the present Little Colorado. Then the ancestral Hualapai River, which drained the Kaibab plateau on the west, chewed its way eastward, captured the ancient Colorado, pulled it west, and transformed it into a mighty carver of canyons.

MAP BY TIBOR TOTH

OVERLEAF: *Gullies etch the rimrock of Marble Canyon (foreground). Beyond Grand Canyon to the south rise the San Francisco Peaks.*

WILLIAM A. GARNETT

| 0 | STATUTE MILES | 75 |
| --- | --- | --- |
| 0 | KILOMETERS | 100 |

Dinosaur National Monument

ROAN CLIFFS

White

Desolation Canyon

San Rafael

BOOK CLIFFS

Gunnison

Arches National Park

Moab

LA SAL MTS.

Green

San Miguel

Fremont

Dirty Devil

HENRY MTS.

Canyonlands National Park

Capitol Reef National Park

ABAJO MOUNTAINS

Bryce Canyon National Park

KAIPAROWITS PLATEAU

Escalante

Cataract Canyon

SAN MIGUEL MOUNTAINS

Cedar Breaks National Monument

PAUNSAGUNT PLATEAU

Lake Powell

Johns Canyon

Mesa Verde National Park

Zion National Park

Virgin

Parla

Kanab Creek

San Juan

UTAH

COLORADO

Navajo Mt.

Monument Valley

ARIZONA

NEW MEXICO

Glen Canyon Dam

Rainbow Bridge National Monument

Lees Ferry

Marble Canyon

GRAND WASH CLIFFS

Ship Rock

Farmington

UINKARET PLATEAU

Chaco

SAN JUAN BASIN

Colorado

Grand Canyon

KAIBAB PLATEAU

Canyon de Chelly National Monument

COCONINO PLATEAU

Grand Canyon Village

BLACK MESA

PAINTED DESERT

Little Colorado

SAN FRANCISCO PEAKS

Gallup

Sunset Crater National Monument

Flagstaff

Verde

Meteor Crater

Petrified Forest National Park

Holbrook

San Jose

Oak Creek Canyon

MOGOLLON RIM

## Cliffs and Canyons Bare Earth's Past

*Gigantic gashes expose 1.7 billion years of geologic time on the Colorado Plateau. The walls of Grand Canyon, shown below in a 250° panorama from Powell Point on the South Rim, climb from mile-deep bedrock through 300 million years of the Paleozoic Era. In the diagram, trace the layers to Zion. There the walls pick up the record for another 120 million years through the Mesozoic Era. Bryce Canyon and Cedar Breaks reveal rocks of the present Cenozoic Era, which began about 65 million years ago. A layer 26*

*million years old caps Brian Head.*

*Uplift in Cenozoic times loosed the might of running water seeking the level of the sea. Erosion stripped parts of layers, forming the "Great Rock Stairway" of cliffs—Vermilion, White, Gray, Pink—and fashioned the myriad formations we marvel at today.*

*Late in the era, lava welled up, squeezed between layers at various levels as sills, broke through the surface to cap the Mogollon Rim, then burst free to form the San Francisco Peaks and, only 900 years ago, Sunset Crater.*

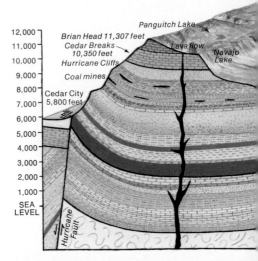

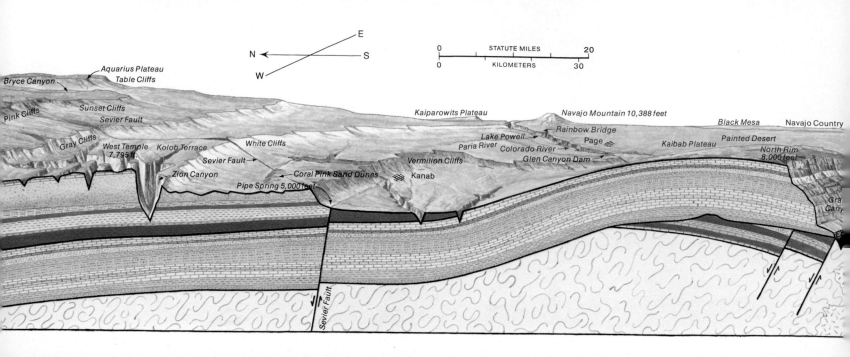

N ← S → E / W

STATUTE MILES 0 — 20
KILOMETERS 0 — 30

Bryce Canyon
Aquarius Plateau
Table Cliffs
Pink Cliffs
Sunset Cliffs
Sevier Fault
Kaiparowits Plateau
Navajo Mountain 10,388 feet
Black Mesa
Navajo Country
Gray Cliffs
West Temple 7,795 ft.
Kolob Terrace
White Cliffs
Rainbow Bridge
Lake Powell
Page
Kaibab Plateau
Painted Desert
Zion Canyon
Sevier Fault
Paria River
Colorado River
North Rim 8,000 feet
Coral Pink Sand Dunes
Vermilion Cliffs
Glen Canyon Dam
Pipe Spring 5,000 feet
Kanab
Grand Canyon
Sevier Fault

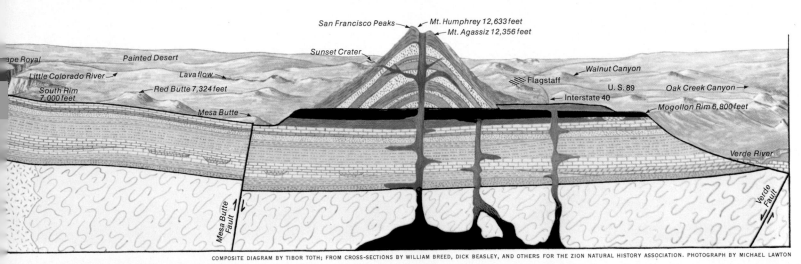

San Francisco Peaks → Mt. Humphrey 12,633 feet
→ Mt. Agassiz 12,356 feet

ape Royal   Painted Desert       Sunset Crater

Little Colorado River →       Lava flow →                        Walnut Canyon

South Rim
7,000 feet       Red Butte 7,324 feet                          Flagstaff       U. S. 89       Oak Creek Canyon →

                Mesa Butte →              ← Interstate 40       Mogollon Rim 6,800 feet →

Mesa Butte                                                                    Verde River

Mesa Butte Fault                                                             Verde Fault

COMPOSITE DIAGRAM BY TIBOR TOTH; FROM CROSS-SECTIONS BY WILLIAM BREED, DICK BEASLEY, AND OTHERS FOR THE ZION NATURAL HISTORY ASSOCIATION. PHOTOGRAPH BY MICHAEL LAWTON

Grand Canyon seems to bleed as flash flood waters rasp its walls. Iron oxides leached from sandstone layers higher up tint the cascade abrading this limestone terrace.

Elevation affects precipitation. The South Rim, 7,000 feet above sea level, and the North Rim, at 8,000, receive 16 to 26 inches a year. The hot canyon floor at 2,500 feet gets less than 10 inches. In this diverse climate thrives a galaxy of life. Mule deer, browsers of the rims, also range down to the rivers. Migrant black-necked stilts search the shallows for food. A toad waits on a bare rock for insects. A foot-long collared lizard lurks in a crevice; when threatened, it runs on hind legs— like many of its ancient dinosaur kin—and can reach 16 mph.

River rafters, like those dwarfed in Marble Canyon above, may even spot desert bighorn sheep vaulting to lofty crags and bobcats padding the beaches. All told, some 67 kinds of mammals, 240 birds, and 43 amphibians and reptiles depend on wild waters that feed the red river of life.

DON BRIGGS

*Creature of evolutionary isolation, the Kaibab squirrel (above) lives in a 350-square-mile forest island on Grand Canyon's North Rim. Except for different markings on tail and belly, the Kaibab is identical with the South Rim's abundant Abert (below). Both measure some 20 inches, weigh nearly two pounds. Both are tied to ponderosa pine, eating its seeds and branch tips. Yet the two never meet, for no ponderosas grow in the desertlike depths of the canyon. The two squirrel species were one, however, until uplift and the Colorado River cut the Kaibab plateau into two widely separated sections.*
WILLIS PETERSON

silt and mud and clay and sand. The region remained flat, sometimes above sea level, sometimes below, as the layers piled up thousands of feet deep. Laid bare through a depth of one mile by the cutting action of the Colorado River, these layered rocks make Grand Canyon unlike any other canyon on the continent.

The study of these rocks has been the lifetime occupation of such men as Edwin D. McKee of the United States Geological Survey. Eddie McKee has become somewhat of a legend, not only for his knowledge of the canyon but also for his hiking exploits there. One evening he was complaining to me that there were no characters like John Hance in the canyon anymore. Then he went on to tell about the time he needed an assistant to help him collect rock samples.

It was during a study that established the boundary between major rock formations in the canyon. In his project he had funds enough only for a packer-guide, none for a pack animal. So Eddie—he was around 60 years old at the time—hired a college student. Summer temperatures in the canyon can soar above 100° F., and after a hot day's work the student began to drag on the trail out. Eddie shouldered the pack full of rocks and climbed to the rim. The student was nowhere in sight. Worried as night approached, Eddie took a flashlight down the trail and helped the exhausted student to the top. The packer-guide had to be packed and guided, so to speak, by McKee. Yet he says there are no characters left in the canyon!

Discoveries by McKee and other dedicated scientists reveal that a lot happened in the canyon area during 300 million years of the Paleozoic Era. Each layer holds its own clues. Limestone commonly forms when the calcium from aquatic animals collects as ooze and is left behind when the waters recede. The climate changes; deserts form, leaving sand which will be compacted into sandstone under succeeding layers. The region rises and falls, rivers and lakes and seas come and go. Deposits of mud and clay become shale. Layers that can be identified as distinctive beds geologists call "formations." The different kinds of rock come in various combinations—sandy shale, silty shale, sandy clay. Conglomerate is a sedimentary rock made up of rounded fragments varying in size from pebbles to boulders. Minerals in rock refine classifications even further. Dolomite, for example, is essentially a limestone, but one rich in the element magnesium.

Limestones in the walls of Grand Canyon tell of at least five invasions by the sea. These layers—named from the lowest to the highest the Muav, Temple Butte, Redwall, Toroweap, and Kaibab formations—contain fossils of trilobites, sharks, corals, and primitive shellfish. Sandwiched between these strata are the red sandstone and shales of the Supai Group and Hermit Shale. They record mighty rivers that once flowed into the area, streams turbid with sediment that formed a huge delta. Tracks preserved in those sediments make you feel that you have just missed seeing giant amphibians lumbering out of the rivers and onto the land.

The same sediments gave some clues that helped start geologists re-evaluating the theory of continental drift. English physicist S. Keith Runcorn studied the magnetism of the red rocks of the canyon and compared them with rocks of a similar age in England. Tiny bits of iron in the canyon rocks acted like compass needles frozen in time, pointing to where the North Pole was more than 200 million years ago. Runcorn's study placed the Grand Canyon area along the Equator and put the North Pole in the Pacific. The rocks that were studied in England also gave a location for the pole. But the polar position from England and America only made sense if the two countries were geographically closer together at the time the rocks were being formed.

Another rich page in the canyon's book of earth history is the Coconino Sandstone, a 300-foot-thick layer just above the Hermit Shale. It is formed of layers of what used to be sand dunes; its extent suggests that a desert of at least 32,000 square miles once covered the southern part of the Colorado Plateau. Perhaps this desert looked like the Sahara—but without Arabs or camels. It did sustain life, however.

Tracks in these fossil sand dunes show the presence of scorpions, spiders, and small reptiles, creatures similar to some inhabitants of present-day deserts. Geologists who observed these early tracks also uncovered something of a mystery. Almost all the tracks ran uphill. Were the animals all going toward waterholes? Were larger animals chasing them? Were they fleeing some catastrophe? Experiments finally solved the riddle: When lizards travel downhill, sliding sand obscures their tracks; permanent tracks occur only on level ground or when the animals go uphill.

While the limestone layers in the Toroweap and Kaibab formations at the top of Grand Canyon record the invasions of seas and preserve a picture of marine life, they also demonstrate the effect of climate on limestone. In a humid climate, rain soon dissolves limestone, which quickly weathers into valleys and lowlands. But in arid regions like the Colorado Plateau, limestone remains a hard rock extremely resistant to erosion. Its strength is reflected in the cliffs it forms, while softer shale and some sandstones erode into slopes. Limestone provides the protective cap of many mesas and buttes and smaller plateaus, as well as Grand Canyon's rimrock.

It is not generally recognized, other than by geologists, that many of the scenic features of the plateau are related. The red rocks in Oak Creek Canyon south of Flagstaff and those in Monument Valley 180 miles to the north represent the same geologic time period as rock layers found in the middle of the Grand Canyon. Sandstones of desert origin similar to the Coconino Sandstone in the Grand Canyon are also found at Canyon de Chelly a hundred miles to the east.

The limestones at the top of the Grand Canyon were laid down near the end of one great chapter of earth history—the Paleozoic Era—which came to a close 225 million years ago. To learn more completely what happened during the succeeding era—the Mesozoic, the heyday of the dinosaurs—we must travel from the Grand Canyon north toward younger Zion Canyon. This journey reveals early stages of deposition now marked by nearly vertical cliffs, mesas, and extremely narrow gorges carved by the Virgin River. Here the Kaibab Limestone that caps Grand Canyon is deep, buried under the Moenkopi Formation, Shinarump Conglomerate,

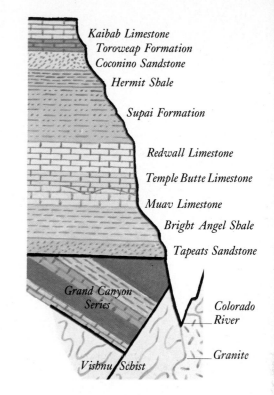

Slice of life of the Paleozoic past—Grand Canyon in cross section. In each stratum, a fossil, track, or fragment hints at life's procession: Tapeats Sandstone, algae; Bright Angel Shale and Muav Limestone, brachiopods and trilobites; Temple Butte Limestone, armored fish; Redwall Limestone, snails and sea lilies; Supai Formation, primitive reptiles; Hermit Shale, insects and ferns; Coconino Sandstone, scorpions and worms; Toroweap Formation, mollusks; Kaibab Limestone, sponges and sharks. Younger deposits that once towered above the Kaibab washed away during the last ten million years.
DIAGRAM BY TIBOR TOTH

OVERLEAF: Temples and palaces create an exotic city of stone at Sunset Point in Bryce Canyon. Rain, frost, and gravity carved the delicate features from limestone laid down 60 million years ago.
WILLIAM A. GARNETT

Chinle Formation, Navajo Sandstone, and several others. The Moenkopi, deposited as broad mudflats interbedded with thin layers of limestone and gypsum from ebbing seas, is another red shale and sandstone layer, similar to the Supai Formation in appearance. During the Mesozoic Era the Moenkopi piled up hundreds of feet deep, but this material in many places, including the Grand Canyon, has been removed by erosion from the top of the Kaibab Limestone almost as easily as a garden hose washes mud off concrete. How then do we know the Moenkopi rocks once rested atop Grand Canyon? Nearby features are remnants of the same red shale and sandstone: Cedar Mountain, a lone mesa rising just east of the canyon rim, survives because it is capped by a protective layer of harder rock, the Shinarump Conglomerate; Red Butte, south of Grand Canyon Village, remains because of a resistant lava cap.

Some of the most fascinating strata deposited during the Mesozoic Era are found in the Chinle Formation. In the Painted Desert near Holbrook, Arizona, the Chinle has weathered into cones and pyramids banded in reds, grays, greens, and yellows that are due to the presence of minerals in the rock—iron and manganese oxides and carbon. Of more interest to the casual observer, however, are the tons of petrified wood scattered in and around Petrified Forest National Park.

Early in the Mesozoic Era 200 million years ago, this fossil wood grew as coniferous trees. Washed by floods into swampy bogs and buried in and under successive layers of mud, the fallen trunks underwent a cell-by-cell mineral replacement process that changed them into quartz (page 89). Erosion has bared acres of the gemlike rock, but much more lies deep underground.

Younger than the Chinle Formation is the Navajo Sandstone. It forms the sheer white cliffs at Zion and also caps Glen Canyon, where the Federal Government dammed the Colorado River in the 1960's to create Lake Powell and produce electricity. Deposited as dune sand, the Navajo Sandstone has an unusual capacity for absorbing water. Because the sand grains are rounded and all about the same size, they are surrounded by numerous pore spaces that allow the formation to act like a giant sponge. During the first year after Glen Canyon Dam was built, the sandstone bed of Lake Powell sucked up some 285 billion gallons of water, enough to supply for a year ten million Americans with the national average of 70 gallons a day.

Erosion of its many sandstone layers has produced much of the Colorado Plateau's sculptured scenery, especially the natural bridges, fanciful arches, and strange spires in southeastern Utah. Rainbow Bridge, one of the most famous carvings, arches 309 feet above the bed of Bridge Creek and spans 278 feet on the flank of Navajo Mountain. The bridge formed when a stream, undercutting its walls, broke through the neck of a loop in the meandering watercourse. Some Indians who hold the bridge sacred call it *Nageelid nonnezoshi*, which means "the-hole-in-the-rock-shaped-like-a-rainbow." Oxides in the rock stripe the bridge red and brown, but even though it lacks the full range of color the feature is still a worthy rival of the rainbow in its great size and symmetrical proportions. *(continued on page 318)*

*Branches crowding the tops of the trunks, Douglas firs reach for the fleeting sun from a stone prison at Bryce Canyon. Vegetation grows on seemingly sterile surfaces by sinking tap roots to ground water. Some grasses, in the manner of these trees, reach down ten feet or more. Where vegetation does not take hold to provide a protective covering, exposed rock suffers the ravages of running water and frost. Water seeps into the tiniest cracks; as the sun sets, it freezes and expands, chipping off pieces of rock. The same process crumbles man-made streets.*
ENTHEOS

## Wonders of a Plateau Pothole

*A microcosmic community of fleas and gnats, mosquitoes and shrimps, beetles and snails miraculously thrives in the ever-dying rock pools of Utah's canyon country. Fierce predator of this realm is the pothole beetle (opposite, top). It sucks the juices from a tadpole that it first disabled by biting off the tail. Needlelike jabbers in its mouth prepared the meal by injecting substances that dissolved the victim's insides.*

*An air breather, the beetle expels a bubble from under its wing case after taking in fresh air; this ability enables it to hunt underwater with rear legs adapted for swimming (far right). If the pothole dries up, wings permit the "water tiger" to escape, perhaps to be gobbled in turn by a waiting toad.*

*Less marvelously endowed residents face disaster even without the beetle—flushing downpours, temperature extremes that may reach 150 degrees in summer and zero in winter, and eventual evaporation of their watery home.*

*Yet even in dried-up potholes, tiny time bombs of life tick on. Showing an amazing versatility in adapting to change, fairy shrimp (opposite, bottom) lay two types of eggs: thin-shelled summer eggs that pop open immediately; thick-shelled winter eggs that lie in the dry sandy bottom and hatch when the pothole refills. Gill-like plates on the shrimps' legs capture oxygen from the water or from the air and give them another name, branchiopod, or "foot-breather." They are the oldest crustaceans known. Fossils of female fairy shrimp containing eggs have been found in the Mojave Desert, where they have rested 26 million years.*

ROBERT F. SISSON, NATIONAL GEOGRAPHIC PHOTOGRAPHER

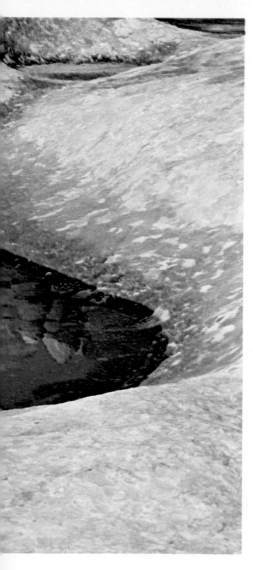

315

*Sandstorm in Utah's Canyonlands National Park adds another "finishing" touch to monuments 250 million years in the making. A classic example of differential erosion, Monument Basin owes its statuary to two sandstones of varied strengths. The soft Organ Rock Tongue layer that forms the spires is held together with weak calcareous cement. Freezing and thawing crack the rock, rain dissolves the cement, and storms like this blow away loose grains of sand. More resistant White Rim Sandstone caps the pillars, sometimes with an umbrella effect.*

DAVID MUENCH

Rocks of the Mesozoic Era offer more than the artistry of stone and the miracle of petrified wood, however. Giant dinosaurs populated much of the plateau, and on its northern edge Dinosaur National Monument preserves an exciting array of bones. They lie partially exposed in the entombing rock of the Morrison Formation, one of the best sources on the continent for the remains of these mighty reptiles.

During the last part of the age, another sea washed over the plateau, leaving behind bones of huge marine reptiles, plesiosaurs and mosasaurs, as well as giant bony fish, innumerable shark teeth, and oysters. Deposits on land near the shoreline encased duck-billed dinosaurs, horned dinosaurs, armored dinosaurs, and one of the fiercest predators of all time, *Tyrannosaurus rex*. Before these creatures left the stage of earth history, they probably dwelt amid a new kind of vegetation. Conifers had been abundant in the past, but now flowering plants and broadleaf trees enter the scene. Leaf imprints of beeches, birches, alders, walnuts, magnolias, sweet gums, laurel, ebony, and holly have been discovered in the layered rock.

Accumulations of these plants in swamps near the seas resulted in beds of coal found today at such places as Black Mesa in Arizona, the San Juan Basin in New Mexico, the Kaiparowits Plateau in Utah. This is the fuel for power plants being built on the Colorado Plateau in ever-increasing numbers, which are now a controversial issue between environmentalists and industry. The deposits are immense, and the Navajo Mine alone, a stripping operation near Farmington, New Mexico, yielded more than six million tons of subbituminous coal in 1975.

The passing of the dinosaurs closed a major chapter in the life history of the Colorado Plateau and opened another—the Cenozoic Era, which ushered in the Age of Mammals—about 65 million years ago. Fossil records indicate that many denizens of today's plateau shared the land with mammals that became extinct in North America about 10,000 years ago—camels, tapirs, mammoths, mastodons. Perhaps the most interesting record of a fossil mammal on the plateau is that of the ground sloth. In Rampart Cave, high up the side of western Grand Canyon, scientists have found dung as big as softballs belonging to the Shasta ground sloth, a pony-size browser of the Southwest. For many years it was thought the living animal might still be found, for the dung looks and smells fresh. Yet radiocarbon dating showed the youngest dung sample to be 10,780 years old!

Much of the record of plant and animal life during the Age of Mammals is spotty, due in large part to renewed uplift and erosion that began on the plateau with the Cenozoic Era. Some portions of the plateau rose more than two miles, setting the stage for dynamic erosion. For when water falls from high regions, gravity intensifies its power to grind and carry away the softer deposits.

While this water power has been the principal agent in carving the formations we know today, volcanism also played a part in shaping the landscape. Near Flagstaff, Arizona, more than 400 small cinder cones dot the surface like giant anthills. Each cone represents an outpouring of molten rock, gases, and ash in a volcanic episode that culminated in the creation of the San Francisco Peaks. These peaks rise 5,000 feet above the countryside, but as active volcanoes they must have reached several thousand feet higher before they were worn down.

Lava shields cap many plateaus in Utah but we find more spectacular volcanism on the Uinkaret Plateau northwest of Grand Canyon. Cinder cones and jagged flows dot this weird, moonlike landscape. Lava also spilled into the canyon. A hundred years ago John Wesley Powell, the intrepid one-armed explorer of the Colorado River, pictured the spectacle thus: "What a conflict of water and fire there must have been here! Just imagine a river of molten rock running down into a river of melted snow. What a seething and boiling of the waters; what clouds of steam rolled into the heavens!" River runners today know Lava Falls, where the Colorado drops 37 feet in 80 yards, as one of the most thrilling spots in boating the length of the Grand Canyon.

Elevation plays an important role in the life of the Colorado Plateau because it influences temperature and moisture. Plants especially are closely adapted to available moisture. The higher the elevation the more rainfall, the cooler the temperatures, and the shorter the growing season. As a rough rule, every 1,000-foot rise in elevation climatically equals traveling 300 miles northward. Exposure to sunlight, of course, is a factor that controls environment, and in mile-deep Grand Canyon it leads to sharp contrasts. South walls, which face north and get little sun, support spruce and fir and other normally high-elevation plants, while the north walls, which face south, are covered with cactus, yucca, mesquite, and other low-level vegetation.

In fact, it seems impossible to visit any remote area of the plateau without seeing something interesting or exciting in nature. A fully submerged bird, the water ouzel, walks along a stream bottom in search of insect larvae. An ant slides helplessly down a conical sand trap where the waiting jaws of an ant lion protrude from the bottom of the pit. Two rattlesnakes in the underbrush rise up like cobras, staring and testing each other's strength. And how can I forget a walk through a grove of white-barked aspen trees when the leaves have turned gold in the fall—or the same grove in winter with its harsh shadows against the snow on a moonlit night. Or a dry canyon with a small pool filled with tadpoles, and a garden of maidenhair fern nearby. Or the blossoms of a redbud, red-purple against a brown canyon wall.

Some people, however, tend to remember the thorns on a rose, rather than the flower itself. I knew a weatherbeaten old cowboy in Flagstaff who liked to complain that "Everything that moves can bite or sting. Everything else sticks or pricks." An exaggeration, of course. Still, you do have to watch out for cactus and yucca and scorpions and those rattlesnakes. And don't eat the leaves of the sacred datura, a beautiful but potent narcotic plant.

The value of plants and animals, on the other hand, should not be judged solely by their usefulness to man. Two of the most interesting animals on the plateau, the coyote and cougar, compete with man for food, so some consider them "public enemies." But they are necessary to maintain a healthy balance in nature. A classic

*Petrifaction converted this ancient brachiopod into a jewel of a fossil. Found in John's Canyon in southeastern Utah where it inhabited a shallow sea 300 million years ago, the shell is frozen in time as jasper—quartz tinted red by the presence of iron. The shell could easily have been a mold for iron pyrite, or fools' gold, if the minerals that replaced its calcitic cells had contained iron and sulphur.*
DAVID CAVAGNARO

OVERLEAF: *North Fork of the Virgin grinds through Navajo Sandstone walls of Zion Canyon. Rocks from limestone layer atop the Navajo add grist to the river's mill.*
ENTHEOS

example of this began in 1906. To protect the dwindling deer population on the North Rim of Grand Canyon, the Federal Government set up a predator control program aimed at eliminating the cougar—also called mountain lion, puma, or panther—along with other natural enemies of the deer. Eventually, more than 600 cougars were killed, and the deer population did increase. It exploded from 4,000 to an estimated 100,000, a greater number than the forest could support. Controlled deer hunts had to be organized, and the attempted extermination of the cougar finally came to an end.

One day I took a friend to a Grand Canyon overlook where he could see the Colorado River far below. I explained how weathering had broken up the rock, how gravity and running water had propelled the rock to the tributaries and eventually to the Colorado, how all the rock carved out of the Grand Canyon had been carried away by this insignificant-looking stream. My friend looked at me in disbelief. I hadn't the heart to tell him that all the rock eroded from the entire Colorado Plateau had been removed by this same river system.

Fifty years ago the river ran wild. Fed by meltwater from the mountains of Wyoming and Colorado, it roared through the numerous canyons cut along its 1,450-mile length. Storm-fed floods would raise the river level 40 to 60 feet above low-water mark. The free-running Colorado, named by the Spaniards for its red color, transported an average of 500,000 tons of sand, silt, and mud through the Grand Canyon every day—enough solid material to fill two million quarter-ton pickup trucks. Like many another wild river, the Colorado was "too thin to plow and too thick to drink."

This is still the case in some parts of the upper river system but no longer true below Glen Canyon Dam. Where the Colorado once experienced torrential floods at the whim of nature, it now gently rises and falls daily, depending on the power needs of Phoenix and Los Angeles. It's also not as muddy as before, and riverside beaches are slowly disappearing as silt washes away. Upstream silt that formerly settled on the riverbanks following the floods—thus renewing the beaches—now drifts to the bottom behind the dam, silting up Lake Powell.

Other changes are occurring on the Colorado Plateau. More and more paved roads penetrate once isolated regions. Machines claw the earth for minerals, and power plants pollute once crystal-clear air. Yet for me—and many others—the importance of the Colorado Plateau is not its potential for developing electricity but its still-abundant wild places. Places where one can find rocks and plants and animals in the conditions nature blended, where man has not tried to rearrange or reorganize or tame all that is untamed. In these areas of the plateau, sculptured by nature and untouched by man, we may find the greatest value of all.

*Ship Rock rides out time and the elements in the New Mexico desert. A neck that fed a cone-shaped volcano in Tertiary times, it thrusts 1,600 feet above the surrounding floor of earlier Mancos Shale on the Navajo Indian Reservation. Erosion stripped away the volcano's ash and cinder slopes and perhaps 2,000 feet of softer sedimentary rock through which it burst, leaving this plug a stark sculpture in a lonely setting.*
DAVID MUENCH

# The Patchwork Desert

John S. Shelton

My favorite desert lies in southeastern California, west of the Colorado River. As youngsters my brother and I romped on its sandy surface, chasing rabbits, lizards, and each other. In rocky places we hunted Indian pottery chips, arrowheads, and spirit sticks. We observed with wonder the different tracks left by sidewinders and other rattlesnakes. Sand-colored horned lizards first flattened themselves in the palms of our hands and then, if further aggravated, emitted tiny squirts of blood from glands near their eyes. Almost everything came in shades of brown and gray, even the petrified wood we picked up; the etched knots and abraded ends suggested scraps of driftwood instead of logs. Many people would consider this northwestern slice of the Sonoran Desert a barren place, but we found it full of life, and we loved the freedom and adventure it offered.

The Sonoran Desert reaches into southern Arizona and northern Mexico for 120,000 square miles. Embracing millions of acres of drifting sand dunes, it lives up to the popular notion of what a desert should be. Yet it fills but one dramatic corner of the vast Basin and Range Province—an 1,800-mile stretch from southern Oregon almost to Mexico City. Nearly everything we call desert in the United States and half the dry lands of Mexico fall within the province boundaries.

The Basin and Range is rugged country. Per thousand square miles, it probably has more ups and downs than any other province. (The Rockies with their continuous crests have more ups, but they are short on downs.) At least 60 peaks in the desert province reach 10,000 feet or higher, while the floor of Death Valley near Badwater lies 282 feet below sea level—lowest point on the continent. Between these extremes are valleys and plains flanked by more than 200 ranges and mountainous ridges. Most of the major ranges align roughly north-south in Nevada and New Mexico. In Arizona, west Texas, and south of the border, they trend northwest. These nearly parallel mountain ranges were described years ago by pioneer geologist Clarence E. Dutton as "an army of caterpillars crawling northward out of Mexico."

Because half the area receives an average of less than 10 inches of rain a year, and the other half less than 20 inches, desert conditions dominate the province. Moisture decomposes rock into soil; where rain is scarce, soil and vegetation are too. Bare rock abounds, and temperatures are often extreme. Population density, less than five per square mile in most places, dips to zero over many hundreds of square miles. Compared to most other regions, the Basin and Range Province must be considered inhospitable. But that in itself constitutes both a challenge and an attraction. One develops special feelings for a land that is big, tough, yet open, honest, and—when initial difficulties are overcome—rich and rewarding.

A good way to get acquainted with such a giant landscape is to fly over it at low altitudes—early in the morning, when the air is still, cool, and smooth, and longer shadows emphasize subtle shapes that will be unrecognizable under the high sun of

*Attuned to a land of little rain, the black-tailed jackrabbit seldom drinks but slakes its thirst on succulents, lacks sweat glands yet keeps its cool. Long ears laced with blood vessels help dispel excess body heat.*
FARRELL GREHAN

SAGUARO; DAVID MUENCH

BOOJUM TREE; WALTER MEAYERS EDWARDS

BARREL CACTUS; ENTHEOS

midday. Low sunlight, because it traverses more of the earth's atmosphere, loses some of its wavelengths at the blue end of the spectrum through scattering. The light arrives enriched in reds and yellows, bathing the land in a warm, caressing glow symbolic of earth's dependence on this wondrous source of energy.

One sunny morning my wife and I climb into the small plane that I use for geological photography. Our flight will traverse the Basin and Range where its width narrows to no more than 250 miles—yet we'll sample a broad variety of desert landscapes.

As we take off at Lone Pine, California, the granite wall of the Sierra Nevada towers above us, culminating in jagged peaks against a deep blue sky. Flying eastward toward the mouth of Grand Canyon, we will cross a succession of typical basins and ranges. We have started in Owens Valley, a long, straight, deep depression hemmed in by steep walls rising 10,000 feet above the valley floor on the west, 7,000 feet on the east. Beginning about 150 million years ago, compressive forces within the earth wrinkled the older sedimentary layers into giant folds. Much later, volcanoes spewed lava, ash, and cinders over the land. At about the same time, block faulting occurred; huge mountain blocks were uplifted along fractures in the earth's crust and tilted, while basins like Owens Valley sank. During an earthquake in 1872, as much as 20 feet were added to the difference in height between the bottom of Owens Valley and the crest of the Sierra Nevada. The fault scarp is still visible.

For the next 250 miles we will fly over ten mountain ranges spaced an average of 22 miles apart. From mountaintops to basin floors the average relief is 6,400 feet, well over a vertical mile. Northward into central Nevada and western Utah the rough terrain continues. Nevada serves as the classic model of this "washboard" structure. Paul Bunyan might have sliced off a strip and used it as a file to trim the hooves of his great ox.

What caused this patch of crust to break up the way it did? Faulting and tilting are adjustments of the outer crust to stresses and strains deep in the earth. Mechanically, the Basin and Range type of faulting and tilting requires stretching of the crust—a process that is still going on. In western Nevada, earthquakes in 1915, 1932, and 1954 produced breaks in the ground. A sharp cliff 23 feet high emerged during the 1954 quake. Clearly, the ranges are still rising, the basins sinking. Such stretching also favors volcanic eruptions—the cracks allow molten rock under pressure to escape.

But geologists are puzzled by the fact that this stretching is occurring in the same region that underwent east-west compression less than 150 million years ago. Why this accordion-like reversal? Many geologists search for clues in the theory of plate tectonics. Perhaps the collision of the Pacific and North American plates caused the ancient compression, and the later stretching is associated with the more recent slow splitting off of Baja California. Such ideas involve much speculation; plate tectonics better explains events along plate margins than here in the interior.

As internal forces raise mountains and drop valleys, weathering and erosion are sculpturing the surface shapes. Rains pour down (continued on page 334)

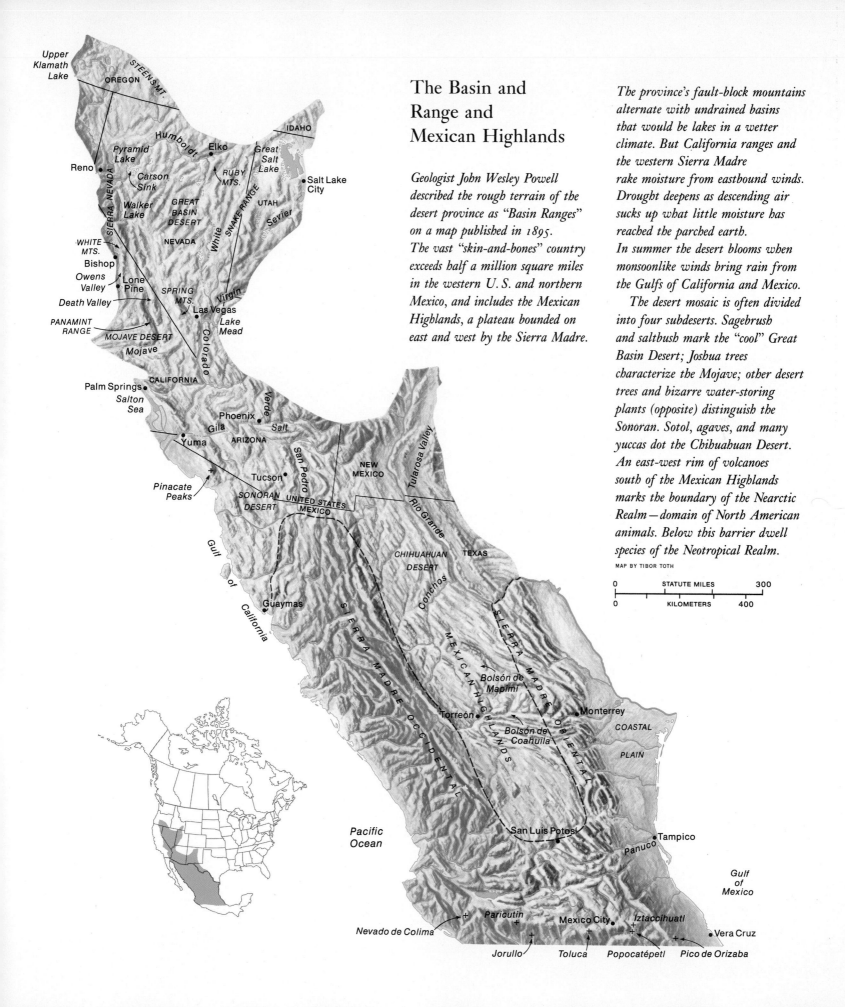

# The Basin and Range and Mexican Highlands

Geologist John Wesley Powell described the rough terrain of the desert province as "Basin Ranges" on a map published in 1895. The vast "skin-and-bones" country exceeds half a million square miles in the western U.S. and northern Mexico, and includes the Mexican Highlands, a plateau bounded on east and west by the Sierra Madre.

The province's fault-block mountains alternate with undrained basins that would be lakes in a wetter climate. But California ranges and the western Sierra Madre rake moisture from eastbound winds. Drought deepens as descending air sucks up what little moisture has reached the parched earth. In summer the desert blooms when monsoonlike winds bring rain from the Gulfs of California and Mexico.

The desert mosaic is often divided into four subdeserts. Sagebrush and saltbush mark the "cool" Great Basin Desert; Joshua trees characterize the Mojave; other desert trees and bizarre water-storing plants (opposite) distinguish the Sonoran. Sotol, agaves, and many yuccas dot the Chihuahuan Desert. An east-west rim of volcanoes south of the Mexican Highlands marks the boundary of the Nearctic Realm—domain of North American animals. Below this barrier dwell species of the Neotropical Realm.

MAP BY TIBOR TOTH

STATUTE MILES
0 — 300
KILOMETERS
0 — 400

mountain canyons, depositing on lower slopes aprons of rock debris—alluvial fans. What the mountains lose through erosion, the valleys gain as infilling sediment. In Owens Valley bedrock lies a mile below sea level, buried under an estimated 8,000 to 9,000 feet of alluvium. Flat depressions on the basin floor called playas ("beaches" in Spanish) collect rain and runoff, forming shallow lakes, most of which dry up in a few weeks. Owens Lake, fed by the Owens River, was 30 feet deep in the 1870's. A small steamboat plied its salty expanse carrying silver bullion mined in nearby Cerro Gordo —Fat Mountain—for delivery in Los Angeles by wagon. After 1913, when the river's waters were diverted to the Los Angeles Aqueduct, the salt sea became a cracked, dusty lake bed—a typical playa.

To clear the Panamint Range, rising almost 10,000 feet in seven miles, we pull the nose up and start a gentle climb, leveling off at 11,500 feet. South of Telescope Peak sharp ridges and deep canyons come into view; here prospectors found silver and lead in the old days. Small pine and juniper trees cover north-facing slopes where evaporation is less severe and winter snows linger a little longer. Just ahead and more than two miles below us lies the most spectacular basin of all—Death Valley.

Author J. Ross Browne described the desolate sink in 1868: "The climate in winter is finer than that of Italy . . . [though] fastidious people might object to the temperature in summer. . . . I have even heard complaint that the thermometer failed to show the true heat because the mercury dried up." Summer air temperatures average 100° F., sometimes soaring to 120°. Ground surface temperatures have risen to 190°. Located just north of the Mojave Desert, an arid patch of land in the rain shadow of the Sierra Nevada and Panamint Range, the valley averages only 1.5 inches of rain a year; potential evaporation—the moisture that would evaporate if it were available—is more than 150 inches—100 times greater. No wonder it is dry and barren down there!

Although Death Valley may go a year without rainfall, underground seepage from higher and wetter ground tends to collect in a few springs, wells, and ponds. The water, rich in dissolved salts, ranges from mildly unpleasant to impossible for drinking. The members of a covered wagon party, trapped in Death Valley in the winter of 1849-50, survived because of these water sources. The pioneers were seeking a southerly route to the California goldfields and failed to get their wagons across the Panamint Range. Two men, William Manly and John Rogers, went ahead to scout the way and bring back supplies. Twenty-six days later they returned to lead the desperate little band to safety. One of the party looked back as they were leaving and murmured, "Goodbye, Death Valley!" christening the "God-forsaken country" where, had it been summer, all might have perished.

This huge depression was formed by block faulting within the last four or five million years, and it is still moving. The United States Geological Survey has installed tiltmeters to measure the continuing motion. Fault scarps across the surfaces of long, coalescing alluvial fans show older, but still geologically recent, activity. Desert varnish—iron and manganese oxide—stains some fans dark brown. Acquired in wetter times when the rock surfaces were moist enough to encourage oxidation, the varnish helps the geologist fix a recent chronology—only dry gravel surfaces more than 2,000 years old show the dark stain.

During the Ice Age, Death Valley was the end puddle for three chains of lakes, and at Mormon Point the delicate shorelines of vanished waters are clearly visible. The Pacific Coast Borax Company drilled wells near Badwater and encountered layers of salt and mud to a depth of 1,000 feet—proof of a long history of wetting and drying in this basin. Each layer of mud represents the sediment that accumulated in a lake, and each layer of salt on top testifies to the drying up of that body of water. More than 10,000 years ago, Indians probably camped along the shores of the one we call Lake Manly, which at times was 100 miles long and 600 feet deep. As the climate grew drier, the lake evaporated, leaving almost 100 square miles of salt-encrusted playa. One of the weary pioneers trying to cross the playa's rough surface joked about the endless supply of the white mineral: "If a man was to die, he would never decay on account of the salt."

Looking down from our altitude of 11,500 feet, we see only a few shrubs and grasses amid the desolation. Actually, more than 1,300 kinds of plants and animals have adjusted to life here. Coyotes lope up and down the fans and may cross the salt pan at night; sidewinders leave their distinctive tracks among the dunes. Mesquite trees up to 20 feet tall thrive where groundwater is near the surface but not too salty. Desert holly, creosote bush, and honeysweet dot the rocky alluvial fans.

Botanists from the Carnegie Institution of Washington, intrigued by the ability of honeysweet to grow during the hot, rainless summer, took a mobile laboratory into Death Valley to probe the shrub's secrets. A study of the plant's photosynthesis—how it uses the sun's energy to power its own chemical factory—showed it to be one of the most efficient in the plant kingdom. A special leaf enzyme allows honeysweet to grab more carbon dioxide from the air in less time than other plants do. Leaf pores open quickly to let the gas in before too much of the leaf's water vapor escapes; the fast-growing honeysweet seedling increases by 90 times in three weeks. Scientists believe that lessons learned from the hardy shrub may be applied to the development of high-yield crops for arid farmland.

Four ridges beyond Death Valley we pass the Nopah Range. Ahead rise the Spring Mountains, almost 12,000 feet high, the largest massif along our route. Long, sweeping, half-shadowed canyons converge toward the summit, Charleston Peak. On the south flank a forest of green pines—bristlecone and ponderosa—gives way through woodland foothills to dusty valley floors. We are flying over an environmental island. About

*The sidewinder's rattle and the spines of a prickly pear cactus fend off foes on Mojave Desert dunes. The rattler's tail, tipped with rings of hard skin left by successive molts, clicks with a menacing sound. Barely touching the torrid sand, the serpent undulates obliquely in search of rodents and lizards. Swallowed whole, a horned lizard may pierce the snake's neck with its spines—a posthumous revenge.*
E. R. DEGGINGER

OVERLEAF: *Follow the Buttermilk Road to California's lofty barrier range, the Sierra Nevada, where moisture-laden westerly winds dump ten times more rain than here in Owens Valley. In the 1870's the valley road wound through irrigated grazing lands, past a dairy farm that sold a creamy thirst quencher.*
GALEN ROWELL

*Etched in a twisted torso, the saga of a single bristlecone pine may span nearly 5,000 years. On rocky heights in California's White Mountains, gnarled skeletons cling to life with a narrow strip of live tissue; resin-rich wood resists decay. Exposed roots show that erosion may scour a foot from the tree's windy perch every thousand years.*

*The beleaguered ancients, relics of 50,000,000-year-old conifer forests, store data from the planet's past. Scientists date the tree by counting annual growth rings. Ring-dated bristlecones revealed fluctuations in radioactive carbon as amounts in the atmosphere varied. This so changed the radiocarbon dating scale that archeologists had to redate man's early monuments—with strange results. Some European cultures now appear to be more ancient than those from which they supposedly derived.*

31 kinds of plants, a ground squirrel, a chipmunk, and a wood rat are marooned on the slopes, unable to survive a crossing of the surrounding desert. In winter, people are skiing on mountain trails, while others are basking in the broiling sun of Las Vegas Valley less than an hour's drive away.

As we wing away from the east slope, sunlight falls on the full spectrum of plant life that girdles this island mountain, from the summit through pine forest, juniper and piñon woodland, Joshua tree and Mojave yucca, creosote bush and cacti, down to the shrubby desert floor. Within the desert biome—an arid-climate assemblage—different plant and animal habitats exist, influenced by varying temperature, rainfall, soil composition, amount of sun, and angle of slope, but most of all by elevation. Climate changes faster vertically than horizontally.

North of the latitude of Las Vegas, forested belts cover only about 5 percent of the Basin and Range Province. Sagebrush blankets 80 percent of the land, climbing slopes where it mixes with Utah juniper and pine trees. Aromatic juniper wood, much used by Indians, makes a good campfire; the brown foliage at the tree's base is one of the better places to put a sleeping bag in this rocky land. In drier desert areas of southern Nevada and farther south, sagebrush gives way to cacti and creosote bush.

Did the Basin and Range Province look very different during the Pleistocene? The shape of the land—high ranges and low basins—was essentially the same as it is today, but there were marked alternations between cool, wet periods and warm, dry ones. Though the ice sheets never covered the Southwest, Ice Age meltwater and heavy rains filled the basins, as in Death Valley. Abundant vegetation offered food to giant ground sloths, mammoths, and other mammals now extinct. In response to the climatic swings of the Pleistocene, the lakes formed and dried up again and again. With each change plants and animals were forced to adapt or to move on—upslope or north during drought, downslope or south in cool, wet times. In strange territories they faced new competition, new predators, and more—or less—crowding. The results surely led to hybridization and new species, or extinction.

A tiny vegetarian, the pack rat, left a record of some of these changes. The rodent's mummified nests—ancient middens consisting of twigs, bark, cactus joints, fruits and seeds—have been found in caves and rock shelters. Dated by the carbon-14 method, the middens range in age from 7,800 to over 40,000 years, and contain some plant products no longer found close to the sites. From this and other evidence we know that plant zones during the very late Pleistocene were located 1,000 to 2,000 feet lower than they are today. This process may be still going on; plants and animals marooned on high mountains have an uncertain future. During a dry cycle, some habitats may be eliminated—squeezed upward off the summits.

All over the Basin and Range Province are plants and animals with restricted habitats. Some, like the bristlecone pine, seem to hang on wherever conditions are right. Others, like the desert pupfish, have evolved species that may be unique to a single spring—creatures confined to "islands of water in a sea of sand."

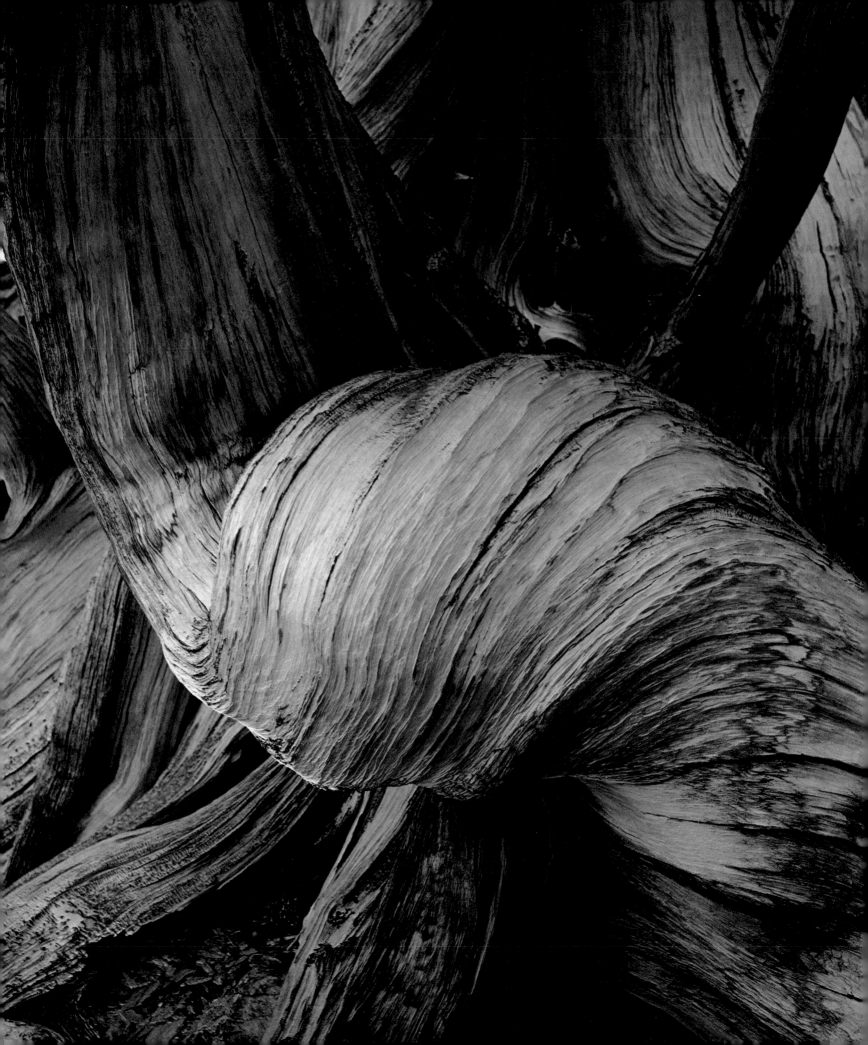

# Made for Each Other: Yucca and Yucca Moth

The Mojave yucca aims daggerlike leaves at the sun in a cluster that shields flat leaf surfaces from the burning rays. Plants bloom in bright profusion, unconquered by the upland desert of the Spring Mountains. Desert marigolds nudge beavertail cacti, succulents without leaves; waxy stems retain moisture, and shallow, wide-spreading roots suck water after the briefest sprinkle.

The desert's tangled skein often unites plants and animals in the struggle for life. Some yuccas and yucca moths cannot survive without each other. Visiting a yucca plant by night, a pronuba moth trysts with her mate on a creamy blossom (A). Scraping pollen from an anther (B), she rolls a ball much larger than her head and flies to another flower, there to pierce its ovary wall and lay her eggs (C). Then she climbs the pistil and tamps in pollen, ensuring the yucca's pollination (D). As payment, the plant's yield nourishes the moth's offspring, but the hatched larvae eat only a few developing seeds, leaving the rest for propagation (E). In this drama of co-evolution, only one moth species pollinates the yucca, which in turn is the moth's sole egg-laying site. The insect's mouthparts evolved to carry pollen.

Other plant adaptations—sharp spines, toothed leaves, or built-in insecticides like those in poison ivy—repel unwelcome visitors. Botanists wondered: Does nibbling a hallucinogenic plant send the nibbler on a trip? Spiders, doused with marijuana and amphetamines, wove skewed, wacky webs.

By using natural weaponry, scientists suggest, man might breed crops with built-in repellents— thus controlling insects without spraying poisons into the air.

ANDREE ROBINSON. OPPOSITE: DAVID MUENCH

A

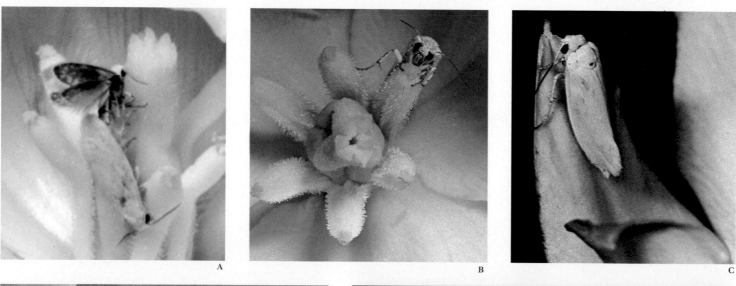

B

C

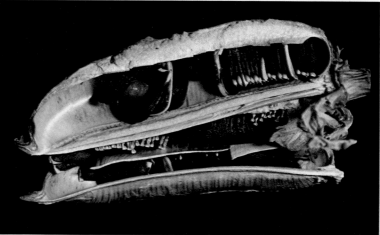

D

E

In the Death Valley region, nine kinds of pupfish occupy a dozen isolated springs, marshes, and streams, often one type per site. These adaptable, inch-long fish have evolved independently since the Ice Age lakes began drying up. But their future is precarious. Small changes in groundwater levels may wipe out their abodes. Many have already become extinct, and 19 species within the Basin and Range Province are listed by the Secretary of the Interior as endangered.

Skimming over a wide valley east of the Spring Mountains, we approach a toy town perfectly delineated in the clear desert air—Las Vegas. Tall hotels cast long shadows; green golf courses and brown desert floor sketch a patchwork design. Like a procession of bugs, automobiles crawl along "The Strip." From this perspective, it is a contrived city, a cluster of artifacts unrelated to its surroundings, built of imported materials for the benefit of imported people—a strange destiny for what was once a single ranch house in a clump of cottonwood trees; later a tent town sprang up when the railroad established a station there. But at night, the incongruity is blacked out and the city sparkles like multicolored jewels.

Seventy miles farther on, the Grand Wash Cliffs appear, and to the right, the Grand Canyon winds toward us between shadowed walls. Gone are the upfaulted mountains and downfaulted basins. Instead the Colorado Plateau stretches as far as the eye can see. We have crossed the Basin and Range Province wall to wall in an hour and a half. Near Las Vegas we flew over the rim of the Great Basin—that huge section of the province that embraces most of Nevada and parts of Oregon, Idaho, Utah, and California, from which there is almost no drainage to the sea.

Although two Spanish priests penetrated the Great Basin in the 18th century, mountain man Jedediah Smith was the first white explorer to cross it. Leaving Cache Valley near Great Salt Lake in August 1826, he and his companions stumbled into California four months later after a grueling journey across the Great Basin and the Mojave Desert. Back in present-day Utah, he reported the country barren: "Some isolated mountains rise from this Plain of Sand, to the region of Perpetual snow, the small streams that flow from these are soon absorbed in the Sand. It contains a few miserable Indians, and but little Game." Two years earlier, Jim Bridger had taken a bullboat down Bear River Canyon to the north end of the Great Salt Lake. Tasting the briny water, he spat it out. "Hell! It's the Pacific Ocean!"

Explorer John C. Frémont revealed the true nature of this little-known region. After a year's reconnaissance that took him from the Wasatch Range to the Sierra Nevada, he wrote that the vast country was "filled with rivers and lakes which have no communication with the sea." Recognizing the land as a huge depression with interior drainage, he named it the "great basin." His insight forever laid to rest the myth that a large river in the area offered a pathway to the Pacific. Emigrants, however, found Frémont's report an unreliable tour guide. He lumped Utah Lake and Great Salt Lake together as one body of water and described the Humboldt River Valley as a "rich alluvium, beautifully covered with... nutritious grasses." Pioneers who believed his

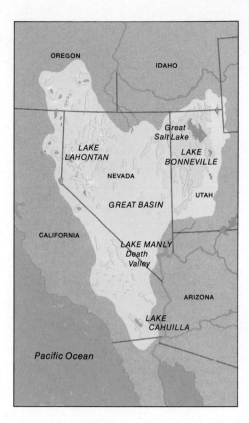

"A vast, waveless ocean stricken dead," wrote Mark Twain when he crossed Utah's salt flats in 1861. But the shriveled wastelands of the Great Basin and adjacent areas once glimmered with lakes (light blue) as glaciers to the north brought wetter weather. Two giants, Lakes Lahontan and Bonneville, flooded parts of Nevada, Idaho, and Utah. The sites of most of Utah's large cities lay underwater. Drought began to shrink the lakes 15,000 years ago—2,000-square-mile Great Salt Lake is but a tiny remnant of 20,000-square-mile Lake Bonneville. On distant heights strandlines mark Bonneville's levels (opposite), which rose and fell more than 20 times in 800,000 years. The briny crust of the salt flats—the ancient lake's evaporated bed—forms crystals in the summer heat, and cracks. Great Salt Lake harbors the salt of the ages—eight billion tons.
BILL RATCLIFFE

343

## True Grit: A Coyote's Tale

*Precocious coyote pups pose for a picture outside their home dug in a hillside. The male, a good provider, brings food, decoys enemies away from the den, and helps teach the youngsters to hunt at the age of two months. Mated for life, a coyote pair may have as many as ten pups in a litter.*

*Relentlessly hunted, this shrewd, adaptable symbol of the West has extended its range north to Alaska and east to the Atlantic Seaboard, replacing its once-numerous kin, the wolf. Coyotes rarely travel in packs as wolves do; loners attract less attention. Off at an incredible 40 miles per hour, they often pursue pronghorns and jackrabbits. One crafty coyote was seen clowning before a spellbound jackrabbit, while another coyote jumped the hare from behind. In the Southwest the animals dig to find water underground—the "Coyote Wells" marked on many desert maps. In a battle that rouses public ire, stockmen slaughter mutton-loving coyotes, whose endurance is legendary. One lived with its jaw shot off, another with broken legs. The coyote, says an Indian tale, will be the last animal on earth.*

JOSEPH VAN WORMER. LEFT: WOLFGANG BAYER, BOTH BRUCE COLEMAN INC.

345

account took their families to settle along the Humboldt River but found in most places only a desert cut by a narrow stream. They renamed it "the Humbug."

Southward from the Great Basin the province changes character. Hot, dry desert replaces "cool" northern desert. Mountain ranges gnawed by erosion stand farther apart in southeastern California and southern Arizona. This part of the province, as in the north, has few drainage outlets. Southern Arizona drains toward the Colorado and Gila rivers, but enclosed sinks scattered from California to west Texas cradle dry beds where runoff collects only during the wet season.

A huge basin in southern California—the Salton Trough—contains the Salton Sea. The Mexicans call it *La Palma de la Mano de Díos*—the Hollow of God's Hand. In photographs taken from space (pages 370-371) it appears as an extension of the Gulf of California, whose waters ten million years ago probably lapped the shore as far north as Palm Springs. By the Pleistocene, the Colorado River had disgorged enough silt into the gulf to build a delta barrier. Since then the Salton Trough has contained a lake or a dried-up sink as the river meandered back and forth, changing course. Lake Cahuilla, an ancient sea that probably dried up about 300 years ago, left shorelines up to 40 feet above present sea level on both sides of the trough.

In 1905 the Colorado River flooded, filling the sink to a depth of 80 feet. Today the Salton Sea, 35 miles long and 40 feet deep near the center, occupies the lowest part of the trough. The sea's surface lies 236 feet below sea level. With its salt floor, salty intake from irrigation drainage, heavy evaporation, and no outlet, the sea in 70 years has become brinier than the ocean. Sport fish introduced in the 1950's probably face extinction, since the salt concentration is approaching a level deadly to embryos.

The San Andreas Fault zone borders the east side of the Salton Trough. More than 15 earthquakes with Richter magnitudes of 6 or greater have jolted the area since 1912. (The 1906 San Francisco quake measured 8.3). The presence of natural hot springs and mudpots along the sea's southeast shore led to drilling in the 1960's. Temperatures 5,000 feet down reach 500° to 600° F., very high for a hot spring area. But the "water" that comes up is a witch's brew, a corrosive brine rich in minerals—barium, gold, silver, manganese, and others—that encrusts pipes. When we learn to handle the fiery liquid and to dispose of its wastes, the hot springs may be a source of geothermal energy. By one estimate, electricity could be generated to meet the needs of four million people for about 8,000 years.

Desert country adjoins the Salton Sea on the east and west; stark mountains rise from sandy plains. Hollywood has long considered

*Fearsome in look and legend, Arizona's hairy tarantula poses little hazard to humans— if provoked, it bites without bane. But to a mouse the big spider is truly a monster: By injecting enzymes, it reduces the prey to mush that can be sucked up with powerful stomach muscles.*

*Nearly blind, the male gropes for his mate or sniffs her scent. After mating, he scrambles away before the female can devour him.*
DAVID CAVAGNARO

the Algodones dune belt a substitute Sahara, where film crews shoot scenes of camel caravans toiling across the sand. The dunes cover more than 200 square miles, a billowing sea up to 400 feet deep. Driven by the wind, the granitic grains come from the floor of the sink to the northwest, carried there earlier by mountain streams.

I have often noticed that sand-moving winds occur when the Pacific coastal belt is cool and overcast, the desert clear. Low pressure is induced over the desert by solar heating; meteorologists call it a "thermal low." The rising air in the thermal low is replaced by cooler air sucked over the west wall of the Salton Trough. Stratus clouds pulled along with it quickly evaporate in fascinating wisps as the torrent of air is warmed in its descent to the desert floor. There it drags plumes of dust and sand in long streamers as it rushes eastward.

Camping in such a desert, where daytime temperatures reach 100° F., is not like camping in the Adirondacks. My parents backpacked in their youth in the eastern mountains, so comparisons were a frequent topic of family conversation. My father thought in terms of tents, dehydrated food ("every ounce counts"), and waterproof coverings, especially for matches. Finding water and firewood was no problem. In the desert, everything was different. Because we had to bring our water, each day's hiking ended back at the car. Canned food was not too heavy, and we never used a tent. Firewood from dead bushes lacked substance, burned poorly, and smoked with an unpleasant odor. We often preferred a gas camp stove.

In later years when I worked in the desert as a geologist for months at a time, I learned to cope with the water problem. I disciplined myself not to drink every time I thought about it, and made it a rule to have some water left in my canteen when I returned to camp—in case I didn't make it on schedule. The key is to avoid panting. I moved slowly with my mouth shut; when climbing, this means taking small steps, standing erect, using as few muscles as possible. I perspired less and could get by on one canteen of water. Try it sometime, hiking in the canyons around Death Valley, or in the wilderness of Arizona's Superstition Mountains.

*Plodding on clubfeet, safe behind a bony shield or snoozing in a winter den—the desert tortoise is one of nature's triumphs, with a reptile pedigree as old as the days of the dinosaurs. Stored fat provides energy during hibernation; by excreting dry wastes the tortoise retains half a pint of water in two sacs under its carapace for rainless months. Humans trying to capture it may get a soaking.*
M. W. LARSON

Like a giant claw, Mexico's lower Sonoran Desert embraces the Gulf of California, including part of the Baja Peninsula; on the mainland side the desert stretches 150 miles near the head of the gulf and tapers to a southern limit south of Guaymas. From the shore the desert floor rises gently inland toward the foot of the Sierra Madre Occidental at about 3,000 feet. Random isolated mountains 3,000 to 5,000 feet high are never out of sight. Most plants are xerophytes—"dry plants" that have adapted to their harsh realm: cacti, such as organ pipe, saguaro, and cardon, a Mexican tree cactus; century plants that flower once in 15 or 20 years and then die; the weird cirio or boojum tree, named by a British botanist for the mysterious "Thing," neither plant nor animal, in Lewis Carroll's *Hunting of the Snark*.

A wild bush growing on shrub-covered slopes of the Sonoran Desert foothills may help save the sperm whale from extinction. The jojoba's seeds consist of 50 percent oil; by an evolutionary coincidence the oil is almost the same chemically as the

347

## Dazzling Chips from the Earth's Crust

*In the rocky kingdom beneath our feet lies a rich hoard of some 3,000 known mineral species. Rare crystallized specimens from the Basin and Range Province reflect the exceptional beauty of color and form prized by collectors.*

*In arid lands, where the water table may be 2,000 feet below the surface, slowly seeping water deposits dissolved minerals at lower levels. In the process, percolating chemical solutions produce a kaleidoscope of brightly colored crystals of minerals; each has a unique atomic structure that admits and reflects light, influencing color. Most of these and other highly colored mineral specimens were formed this way. Impurities may change atom arrays, altering hue. Iron traces color amethyst — a kind of quartz — purple. Volcanic action in Mexico formed this nodule of banded quartz called agate. Quartz is one of the silicates, a group of minerals that makes up 95 percent of the earth's crust. A splinter of calcite, the stuff of many stalactites in limestone caverns, adheres to chalcopyrite, an ore of copper. Crystallized from groundwater charged with copper, this chunk of blue azurite and green malachite was saved from a copper mine's crusher in Arizona. Lead-silver mines in Mexico and Arizona yield vanadinite, an ore of vanadium; galena, chief source of lead; wulfenite, an ore of lead and molybdenum. Legrandite from Mexico, a zinc and arsenic mineral, is too rare to be commercially mined. A mosaic of color that reflects a complex geologic history, the variscite gemstone from a Utah phosphate bed is valued at $25,000.*

SMITHSONIAN INSTITUTION; VICTOR R. BOSWELL, JR., NATIONAL GEOGRAPHIC PHOTOGRAPHER

*Agate nodule*

*Amethyst*

*Vanadinite*

*Chalcopyrite and calcite*

*Wulfenite*

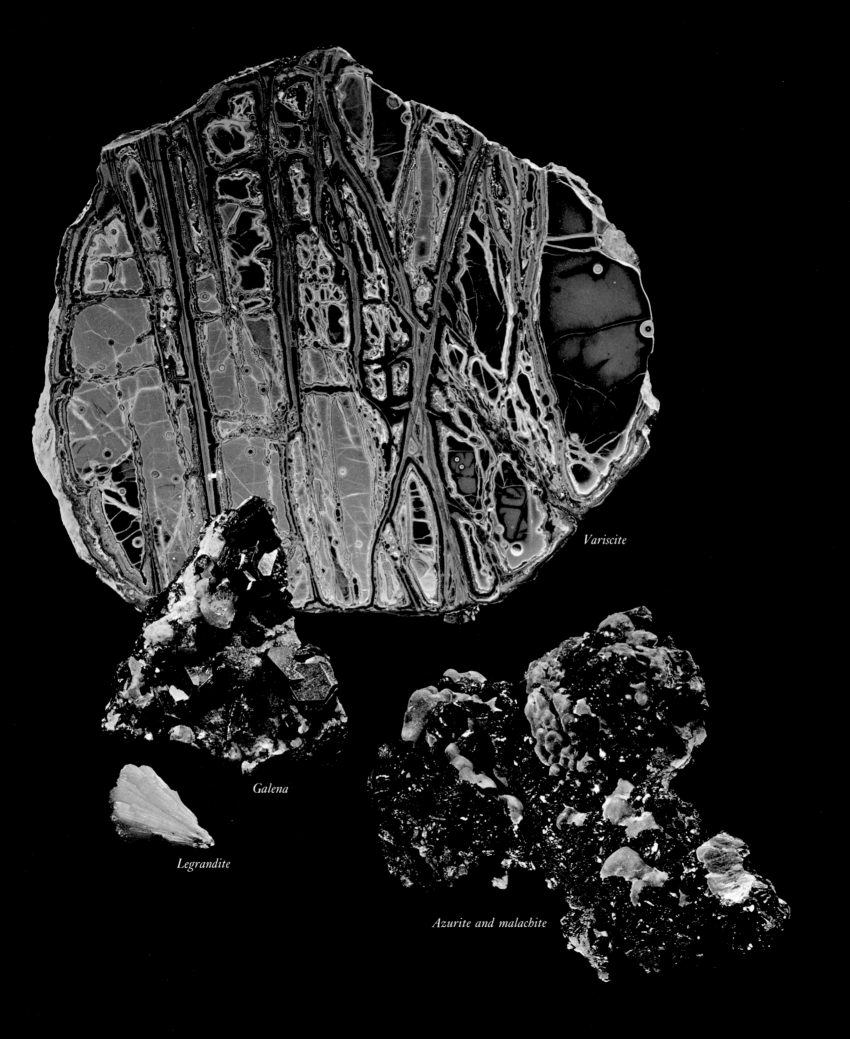

*Variscite*

*Galena*

*Legrandite*

*Azurite and malachite*

sperm whale's. When the United States banned importation of oil from the endangered mammal, interest in the humble desert bush increased; scientists had long been aware of its potential. The National Research Council studied the feasibility of cultivating the plant on southwestern Indian reservations. Their conclusion: The Indians would benefit and so would the sperm whale. Today the Apaches cultivate jojoba on their San Carlos reservation, hoping to market the oil and wax (the hydrogenated form of the oil). Studies show that jojoba oil could replace sperm oil as a lubricant for high-speed machinery and in automobile transmission fluids.

"Hell must have boiled over at Pinacate," exclaimed an observer of the burned-out landscape at the north end of the gulf. A volcanic field covering 600 square miles of cinder cones, lavas, and craters, the Pinacate region first shook with eruptions several million years ago, though some disturbances date from the Pleistocene or later. One small outburst was reported in 1935. Most distinctive are seven steep-walled calderas—circular pits—each half a mile to a mile across and as much as 800 feet deep. After the explosions, molten rock underneath drained away, producing craters by collapse. Pinacate's bleak lunar landscape contains no natural springs. Runoff from thundershowers and flash floods collects in rocky basins called tinajas, the only source of drinking water. To the west, the rolling sand dunes of El Gran Desierto cover more than a thousand square miles.

An extension of Basin and Range topography, the Mexican Highlands, or Central Plateau, stretches for 850 miles through the middle of Mexico. Bounded on the west by the Sierra Madre Occidental, on the east by the Sierra Madre Oriental, and on the south by a chain of volcanoes, the plateau features low mountain ranges alternating with broad, enclosed basins called bolsons. Lower than the mountains that surround it, the tableland rises southward from 2,000 feet near the Rio Grande to 6,200 feet above sea level at San Luis Potosí.

Limestones 100 million years old dominate the eastern Sierra, while the western range is younger—and volcanic. Geologists believe that eruptions beginning some 25 million years ago built up the western Sierra and blocked the westward drainage out of the eastern mountains. Sediment then accumulated between the two ranges, building the plateau. Instead of tilted fault blocks like those north of the border, the plateau's limestone ranges, especially between Torreón and Monterrey, are anticlinal (up-arched) folds—like giant wrinkles in a blanket. With this kind of folding, faulting is not needed to produce the relief, though it may have helped.

A vast desert named for the Mexican state of Chihuahua encompasses most of the Mexican Highlands and extends northward into New Mexico and Texas. Upland

---

*"There were hills and valleys a-many, of piled up hell-fire suddenly grown cold,"* William Hornaday *wrote of Sonora's Pinacate region. Jumbled lava beds ring the Pinacate Peaks—stratified lava, rock, and ash from hundreds of eruptions. Cinder cones pock the desert where craters spewed fire, turning the land to burnt umber. A grace note in a somber scene, chollas glisten like "a million glass toothpicks."*
WALTER MEAYERS EDWARDS

351

grasses and creosote-bush plains mark this arid land; in these latitudes descending winds absorb moisture. Conspicuous plants include the sotol, a yucca-like shrub; the lechuguilla, an agave with spines so stiff they will puncture a thick boot; and candelilla, an asparagus-like stalk coated with wax. The city of Torreón lies within the vast Bolsón de Coahuila, an irrigated agricultural area. Despite light rains, this broad basin receives enough runoff from two streams to maintain a shallow water table.

Forty-niners who took the Mexican route to California had to cross the sere highlands first, then tackle the rugged Sierra Madre Occidental. At the 50,000-square-mile Bolsón de Mapimí, a series of ancient lake bottoms southeast of the Río Conchos, they encountered a sun-blistered realm of saltbush and inkweed, where dust devils rise in the shimmering heat and travel in spiral columns across the parched land. Bandits swooped out of mountain passes, Apaches and Comanches made hit-and-run attacks, heat and thirst took their toll. For many, the quest for gold became a *jornada de la muerte* — a "journey of death."

South of the Central Plateau, majestic, snow-crowned volcanic peaks span the country from the east to the west coast. "A fairyland such as cannot be seen in Spain," Hernán Cortés said of the jagged silhouette in 1519. Part of the "ring of fire" that circles the Pacific, the volcanoes have been building a massive dam across the land for about seven million years, blocking drainage from the north. Eroded debris that filled the Central Plateau cannot reach the south. Geologically, the landscape differs dramatically above and below the volcanic axis. Earthquakes regularly shake the south, while the north is stable. And the mountain barrier draws a rough dividing line between temperate and tropical wildlife realms, the southern edge of the Mexican Highlands and other border areas forming a transition zone for the two.

During the Pleistocene, glaciers crowned the highest volcanoes. Popocatépetl, poetically named "Smoking Mountain" by the Aztecs, and 18,700-foot Orizaba, the nation's highest peak, are still snow-capped. Several vents have come into being within historic times. Jorullo, on the western rim, was born in a burst of fire and smoke in 1759. German scientist Alexander von Humboldt descended the still-smoking crater 45 years later to measure the temperature of volcanic gases, while a companion picked his way through the twisted lava masses, collecting plant specimens.

Mexico's newest vent, Paricutín, erupted in 1943. The ground rumbled for more than a week; then a wisp of vapor appeared from a crack in a cornfield. Soon explosions every six seconds sent a barrage of rocks 3,500 feet into the air, "like a flock of blackbirds escaping from an inferno." Seething golden lava seeped from the base of the cone, and at night a 3,000-foot "candle" illuminated the sky. In nine years Paricutín belched over a billion tons of volcanic ash, burying two villages and building a cone 1,200 feet high. Spectacular though it was to puny man, this display of earth's power was a minor sniffle compared to the giant squeezing, stretching, and heaving of the crust that over hundreds of millions of years have molded the vast sweep of desert and mountain in the Basin and Range Province.

*Oasis in the desert, a grove of fan palms survives in a remote canyon of California's Anza-Borrego State Park. Fanlike fronds often tattered and torn by the wind cloak the West's only native palm species. Dead leaves droop and form a dense mat around the base. Palm trees once thrived in warm, wet lands as far north as Alaska and Greenland, but receded during the Age of Mammals as the climate grew cooler. Surviving in the Southwest and Mexico, where orioles hang nests in its leafy bower, the fan palm sends its roots deep to find the desert's hidden springs.*
ENTHEOS

# The Restless Edge

Bates McKee

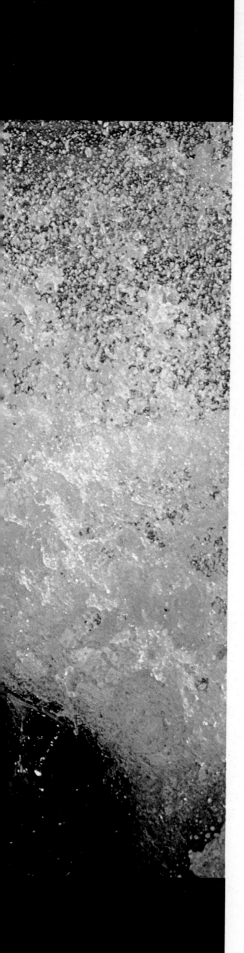

Lituya Bay in southeastern Alaska is one of those places of incredible majesty that photographs never quite seem to capture. It combines scenic splendor with an awesome array of the natural forces that characterize so much of the unquiet Pacific coast. Lituya indents the shore of the Gulf of Alaska, cutting a T-shaped inlet through a narrow coastal plain and foothills backed by the glacier-clad Fairweather Range. Away from storms of the gulf, it provides mariners the only good shelter along the 150-mile open stretch between the Inside Passage and Yakutat Bay.

Fairweather seems a misnomer. Captain James Cook, exulting in a rare clear day in 1778, had so named the 15,300-foot peak that caps the range. He overlooked Lituya's narrow entrance. Eight years later French explorer Jean François de La Pérouse discovered it and entered to reprovision his two ships in "perhaps the most extraordinary place in the world.... a basin of water of a depth in the middle that could not be fathomed, bordered by peaked mountains, of an excessive height, covered with snow. ... I never saw a breath of air ruffle the surface of this water; it is never troubled but by the fall of enormous pieces of ice...."

Trouble had met the explorer at Lituya's mouth. Tidal currents had nearly beached his ships. During his brief stay an iceberg calved from a glacier, causing a wave that upset the captain's boat. Nevertheless, the provisioning went well. The men had laid on wood and water, bartered with the Indians — iron for salmon and sea otter pelts — gone bear hunting, and determined that the bay, no inside passage, dead-ended on the glacier's icy wall. Ending his business, the captain wrote, "No port in the universe could furnish more conveniences," a curious claim for this wild bay. Preparing to leave, he sent three ship's boats to take soundings near the entrance. The ebbing tide swept two of them into the channel, where they capsized, and 21 men perished. La Pérouse and his large ships made it out safely.

Those intrepid early explorers gained firsthand experience not only of Pacific coast scenery, its wealth of forests, fresh water, fish, land and marine mammals, its storms, fogs, tides, and currents, but also of geology's molding hand on the landscape. The Fairweather Glacier that once extended all the way to the gulf gouged out Lituya's great depth. The gravel spit that nearly seals off the bay is the remnant of its moraine. The constricted entrance and the great volume of water enclosed cause the treacherous currents. A trough forming the top of the T at the head of the bay results from glacial erosion along another geologic feature significant to the Pacific coast — a major, active fault, the Fairweather.

La Pérouse and his party may have been the first white men to tangle with the dynamics of Lituya Bay. They were not the last. On the evening of July 9, 1958, three small fishing boats rode at anchor inside the spit. At 10:17 a great roar came from the head of the bay, followed by a moving mountain of water choked with icebergs and uprooted trees. As the gigantic wave that filled the head of the bay swept

---

*Northern sea lion takes a breather from frigid Pacific breakers. Propelling up to a ton of blubber with speed and grace, the agile pinniped can dive 700 feet for a fish; it hauls up on islets to bellow and breed.*
FRED BRUEMMER

ROUGH PHOLIOTAS; ENTHEOS

MYCENA MUSHROOMS; ENTHEOS

SCALY CHANTERELLES; DAVID CAVAGNARO

toward the sea its height diminished to about 50 feet, still adequate to surf two of the boats right over the spit—trees and all—where they foundered in the ocean, with the loss of one full crew. The third vessel rode out the initial wave and a second that followed before safely exiting from the debris-filled bay.

The event held particular interest for the United States Government, which had plans to develop the bay, as it affords small-boat access to Glacier Bay National Monument. Studies of the 1958 wave indicated that 40 million cubic yards of earth and rock had split from the face of the Fairweather Range and fallen 3,000 feet into the northwest arm of the T. The resulting splash rose to an incredible 1,740 feet on the foothill spur opposite, stripping off all the trees and creating a trimline clearly visible today. It then settled down to form the wave that swept out the bay, removing vegetation within an average 110 feet of sea level. Scientists estimated the velocity of the wave between 97 and 130 miles per hour. They also discovered remnants of older trimlines, evidence of similar waves. By counting rings on trees that started growing afterward on the cleared ground, they estimated the dates of those devastating waves as 1854 (395 feet), 1874 (80 feet), 1899 (200 feet), and 1936 (490 feet).

Earthquakes along the Fairweather Fault certainly help make the waves, either by breaking up and loosening rock and glacial masses or by direct displacement of the bottom of the bay. At any rate, the Government dropped its plans to develop Lituya Bay, and sailing into La Pérouse's port of great conveniences still provides some thrill of anticipation beyond the picturesque. All it needs is a dormant volcano to make it a perfect microcosm of Pacific coast geologic hazards.

Attempts of La Pérouse and other explorers of the northwest coast to find an easy passage to the interior of North America met with failure, of course, for one of the world's great mountain systems guards the western edge of the continent. Easy passage to or from the east came only with the development of railroads. The more continuous mountain chain includes the Sierra Nevada, Cascade Range, and Coast Mountains of British Columbia and southeastern Alaska. Its length, more than 2,000 miles, is breached only twice by major rivers—the Columbia and the Fraser—and both have cut spectacular gorges. In general this mountain barrier lies 100 to 200 miles inland. The true coastal range is lower and is breached in more places. It includes the Coast Ranges of California and Oregon, the Olympic Mountains of Washington, and the islands of British Columbia and southern Alaska. A lowland near or below sea level lies between the coastal and inner chains.

Mountains bar the door to weather systems as well as to human travel. They do not stop the onshore flow of moist marine winds, but they do force them to go up and over rather than around or through gaps. The resulting precipitation as rising air cools and condenses brings western slopes a certain fame—100 feet of snow on Mount Rainier in 1974 and 14 feet of wetness in 1975 on the rain forest at Lake Quinault on the southwestern flank of the Olympics, the moss-draped winter home of majestic Roosevelt elk. Markedly drier conditions prevail in the lee (continued on page 364)

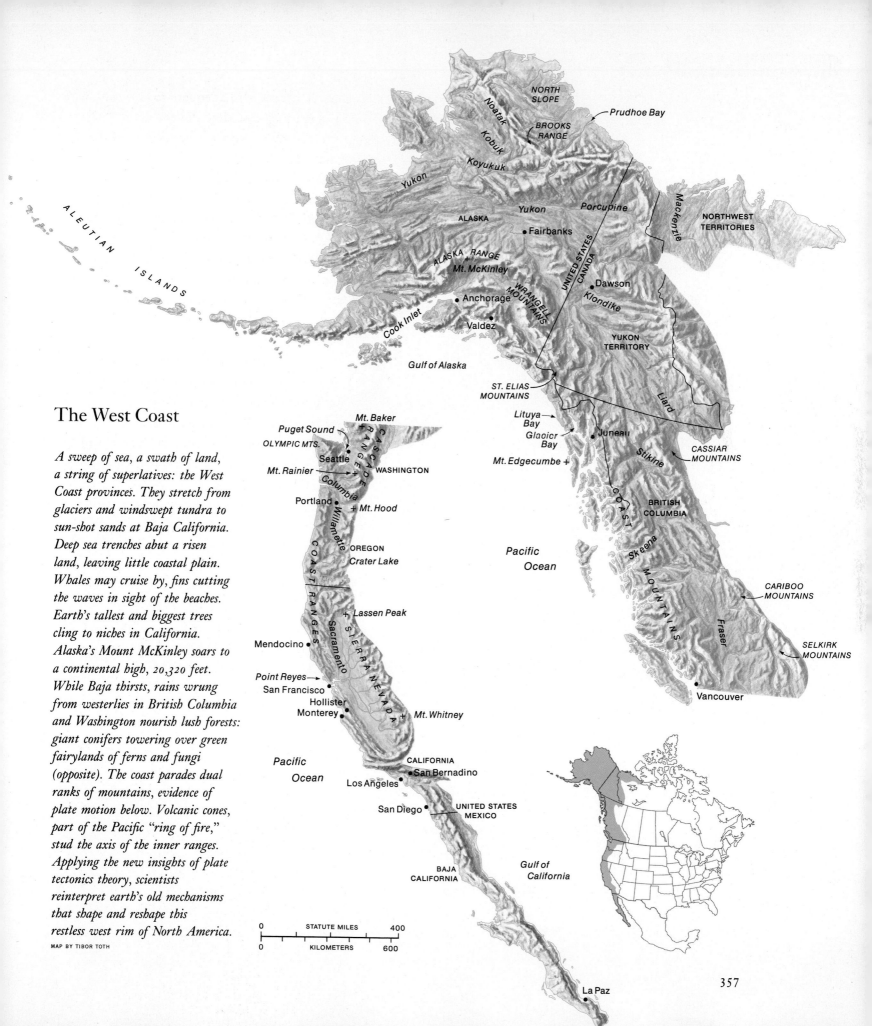

# The West Coast

*A sweep of sea, a swath of land, a string of superlatives: the West Coast provinces. They stretch from glaciers and windswept tundra to sun-shot sands at Baja California. Deep sea trenches abut a risen land, leaving little coastal plain. Whales may cruise by, fins cutting the waves in sight of the beaches. Earth's tallest and biggest trees cling to niches in California. Alaska's Mount McKinley soars to a continental high, 20,320 feet. While Baja thirsts, rains wrung from westerlies in British Columbia and Washington nourish lush forests: giant conifers towering over green fairylands of ferns and fungi (opposite). The coast parades dual ranks of mountains, evidence of plate motion below. Volcanic cones, part of the Pacific "ring of fire," stud the axis of the inner ranges. Applying the new insights of plate tectonics theory, scientists reinterpret earth's old mechanisms that shape and reshape this restless west rim of North America.*

MAP BY TIBOR TOTH

STATUTE MILES

KILOMETERS

357

of the mountains. Rainfall averages but ten inches a year, and cactus grows on the northeast shore of the Olympic Peninsula. The sunniest skiing conditions in the Cascades occur in the lee of Mount Rainier. Dryness prevails all along the rain-shadowed eastern foot of the Sierra Nevada-Cascade chain.

Even to the untrained eye, the Pacific region presents a wide array of ecological environments within short distances. In an hour or so we can drive from cool, damp forests dense with Douglas firs, western hemlocks, red cedars, and ferns on the western slope of the Cascades to pines, grassy meadows, and sagebrush east of the mountains. Rainfall diminishes suddenly as one goes east over the mountains; it decreases more gradually as one goes south along the coast.

California's mosaic includes bits of every life zone in North America, from arctic with its stunted conifers on Sierra heights to semitropical in low, flat valleys. The state, among a mere handful of regions in the world, boasts a mediterranean climate — actually many climates — generally marked by dry summers and mild, moist winters. A writer in the 1880's described sunny California as a place "where the chestnuts of Italy are dropping; where Sicilian lemons are ripening; where the almond trees are shining." A promise realized, the state leads the nation in crops such as grapes, pomegranates, olives, dates, figs, lemons (with a virtual monopoly on the last four), and a vast cornucopia of other fruits, nuts, and vegetables.

Geologists trying to establish the history of a region assemble diverse bits of information from the rock record and translate them into a sequence of events that started millions of years ago and slowly led to the scene we find today. The questions answered first, the easier questions, begin with "when" and "how." Beyond these details looms the harder question: "why?" A chronicler of the Civil War can write down all the names and places in the proper order. But when he considers the causes of the war, he escalates his problem. Suddenly he must be a sociologist, an economist, a psychologist, an anthropologist. So it is in geology. The questions of when the Cascades rose and how they grew pose complex problems, certainly, but easier and less controversial ones than *why* they grew. The earth scientist must also be a physicist, a chemist — some would say a mystic!

The origins of the remarkable mountain chains along the Pacific coast have been objects of serious study for a century, and the histories of the ranges unravel slowly. We cannot answer all the questions. One always leads to another. The pioneer advocates of continental drift regarded the mountains as the result of pressure on the leading edge of the westward-moving continent. At first most scientists scoffed at the early "drifters." Now the "heresy" has become a keystone.

We view the Pacific coast as a long-standing battleground where two plates collide, the ranges and valleys as wrinkles made when crustal slabs jostle each other. The Cascades have come up primarily by folding, or rumpling; others, like the Sierra Nevada, by tilting along a fault. The spreading of the Pacific Ocean floor complicates the problem of too much crust vying for too little space. Volcanism along the East Pacific Rise generates new crust, which pushes the sea floor away along the axis of the ridge. The Pacific plate east of the rise moves toward the American plate.

The oceanic plate, thinner and heavier than the continental plate, loses in the competition for room at the margin. The Pacific plate is stuffed under the edge of the continent, the process known as subduction. The descent not only generates earthquakes but, at depths below some 50 miles, the plate may begin to melt. Molten rock rises to erupt as lava and to build volcanoes. Thus in the processes of continental drift, sea floor spreading, and subduction, we have an explanation for the volcanism, earthquakes, and mountain-building around the Pacific rim.

Twenty years ago, while working for my doctoral dissertation at Stanford, I started mapping the Pacheco Pass area southeast of San Francisco in California's central Coast Ranges. At first glance the country would not appear to hold great secrets. Sunny and picturesque, its rolling hills, covered with grass and live oaks, rise no more than two thousand feet. Rocks lie exposed along stream beds and form curious scattered piles on the upland surfaces, but even a geologist would probably not slow his car much below the speed limit. But the structure of the Pacheco Pass area, it turned out, is representative of much of the Pacific rim.

Rocks in the central Coast Ranges belong for the most part to the Franciscan Formation. They consist of marine sedimentary rocks and altered volcanic rocks. Much of the formation has been altered under high pressure. Internally, it is so folded, fractured, and confused that no single layer can be traced very far before it ends against a fault. The few fossils that have been found indicate that the strata were deposited during the Mesozoic Era, 130 to 80 million years ago, but the chaotic structure mixes rocks of quite different ages.

The Franciscan Formation's great thickness (ten miles or more), the scarcity of fossils, and the general nature of the sediments fit the pattern of birth in an ocean trench. But other features long remained a puzzle: the presence of volcanic rocks and of deep ocean sediments, and the chaotic structure. Further, some rocks of the formation had been metamorphosed under pressures that are only found tens of miles within the earth. We needed the new knowledge that came with plate tectonics to understand what went on to bring the Franciscan deposits into the present state.

The key was subduction—the stuffing of the Pacific plate under the edge of the continent. Now that we know something about that process, we can fit more pieces into the Franciscan puzzle. The confused structure resulted when the oceanic plate went down but its upper sediments became "plate scrapings" shaved off the top and churned against the edge of the continental plate. Deep oceanic sediments and volcanic rocks had ridden in on the oceanic conveyor belt to intermix with sediments washed down the continental slope into the trench. The descending Pacific plate carried some of the rocks under the continent's edge; altered by the pressures there, the rocks ultimately were faulted back up to the surface. Subduction seems able to explain all the features of the Franciscan Formation which 20 years ago were so puzzling; thus this unit has become a world-famous example of the process.

*Sickle teeth harvest a late-summer snack for an Olympic marmot, pudgy denizen of Washington's Olympic National Park. Like its similar, more common relative, the hoary marmot, this 20-pound rodent clambers about rocky heights and alpine meadows, warily sunning or warning its gregarious kin with a piercing whistle. Stored fat sees it through a winter sleep—at eight or nine months probably tops among hibernators. Fossils suggest marmots originated in North America.*
ENTHEOS

## Kid's Play: King of the Mountain

*Nimbly following nanny up a wall, a kid poised* en pointe *shows fine form for a mountain goat. Neither goat nor sheep but an antelope, this native of the northwest and Rockies is adapted for cliff hanging. Its two toes separate, then grip small rock juts for firm footholds. After foraging on grasses, sedges, and alpine plants such as bluebell and lupine, mountain goats pick a spot to rest and ruminate — one with a view, preferably. The nanny and kid opposite cross a heathery ridge draped with fog, a hallmark of northern Pacific coast weather.*

*Both sexes have horns and beards; coats stay white the year round. In winter when many high-slope dwellers move to warmer valleys, these antisocial climbers usually cling to their rocky ramparts.*
ENTHEOS

In Oregon and Washington the celebrities are the Cascade volcanoes, snow-clad cones famed for their majestic beauty. The frequency of veiling clouds and storms seems only to enhance the mountains' appeal; when Mount Rainier or a sister summit does come out of seclusion the event is worth mentioning. The occasional past violence of these sleeping giants has left some notable scars. Mount Mazama's devastating eruption of 6,500 years ago bequeathed us today's lovely Crater Lake. People aware of the melting zone deep beneath these cones know they have hazardous potential. But few can recall the last eruptions of a Cascade volcano—from 1914 to 1917 at Lassen Peak in California—and even though most of the cones rumble a bit and burp minor amounts of steam, only mountaineers notice. The volcanoes seem dead.

But consider Mount Baker, a medium-size giant in the Cascades near the Canadian border. It rises a mile above range level, its icy flanks in stark contrast with the dark tree-clad neighboring hills. On a sunny day you look twice to be sure it's real, for from the distant vantage point of Seattle, 80 miles to the south, it looks like a dense white cloud floating above the Cascades. In a sense the view from afar is superior. As you approach the mountain you pass through deep forested valleys which provide only tantalizing glimpses of the cone, and you feel cheated.

Baker's log is meager, its history rather ordinary. It erupted briefly in 1843 and again in 1854. Since then, it steamed at times, then appeared to cool. In the late 1960's scientists began monitoring various Cascade volcanoes, including Baker, using infrared aerial photography to detect ground thermal activity. In 1972 they installed a seismograph station on Baker's western flank. Meanwhile Baker slept on.

It woke up on March 10, 1975. Without warning, a steam cloud, darkened by fine-grained rock fragments, billowed a quarter of a mile above Sherman Crater, high on the south flank of the mountain. The cloud, visible in Bellingham, 35 miles away, signaled perhaps a hundredfold increase in steam activity. Besides steam, the crater vented hydrogen and hydrogen sulfide. Scientists working in the crater area needed

*Under a scalloped canopy of melting snow, marsh-marigolds make an August debut (opposite and below, center). At 4,700 feet in the North Cascades, subalpine summer allots only a brief period of bloom. Stonecrop (below, left) grows in low mats on rocks. Its fat, waxy leaves save moisture, letting it lie dormant until conditions are right to flower. A belle for all seasons with its shiny evergreen foliage, a mountain huckleberry (below, right) blossoms under the season's fleeting spotlight.*
ENTHEOS

protective breathing apparatus, and the sulfurous "rotten egg" smell at times tinged the air on the volcano's lower flanks.

Mount Baker's heating up constituted the greatest volcanic activity in the Cascades in half a century. An eruption was possible, but by no means certain. Baker might slowly cool down again, but so long as the threat of an outburst continued, close monitoring would also continue. In addition to seismometers to capture the smallest tremors, scientists installed instruments that record the temperature and composition of gases, and tiltmeters and gravity meters that respond to physical signs of lava swelling up within the cone. In a sense, a monitored volcano is like a patient in the intensive care unit of a hospital. Every vital sign is being checked, every change analyzed. But unlike most patients, the volcano is in charge of its own case, and the "doctors" can only observe. Isolation is the best treatment.

Judging by Baker's history, debris avalanches and mudflows triggered by eruption would pose the greatest risk to human life. Avalanches can travel at 100 miles an hour, and mudflows slide fast enough to make evacuation impossible. Most visitors camp in valley bottoms, where the greatest danger lies. At Baker, the likely course of debris from Sherman Crater would be toward Baker Lake, at the foot of the flank. A

sudden influx of debris could cause waves that would not only devastate lakeside campgrounds but might top Baker Dam, creating floods downstream. As a precaution, these campgrounds were closed and the lake held below the top of the dam.

All the Cascade volcanoes are geologically "young"—their initial eruptions occurred less than a million years ago. However, they are only the latest generation of an old volcanic lineage. The eroded roots of old volcanoes bolster almost all the mountain systems on the coast. The great granite cliffs, domes, and spires of the Sierra consist of lava that congealed slowly underground 100 million years ago, essentially in the same chamber as the flows that built earlier Mesozoic volcanoes. The rocky capes and headlands of Oregon are composed of dark lavas poured out 40 to 15 million years ago, in a setting not unlike the present Aleutian Islands. Related outpourings many miles thick, followed by uplift and erosion, produced the sheer eastern and northern flanks of the Olympic Mountains. Even older, the dark lavas that form the backbone of Vancouver Island date back almost 200 million years. Volcanism has dominated the history of the coast for as far back as we can see. Through the study of modern volcanoes and processes like continental drift, sea-floor spreading, and subduction, we can produce the models that explain this fiery record.

*Long view of a future sea: the Gulf of California from a vantage of 570 miles. An automatic scanner aboard Landsat, orbiting the earth every 90 minutes, sent back a continuous stream of image data fused into the panorama below. The view extends from the mainland of Mexico across the gulf, and the wavy peninsula of Baja California to the Pacific. Spreading of the sea floor made this breach in the land. Volcanism of the underlying Pacific plate ruptured the continent's edge. An arm of the sea fills the 700-mile rift. As plates shift along the fault zone running north from the gulf, sundered Baja may in time ride the ocean slab into northern climes.*

NASA

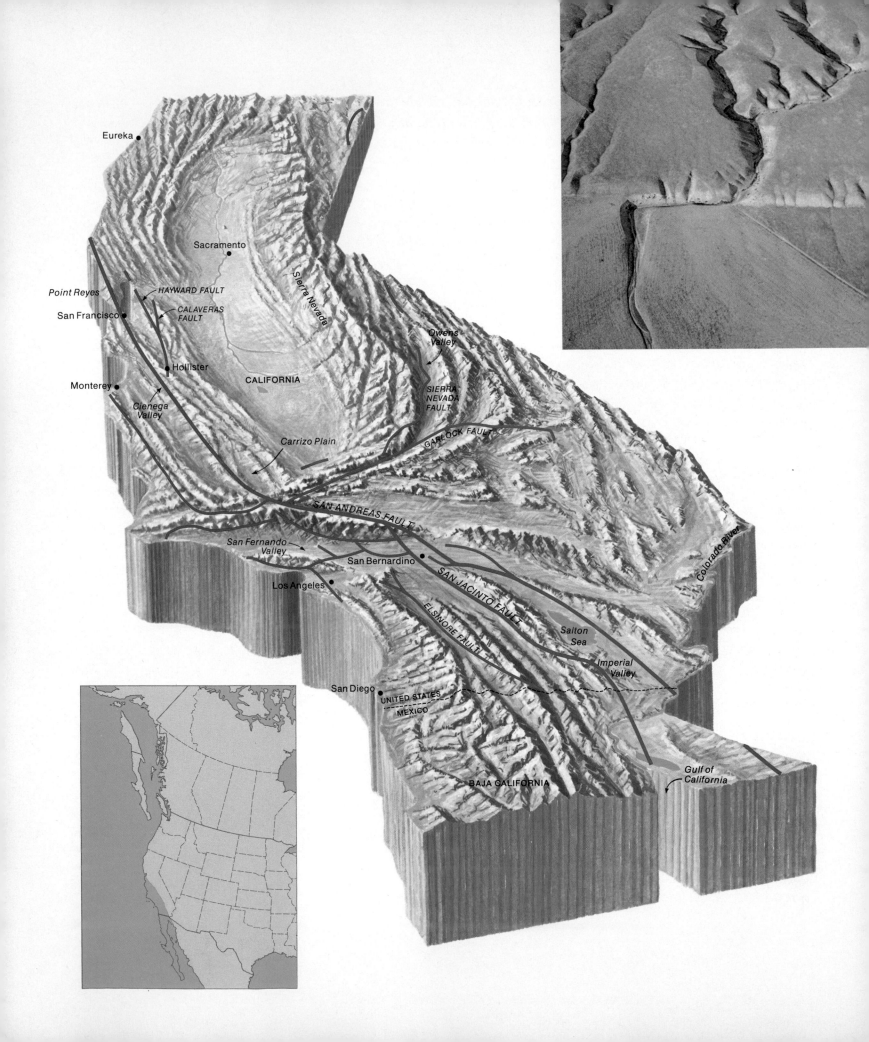

Eureka

Point Reyes

San Francisco

Monterey

Sacramento

*HAYWARD FAULT*

*CALAVERAS FAULT*

Hollister

*Sierra Nevada*

*Cienega Valley*

CALIFORNIA

Carrizo Plain

*Owens Valley*

*SIERRA NEVADA FAULT*

*GARLOCK FAULT*

SAN ANDREAS FAULT

San Fernando Valley

San Bernardino

Los Angeles

SAN JACINTO FAULT

*ELSINORE FAULT*

*Colorado River*

*Salton Sea*

*Imperial Valley*

San Diego

UNITED STATES

MEXICO

BAJA CALIFORNIA

*Gulf of California*

## Faults Line the Face of California

*Lacework of lines tells where the action is—and was—in California: the earthquake-prone San Andreas Fault system. The south end of the San Jacinto is among its most active branches. Thinner lines mark less active faults. Near notch at bottom on the relief map (opposite), the East Pacific Rise that bulges under the Gulf of California is offset along a transform fault system; these cracks in the crust result from shifting of adjoining plates. The Pacific plate, moving northwest, slides horizontally by the American plate. Friction prevents a smooth passage.*

*Rocks lock edges, bending until the pent-up strain overcomes the friction, then move suddenly and violently—an earthquake. As the rock masses jolt past each other, released energy travels in waves through the ground. Magnitude of an earthquake, its number on the Richter Scale, is the measure of that energy. Each higher unit on the scale marks a 31-fold increase in earthquake energy. An 1857 quake (about 8 on the scale) offset a river channel on Carrizo Plain by 33 feet, a near-record for a single jolt. The 450-foot zigzag in the aerial view of this stream (upper) results from recurrent earthquakes over thousands of years. Experts plot ways to ease friction; the plates, it seems, must move. If present motion continues for the next 50 million years, some scientists predict, the land west of the San Andreas will have split off and moved to the Aleutians.*

JAMES P. BLAIR, NATIONAL GEOGRAPHIC PHOTOGRAPHER. MAP BY TIBOR TOTH

Cienega Valley, south of Hollister in the central Coast Range of California, is a peaceful vale far from major roads and urban sprawl. Grass and live oaks cover the low hills on either side, and the valley floor and lower slopes are planted in grapes. This has long been a good producing valley for the Almaden wine district. Sheds and buildings belonging to a modest winery have stood beside the Cienega Road for many decades. The San Francisco earthquake and resulting fire of 1906 brought members of at least one new family to the valley. After losing their city home in that disaster they settled down to the peaceful, quiet life of vintner. They built a new house—right over the San Andreas Fault.

California is laced with faults, most of which run north to northwest along linear valleys like the Cienega. Slippage on these faults generates most of the state's earthquakes. Since the 1906 disaster, the San Andreas Fault system has become the most studied earth feature in California, and the Cienega Valley has become the most studied segment of the San Andreas. The reason for the popularity of this locale is, of course, the winery—not for its product (for scientists don't drink), but because the fault has had such an interesting effect on the buildings. One of the original buildings fell down in 1939 and was replaced by a stronger one with massive concrete floors and walls. Once again, the employees of the winery found that part of their job consisted of patching cracks in the floor and walls and shoring up studs that kept slipping off their foundations. In 1956 scientists "discovered" what the owners had probably known for a long time, that the winery was slowly being wrenched apart by the San Andreas Fault, which passes under the main building. There are other signs of slippage: the offset rows of grapevines just south of the building, and the repeated breaking of the concrete walls of a nearby drainage channel. Since 1956 geophysicists have been carefully measuring the displacements, and much of our knowledge of the mechanics of creep along a fault zone comes from this study.

The Pacific plate is moving an average of two inches per year to the northwest. Scientists have arrived at this rate by direct measurements in recent years along the San Andreas Fault, by a study of magnetic stripes embedded in the oceanic crust, and by comparing the offset along the San Andreas of rock formations of varying ages. When we realize that the movement has been going on for millions of years, this all but eliminates the hope that it will suddenly stop. It behooves us to plan accordingly. Future earthquakes are inevitable. During recorded history fatalities in the United States have numbered a few thousand compared to a worldwide toll of perhaps four million, but experts shudder at the possible consequences of an earthquake as powerful as the San Francisco quake of 1906 recurring there today.

Stopping the Pacific plate may be impossible, but we can minimize the hazards. The day of accurate prediction is dawning. Scientists in the United States, not quite believing their newfound skills, have played down some anticipated earthquakes until after the event. Not so in China, where full-time specialists in earthquake research number 10,000. On February 4, 1975, authorities issued a warning for an area around the town of Haich'eng to expect a major earthquake within *(continued on page 379)*

Oregon sea stacks sentinel a gilded
battleground. Onshore winds drive
ocean and land to ceaseless combat.
These eroded, surf-sawed islets
of greenstone are all that remain
of an old shore level. Waves attack
hardest on jutting outposts of land.
In time headlands are cut back,
islets disappear. Much of the west
coast has been lifted (while Maine's
coast "drowned"). Along undulating
roads that skirt the shoreline,
motorists drive to lovely distractions
—broad beaches, coves, inlets, pods
of sea lions, firs, grassy vales,
wild flowers—beauty by the mile.
DAVID MUENCH

375

## Turbulent Realm Between the Tides

At the time of the month when the moon's magnet pulls strongest, Pacific tides ebb low and far out. Into view comes an otherworldly habitat usually roofed by the waves. Broad, olive blades of kelp dangle from rocks patched with bright-green sea lettuce (*opposite*). Spiny purple urchins, akin to seastars, cluster in the channel. The knobby shell in the foreground is an urchin's bleached skeleton. Algae, related to the world's most ancient plant forms, ease wave shock, feed hosts of intertidal species. Bladderlike Halosaccion, purplish Gigartina, *and greenish*

Ulva *are among the algae (right, upper). Not random sea rovers, many intertidal fauna inhabit distinct zones. Rock space is tight. Acorn barnacles (below) are free floaters as larvae, later cement their limy shells to rocks in the splash zone. Mussels also affix their blue-black shells for life — which may end abruptly if a seastar comes to dine. Many rays and tube feet let the sunflower star (lower) move or cling tenaciously. Sea anemones (middle) may find a niche in an exquisite rock-walled aquarium, a tidepool, that never dries up. For others, when left high and dry, the game plan is to draw in tentacles, like a flower folding its petals, until the sea washes in.*

ENTHEOS

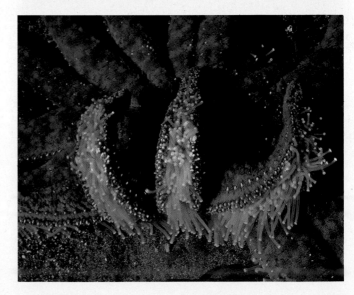

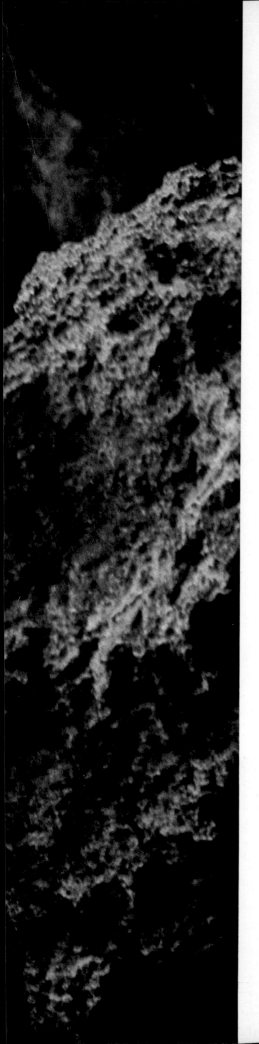

two days. In industrial communes of a few thousand persons, outdoor theaters were set up to entertain residents told to leave their homes and move into the open. During the show, some 5½ hours after the warning, a strong earthquake did occur, destroying many of the buildings. The casualties were a minute fraction of what they would have been without the warning. You have to believe that the next time Chinese authorities set up an outdoor theater, attendance will be near-perfect.

The rocks along a fault about to move change in measurable ways. They expand slightly as minute cracks and cavities open, a phenomenon known as dilatancy. This alters the speed at which seismic waves travel through the rock and its resistance to electrical currents. Also, the ground near the fault may be lifted or tilted, the water level may change in nearby wells, and local changes may occur in the earth's magnetic and gravity fields. Microseisms, or tiny earthquakes, may happen. These can be detected by seismometers and perhaps by animals in some instances. Livestock and zoo animals have been known to act strangely just before an earthquake.

Although we can in retrospect tell what occurred prior to an earthquake, we do not yet know which changes are most reliable. We must continue to monitor, wait for the slip and the quake, and then analyze the data. Once we know the most reliable criteria, networks of instruments could be set to monitor the major active surface faults, like those of the San Andreas system or the Denali system in southeast Alaska.

Given the ability to pinpoint the time of a major earthquake, few scientists would care to call a press conference, announce a prediction, and then stand up to the furor. According to one plan, scientists would report to a review council, which would weigh the findings and, if warranted, issue a formal warning to the state. The state then might take precautionary measures—presumably, some practical compromise between what is safe (total evacuation) and what we do now (nothing).

Even more intriguing than the improvement in predicting earthquakes is the possibility of controlling them. A few years ago the suggestion would have seemed ludicrous. We have since learned that we can reduce the friction along a fault by increasing the water pressure in the pores and cracks. Perhaps a fault can be "vaccinated" against large and destructive earthquakes by inducing numerous small, harmless quakes. This would involve pumping water under pressure into the fault.

Unfortunately this method has built-in legal drawbacks. Suppose a generated earthquake damaged your house. Would you accept the scientists' statement that triggering the quake had prevented a worse one at some future date? Before we write the plan off as too risky, we must realize that major earthquakes in California are inevitable unless we can somehow help Los Angeles to reach its long-desired position opposite the Golden Gate without too many hang-ups along the way.

---

*In sooty suits and vivid accent, pigeon guillemots dress a cliff ledge on Oregon's coast. Basic black is breeding plumage; pre-winter molt changes body and head to mottled white. Diving for food, guillemots "fly" through the water; feet trail to steer rather than propel. The stubby "sea pigeons" and their kin —including the extinct great auk—are northern counterparts of the Southern Hemisphere's penguins.*
ERWIN A. BAUER

379

The United States Geological Survey, whose tasks include devising earthquake prediction and control techniques, is developing a model to simulate earthquake movement and, among other things, to test the possible effects of control methods. A three-ton granite block, five feet on a side and 16 inches thick, has been placed on a special base; a saw-cut through the granite simulates a fault. Lateral pressures of up to five million pounds can be applied by hydraulic jacks to simulate conditions deep underground as well as external stress. Tiny "wells" have been drilled along the fault, and water can be injected under pressure to study the effects. The model study should test the feasibility of fluid injection to produce slippage, and help indicate the safest and most economical way to accomplish the task.

The difference in population between California and Alaska suggests that if experimentation on triggering real earthquakes were to be carried on, it might well be in the Denali Fault system rather than in the San Andreas. The logistics of injecting fluid and monitoring faults in Alaska are much more complex than in California, but the hazard from miscalculation would be very much less. The Alaska earthquake of 1964 claimed 131 lives; experts have said that a quake of such magnitude hitting an unprepared Los Angeles might kill 20,000 people and injure half a million more.

To glance from one end of our coast to the other, we see rifting in the Gulf of California due to the placement of the East Pacific Rise under the edge of the continent; major horizontal faulting in California (west side moving northward); subduction off the coasts of Oregon, Washington, and British Columbia, because the rise is again offshore; horizontal faulting in southeast Alaska north of where the rise again comes ashore; and subduction in southern Alaska and the Aleutians. This represents almost the full spectrum of plate margin types, and is a marvelous laboratory for studying and experimenting with the major forces that are reshaping the earth's surface.

Irregular and complex as it is magnificent, the Pacific coastline reflects the work of many dynamic forces. Waves pummel the shore. Currents erode in one place and deposit in another. Rivers modify the land's edge, as they deposit sediments in the quiet waters of bays and lagoons. These forces tend to straighten the shoreline, but the ups and downs of the land and sea relative to each other quickly destroy such regularity. Sea level goes down during periods of glaciation when more water is stored on land in the form of ice and snow. In warmer periods, glaciers and ice caps melt and sea level rises. The level of the land changes by folding and faulting. Of great significance in the higher latitudes, the earth's surface sinks under the weight of glaciers and slowly rebounds when the ice melts away. The magnitude of these changes in elevation can be hundreds of feet.

*Volcanic fires gone out, snow drapes a cone, clouds pillow a caldera on Alaska's southeastern coast. On Captain Cook's third voyage in 1778, he called the 3,467-foot cone Edgecumbe, the name of a British peer. Another name never made the map. Cook's officer, John Gore, judged the volcano "the most Remarkable of any Ive yet seen on this whight Coast of America, And for Distintion Sake I Call it Mount Beautifull."*
WILLIAM A. GARNETT

Summertime and the salmon fishing
is easy in Alaska's coastal streams.
A sharp-eyed brown bear braves the
rapids of McNeil River to land
a slippery catch. Spawning salmon,
mainstay of early coastal Indians,
lure normally solitary brown bears
in hordes. Size and rank decide which
gets the choicest fishing hole.
Youngsters like the one below may
have to scavenge an adult's reject,
but no one goes hungry. Early in the
season bears eat fish from head
to tail; later they may insist on
a gourmet meal of roe. Cubs weigh
a pound at birth; mature males can
reach 1,400 pounds and tower ten
feet on hind legs—neck and neck
with Arctic polar bears for the
title of world's largest land
carnivore. Ice Age ancestors dwarfed
them all. About 8,000 browns still
prowl Alaska's coast but rapid
land development may spell the end
of summer streamside picnics.

ALLAN L. EGBERT

Upraised wave-cut benches terrace much of the California shore. Along such terraces, coastal roads dip and climb and swerve, giving motorists grandstand views—and sometimes vertigo—where they hover high above sea level. The uplift that raised these "gray granite ridges over swinging pits of sea" has not been uniform. In areas like Big Sur where poet Robinson Jeffers lived, often a terrace that was level when formed by the waves now varies hundreds of feet in its height above the pounding waves. These are very young features geologically; the folding still goes on today.

The Point Reyes Peninsula, north of San Francisco, is a small sliver of the Pacific plate. The San Andreas Fault runs along the trough that divides it from the mainland. The largest displacement measured in the 1906 earthquake occurred near the town of Point Reyes, an offset of 21 feet. Thus the Point Reyes Peninsula is a small "island" drifting north with the Pacific plate. An even smaller piece moving north is nearby Bodega Head, which almost became the site of a nuclear power plant.

A mariner sailing up the coast of California, Oregon, and Washington has little protection. Larger harbors, like those of San Francisco and Astoria, lie at the mouths of "drowned" river valleys (the Sacramento and Columbia) whose channels open to the sea. But bars and spits almost seal off the smaller anchorages like Humboldt Bay and Coos Bay. In storms, crossing the bar can be more dangerous than staying offshore. From Puget Sound north, the sailing is different. One can travel a thousand miles through channels and islands of the Inside Passage with hardly a glimpse of the open ocean. This is largely a glacial heritage.

Glaciers of the past have given us much of the spectacular scenery for which the Pacific coastal region is famous. The deposits the glaciers left behind in this area are seldom so striking as what they removed. Erosion in a moist climate usually means a wearing down of mountains and a smoothing out of topographic relief as the landscape slowly passes through stages of youth, maturity, and old age. We regard the processes of weathering, erosion by running water, and downslope movement of loose material as the great levelers of the land.

In much of northern and northeastern North America, glaciation has allied with the levelers, but in mountainous regions of the west coast the effect is much different. Alpine glaciers have deepened valleys and steepened their walls, creating cliffs and waterfalls, cirques and lakes. Glaciers can transform a coastline into an incredibly complex maze of rocks and islands and inlets. Glaciers probe linear weaknesses; they excavate relentlessly. What were once simple joints in the crystalline rocks of the British Columbia coast became today's narrow inlets and fjords tens of miles long, with near-vertical valley walls and water depths of a thousand feet or more.

Sometimes the reasons a glacier erodes in one place and not in another are not easy to see. Until about 15,000 years ago, the Puget lowland near Seattle was a gentle valley floor mantled with soft sediments. Then a lobe of glacial ice spawned in the Coast Mountains of British Columbia moved south, covering what is now Seattle with as much as 3,000 feet of ice. It didn't last long, perhaps a thousand years, but it

*Gold worth more than the ore of men's dreams sheens a spruce-plumed river valley in the Yukon. In season, salmon are the flash in the stream, the gleam in a grizzly's eye. By October, winter subzeroes in. Blizzards of southbound geese have vacated Arctic skies; caribou have left the frigid barrens. Underground wells warm these Porcupine River headwaters to 32° F.—steaming heat on this minus 10° morning. Hardy white spruces, their claim staked here where gold is a no-rush thing, glean the bonanza of the day.*

transformed the lowland. After the ice melted, north-south trending hills and lakes emerged in what had been a smooth valley, and the ice had eroded it below sea level so the ocean could enter to form Puget Sound. Offshore at Seattle the sound is a thousand feet deep. How the ice carved such irregular topography out of uniformly soft sediment, we do not know. Fifteen thousand years of non-glacial erosion have made nary a dent in the terrain sculptured so rapidly by the ice. The geologically young glaciation in the Pacific northwest, given the slow pace of leveling processes, has left us with some of the most glorious scenery in the world.

By viewing our continent through the great span of geologic time, we can with some confidence expand our time framework into the future. By seeing that certain processes going on today have continued for millions of years, we can assume that they will continue for a while—safe enough, at least, to make long-range predictions and plans. As the philosopher Sören Kierkegaard put it, "Life can only be understood backwards; but it must be lived forwards."

A better understanding of why the crustal pieces of the earth move around would make our predictions more comfortable, but that knowledge probably lies just outside our grasp. So for the next few million years, at least, we predict that the Pacific plate will continue to drift to the northwest relative to the continent, which will move on westward. The volcanism and earthquake activity of the Aleutians and Cook Inlet will persist as the Pacific plate is subducted.

To the south, the leading edge of the American plate will override more of the East Pacific Rise. As it does, the Gulf of California will grow wider, and new rifts may open. As the northwest coast overrides the offshore ridges, the Cascade volcanism may largely cease, and there should develop a great master horizontal fault system to tie together the San Andreas and Denali fault systems and accommodate the relative shift of the American and Pacific plates. In approximately ten million years the Los Angeles smog should be rolling in through the Golden Gate.

Ups and downs are harder to foresee than the horizontal shifts. Presumably, as plates continue to interact and collide, mountains will rise as fast as erosion wears them down. The West should continue as a scenic magnet of the continent.

Vexing problems come to the fore when we try to predict long-range changes in climate. Newspapers these days carry much educated speculation by scientists about whether we are or are not entering a new ice age. Lack of full understanding of the factors that control global climatic conditions hampers logical prediction. We are in an age that cannot reach a common mind on the broad effects of flying SST's or of using spray deodorants. At times it seems we have almost limitless ability to control our environment, once we can agree on what is desirable.

Perhaps the day will come when we can turn off volcanoes, control plate motion, or set a sensitive thermostat on world climate—pretty heady stuff! For the time being, we can justly exult in the incredible advances we have made in recent years in understanding our continent, its past and its possibilities.

# Notes on Authors

WILLIAM J. BREED, curator of geology at the Museum of Northern Arizona, is a specialist in the geology of northern Arizona and the Grand Canyon. His many contributions include *Geology of the Grand Canyon* as well as a newly published geologic map of the canyon.

ARCHIE CARR is graduate research professor at the University of Florida and a contributing editor to *Audubon* and *Biological Conservation* magazines. He is the author of more than 125 articles and papers; his books include *So Excellent a Fishe: a Natural History of Sea Turtles*, *The Windward Road*, and *Ulendo*.

EDWIN H. COLBERT is curator of vertebrate paleontology at the Museum of Northern Arizona, curator emeritus at the American Museum of Natural History, and professor emeritus at Columbia University. He is the author of some 300 scientific papers and several books, including *Wandering Lands and Animals*, *Dinosaurs, Men & Dinosaurs*, *The Age of Reptiles*, and *Evolution of the Vertebrates*.

EDWARD S. DEEVEY, JR., is graduate research curator at the Florida State Museum and professor of zoology and geology at the University of Florida. A past president of the Ecological Society of America, he serves on the editorial board of several scientific journals.

STEPHEN JAY GOULD is professor of geology at Harvard University, where he also teaches biology and the history of science. His widely known column, "This View of Life," appears monthly in *Natural History* magazine. He is the author of *Ontogeny and Phylogeny*.

CHARLES B. HUNT, adjunct professor of earth science at New Mexico State University, taught 12 years at Johns Hopkins University and served 34 years with the U. S. Geological Survey. His many books include *Death Valley*, *The Henry Mountains*, *Geology of Soils*, and *Natural Regions of the United States and Canada*.

PAUL A. JOHNSGARD is professor of zoology at the University of Nebraska (Lincoln). Among his books, *Grouse and Quails of North America* and *Waterfowl: Their Biology and Natural History* have won honors from conservation groups.

BJÖRN KURTÉN is professor of paleontology at Finland's University of Helsinki. A former visiting lecturer at Harvard and the University of Florida, he is the author of several books, including *The Ice Age*, *Not From the Apes*, and *The Age of Mammals*.

BATES MCKEE, affiliate professor of geological sciences at the University of Washington in Seattle, is past president of the Northwest Geological Society and author of *Cascadia: The Geologic Evolution of the Pacific Northwest*.

JOHN H. OSTROM, professor of geology at Yale, is curator of vertebrate paleontology at the Peabody Museum. An editor of the museum's publications and of the *American Journal of Science*, he is also a research associate with the American Museum of Natural History. He is author of *The Strange World of Dinosaurs*, and co-author of *Marsh's Dinosaurs*.

ROBERT O. PETTY, associate professor of biology at Wabash College, is an Indiana Academy of Science fellow, author of a number of technical papers, and co-author of *Deciduous Forest*.

JOHN S. SHELTON, a consultant in geology, formerly taught at Pomona College. He has written many articles on geology, helped prepare numerous films and filmstrips, and is the author of *Geology Illustrated*.

GEORGE E. WATSON is curator of birds at the Smithsonian Institution and an associate in pathobiology with Johns Hopkins University. Secretary of the American Ornithologists' Union, he is a member of the National Geographic Society's committee for research and exploration. His books include *Birds of the Antarctic and Sub-Antarctic* and *Seabirds of the Tropical Atlantic Ocean*.

J. TUZO WILSON, director general of the Ontario Science Centre in Canada, is a former professor of geophysics at the University of Toronto. He has lectured on every continent and was president of the International Union of Geodesy and Geophysics. He has written extensively on continental drift, and is the author of *IGY: Year of the New Moons*, and co-author of *Physics and Geology*.

# Acknowledgments and References

The editors are grateful to many people and organizations for their help in the preparation of this book. We are indebted to the Smithsonian Institution and particularly to Paul E. Desautels, Francis M. Hueber, Clayton E. Ray, Stanwyn G. Shetler, and John S. White, Jr. We thank, too, Robert I. Gait of the Royal Ontario Museum and Ronald Thorpe of the Ontario Science Centre.

Other scholars who assisted include: Farish A. Jenkins, Jr., and Charles R. Schaff of Harvard University; Richard W. Hutchinson, University of Western Ontario; Zoltan de Cserna, Universidad Nacional Autónoma de México; John T. Andrews, University of Colorado; Thomas Barr, University of Kentucky; Lyman Benson, Pomona College; and Richard W. Coles, Washington University, St. Louis, Missouri.

We thank William L. Newman and his colleagues at the U. S. Geological Survey and Herbert A. Tiedemann of the National Aeronautics and Space Administration's Goddard Space Flight Center. T. R. Dudley of the National Arboretum, Steven Q. Smith and John C. O'Brien of the National Park Service, John Kempton of the Illinois State Geological Survey, and J. Ponder Henley of the U. S. Army Engineer Topographic Laboratories gave unstintingly of their time and knowledge.

Books of wide scope we found useful include *Natural Regions of the United States and Canada* by Charles B. Hunt, *The Earth Beneath Us* by Kirtley F. Mather, *Face of North America* by Peter Farb, *Rock, Time, and Landforms* by Jerome Wyckoff, *The Earth Sciences* by Arthur N. Strahler, *Earth* by Frank Press and Raymond Siever, Rand McNally's *The Magnificent Continent*, the Reader's Digest *Scenic Wonders of America*, the 13-volume *Grzimek's Animal Life Encyclopedia*, and *The Illustrated Natural History of Canada* in 9 volumes.

Also, *Adventures in Earth History* edited by Preston Cloud, *Evolution of the Earth* by Robert H. Dott, Jr., and Roger L. Batten, *Essentials of Earth History* by William L. Stokes, *The Procession of Life* by Alfred S. Romer, *Life Before Man* by Zdenek V. Spinar, *Prehistoric Animals* by Joseph Augusta, *The Evidence of Evolution* by Nicholas Hotton III, and *The Fossil Book* by Carroll L. Fenton and Mildred A. Fenton.

For current accounts in the field of geophysics we turned to *Continents Adrift* (Readings from *Scientific American*) edited by J. Tuzo Wilson, *Continental Drift and Plate Tectonics* by William Glen, *Planet Earth* (Readings from *Scientific American*) edited by Frank Press and Raymond Siever, and *Continents in Motion* by Walter Sullivan.

Works about earliest life forms included *Animals Without Backbones* by Ralph Buchsbaum, *The History of Life* by A. Lee McAlester, and *Invertebrate Fossils* by Raymond C. Moore and others.

The reptile chapter benefited from books by Edwin H. Colbert and John H. Ostrom listed in the authors' notes opposite, *Dinosaurs* by Nicholas Hotton III, *The Hot-Blooded Dinosaurs* by Adrian J. Desmond, and *Before the Ark* by Alan Charig and Brenda Horsfield.

References for birds and flowers included *Prehistoric Reptiles and Birds* by Joseph Augusta, *Fossil Birds* by W. E. Swinton, *Birds of the World* by Oliver L. Austin, Jr., and Arthur Singer, *The World of Birds* by James Fisher and Roger Tory Peterson, *Biology of Plants* by Peter H. Raven, Ray F. Evert, and Helena Curtis, and *Because of a Flower* by Lorus and Margery Milne.

Insights into prehistoric mammals and life in the Ice Age came from *Evolution of the Vertebrates* by Edwin H. Colbert, *Vertebrate Paleontology* by Alfred S. Romer, *A History of Land Mammals in the Western Hemisphere* by W. B. Scott, Björn Kurtén's books listed in the authors' notes, *Pleistocene Extinctions* edited by Paul S. Martin and H. E. Wright, Jr., and *Glacial and Quaternary Geology* by Richard F. Flint.

Canadian Shield readings included *The Natural Landscapes of Canada* by J. Brian Bird, *The Mammals of Canada* by A. W. F. Banfield, and *The Flight of the Snow Geese* by Des and Jen Bartlett.

Supplementary sources for Appalachia included *The Appalachians* by Maurice Brooks and *The Americans: The Colonial Experience* by Daniel J. Boorstin.

Helpful works on the plains and prairies included *The Life of Prairies and Plains* by Durward L. Allen, *The Prairie World* by David F. Costello, *Alberta: A Natural History* edited by W. G. Hardy, and *Floor of the Sky* by David Plowden.

Rockies sources included *The Rocky Mountains* by Wallace W. Atwood, *Land Above the Trees* by Ann H. Zwinger and Beatrice E. Willard, *The Rockies* by David Lavender, and *The Mountain World* by David F. Costello.

Assistance with the canyon chapter came from *Geology of the Grand Canyon* edited by William J. Breed and Evelyn C. Roat, *Ancient Landscapes of the Grand Canyon Region* by Edwin D. McKee, and *Red Rock Country: The Geologic History of the Colorado Plateau* by Donald L. Baars.

Desert country aids were *The North American Deserts* by Edmund C. Jaeger, *Desert: The American Southwest* by Ruth Kirk, *Death Valley* by Charles B. Hunt, *The Mineral Kingdom* by Paul E. Desautels, and *Geology: Field Guide to Southern California* by Robert P. Sharp.

Helpful on the Pacific coast were Bates McKee's book listed in the authors' notes, *California's Changing Landscapes* by Gordon B. Oakeshott, *An Island Called California* by Elna Bakker, and *Our Changing Coastlines* by Francis P. Shepard and Harold R. Wanless.

The editors gratefully acknowledge permission to reprint extracts from the following: *Living Water* by David Cavagnaro and Ernest Braun, copyright © 1971 by American West Publishing Company, Palo Alto, California; and "Year's End," copyright © 1949 by Richard Wilbur, reprinted from his volume, *Ceremony and Other Poems*, published by Harcourt Brace Jovanovich, Inc. Alfred S. Romer's *The Vertebrate Story*, copyright © 1959, University of Chicago Press, provided the basis for the diagram on page 60. The editors also thank the Czechoslovakian publishers, Artia, for making available the paintings of Zdenek Burian. His works appear in *Prehistoric Reptiles and Birds* and *Prehistoric Animals*, both by Joseph Augusta, and in *Life Before Man* by Zdenek V. Spinar, copyright © 1972, Artia, Prague.

# Index

Text references appear in lightface type, illustrations in **boldface**.

Type composition by National Geographic's Photographic Services. Color separations by Progressive Color Corporation, Rockville, Md.; J. Wm. Reed Company, Alexandria, Va.; and Chanticleer Company, Inc., New York, N.Y. Printed and bound by Fawcett Printing Corporation, Rockville, Md. Paper by Oxford Paper Company, New York, and Weyerhauser Company, Miquon, Pa. Cover and Wheel of Time: Federated Lithographers, Providence, R.I.

Library of Congress CIP Data

Main entry under title:
Our Continent.

Includes bibliographical references and index.
 1. Natural history—North America.
I. National Geographic Society, Washington, D. C.
QH102.095    500.9'7    76-26633
ISBN 0-87044-153-1